Best regards to
Gerry York

Paul H. Stockdale

The Death of an Army

The Battle of Nashville

and

Hood's Retreat

By
Paul H. Stockdale

Edited
by
John McGlone

Southern Heritage Press
P.O. Box 1615
Murfreesboro, TN 37133-1615

The Death of An Army:
The Battle of Nashville
and
Hood's Retreat
by
Paul H. Stockdale

©1992 by Paul Stockdale
Chappell Hill, Texas 77426

Library of Congress Cataloging-in-Publication
91-068326
Stockdale, Paul H.

The Death of An Army

p. cm

Bibliography: p.
Includes Index
ISBN 0-9631963-0-8

Dedicated
To:
The United Daughters of the Confederacy
And
The Sons of Confederate Veterans
Who
Do So Much To Keep Green
The Memory of Our Southern Heroes.

Contents

Library of Congress Cataloging-in-Publication
91-068326
Stockdale, Paul H.

The Death of An Army

p. cm

Bibliography: p.
Includes Index
ISBN 0-9631963-0-8

Illustrations

Preface

Walt Whitman, who was in the war on the Federal side as a male nurse once wrote:

Do we not think victory great?
So, indeed it is!
But now it seems to me,
When it cannot be helped,
That defeat is great.

One day in late summer, on the Nashville battleground, I climbed to the top of Shy's Hill. I was all alone. The city was all around, yet there was a feeling of remoteness and solitude, and one felt the strong presence of history and a slow passage of time. December 16, 1864 seemed somehow close at hand. There on that "holy spot of ground," high above the city, there was a realization of bustling, materialistic today intermixed with heroic, idealistic yesterday.

Ernie Pyle, the famous war correspondent of World War II in a dispatch from the front lines in Italy wrote: "You feel small in the presence of the dead men, and ashamed at being alive. . . ." The day I scaled the heights of Shy's Hill, and stood on that summit, all alone, I felt small. I felt the presence of those brave Tennesseans who fought and died there for me on that dismal December day so long ago. Lines from the beautiful and touching ode written by Henry Timrod came to mind:

Stoop angels hither from the skies,
There is no holier spot of ground
Than where defeated valor lies. . . .

I stood there in the hushed silence for a long time, and looked about me. I thought of the young officers, Colonel Shy and Brigadier General Smith, inspiring their men by brave example. Colonel Shy was killed at close range by a bullet through his forehead, and General Smith was doomed to a living death due to the cowardly act of a Union colonel.

Nashville was sprawled below, but up there the deathlike silence hung soft, yet heavy. I reached down and took a handful of the sacred and once reeking soil which had been soaked by Tennessee blood on that dark December day of defeat. The thirsty mouth of earth had long since fed upon that sacrifice. I said a silent prayer for the souls of all those faithful heroes. May their souls rest in peace; may light perpetual shine upon them; God grant them eternal rest!

I then turned and walked slowly away from the now gentle stillness to the long flight of crude steps that led down the hill, and left the battle-grieved ghosts of those star-crowned heroes there in nature's cathedral to hold communion at their altar of immortality. Their spiritual presence looked down from their hall of the slain—their Valhalla. The leaves of the trees on that shell-tortured hill whispered softly and gently, rocked by the caressing Southern breeze as if in perpetual remembrance. No other sound. I stood briefly and looked back at the once battle-scarred and timeless crest, then walked on. I left the ghosts of gray "alone with their glory." "Even the wind had a melancholy sound through the woods as if lamenting with us o'er our buried hopes, and the graves of that unconquered band of heroes, whose names are radiant with immortality. . . ."

There was a refusal in the recesses of my mind at that time to picture the body of our hero, Colonel Shy, naked and bayonetted to a tree by the victors, or the exposed brain of General Thomas Benton Smith, the victim of an unwarranted attack after he had surrendered and was unarmed. Sometimes we do not like to admit atrocities if done by American soldiers. But—*Vae victis!* Woe to the vanquished! Woe to the conquered provinces. "That's the hymn of the conquered . . . of the wounded, the beaten, who died overwhelmed in the strife."

"Look down, and swear by the slain of the war that you'll never forget. . . .Look up and swear by the green of the spring that you'll never forget." ("Aftermath," Siefried Sassoon)

Professor Richard Weaver, professor of rhetoric at the University of Chicago, was a Southerner. He was an apologist for the Vanderbilt Agrarians, and defended the Southern philosophy. His was always a "defense of the higher culture of Western Civilization against those who would shatter it." Professor Ralph T. Eubanks wrote: "His defense of orthodoxy began and ended with the Southern idea of life. Weaver was a man of the South." He recognized "the presence of tragedy in life," and wrote that "The South is the region where history has happened. People who have never experienced tragedy are the deviants." He says further that the average American is the "victorious man," and has never faced defeat, while the Southerner "Has had to taste a bitter cup which no American is supposed to know anything about, the cup of defeat." The Civil War ". . . a supreme act of his will was frustrated and that as a consequence of that defeat he had to accommodate himself to an unwanted circumstance, and that, of course, is the meaning of failure. Therefore in the national legend the typical American owes his position to a virtuous and effective act of his will; but the Southerner owes his to the fact that his will was denied; and this leaves a kind of inequality which no amount of political blandishment can remove entirely."

No other defeated enemy of the United States has ever suffered the humiliation and deliberate continued oppression that the South has endured. Weaver says: "But perhaps most important of all is the Southerner's discipline in tragedy. Belief in tragedy is essentialy un-American; it is, in fact, one of the heresies against Americanism; but in the world as a whole this heresy is more widely received than the dogma and is more regularly taught by experience."

I grew up in Army of Tennessee country. Not far away were Forts Henry and Donelson. Up river a little ways was Johnsonville, and a little further up river was Shiloh. At an early age I knew about and felt our defeat. My grandmother had told me that my great-grandfather had been in "Bragg's Army." I knew that we had lost.

This brings to mind Father Ryan's "A Land Without Ruins:" (from *History of the Twentieth Tennessee Regiment* (pp. 473-474:)

"A land without ruins is a land without memories; a land without memories is a land without history. A land that wears a laurel crown may be fair to see; but twine a few sad cypress leaves around the brow of any land, and be that land barren, beautiless, and bleak, it becomes lovely in its consecrated coronet of sorrow, and it wins the sympathy of the heart and of history. Crowns of rose fade; crowns of thorns endure. Calvarys and crucifixions take deepest hold of humanity. The triumphs of might are transient— they pass and are forgotten; the sufferings of right are graven deepest on the chronicle of nations."

> Yes, give me the land where the ruins are spread,
> And the living tread light on the hearts of the dead;
> Yes, give me a land that is blest by the dust,
> And bright with the deeds of the down-trodden just.
> Yes, give me the land where the battle's red blast
> Has flashed to the future the fame of the past;
> Yes, give me the land that hath legends and lays,
> That tell of the memories of long vanished days;
> Yes, give me the land that story and song!
> Enshrine the strife of the right with the wrong!
> Yes, give me the land with a grave in each spot,
> And the names on the graves that shall ne'er be forgot,
> Yes, give me the land of the wreck and the tomb;
> There is grandeur in graves, there is glory in gloom,
> For out of the gloom, future brightness is born,
> As after the night comes the sunrise of morn;
> And the graves of the dead with the grass overgrown,
> May yet form the footstool of liberty's throne;
> And each single wreck in the war-path of might,
> Shall yet be a rock in the temple of right.

Paul H. Stockdale
Waverly Plantation
Chappel Hill, Texas
1991

Foreword

In July 1864, when John Bell Hood took command of the Army of Tennessee, it was still a viable fighting unit. To be sure, it had been on the defensive under Joseph E. Johnston and mishandled under Braxton Bragg, but it was still as dangerous as a wounded panther and capable of inflicting great harm upon its enemies. After six months under the command of Hood, a mere handful of ragged, bleeding survivors showed the world what it meant to maintain dignity even in defeat as they plodded their way south after the Battle of Nashville. In the words of the the participants, Paul Stockdale tells the story of that last major battle through ice, snow, mud, and despair. He also investigates in detail the atrocities committed against Colonel Shy and General Smith, and he tells the heart-rending story of the retreat where leaders like Forrest and Walthall inspired their seemingly beaten men to turn and once more defeat their tormentors at places like Anthony's Hill, the Battle of the Barricades, and Rutherford Creek. Even in retreat, they added laurels to an army already crowned in glory.

Most histories of the Army of Tennessee describe the Battle of Nashville and then make the transition to the survivors surrendering with Johnston in North Carolina. In fact, most of the survivors never made it to the East Coast. They fought and were captured during the retreat from Nashville toward Alabama. They were furloughed home, they served and died in the defense of Mobile, or they surrendered in Mississippi or Louisiana. Paul Stockdale also tells the forgotten but fascinating story of the last days of this other great Confederate Army and in so doing fills in a gap in Confederate historigraphy.

Historians, sophisticated students of the Confederacy, and general readers have shown an increasing interest in reading first-person accounts of the War period. Stockdale has provided a virtual diary of the period by weaving together many eyewitness accounts of the story of the Battle of Nashville, the final retreat, and the people who participated in these events. He also refreshes memories with brief biographies of the principal actors in this drama. Perhaps the leading character in this living mortality play—aside from the common soldiers of the Army of Tennessee—was John Bell Hood.

In April 1861, Hood was a First Lieutenant in the "old Army." By 1865 he was a full General in the Confederate Army. At the end he was a broken shell of a man but it is well to remember that he had gotten that

I

way in the service of the Confederacy. He had lost the use of an arm at Gettysburg, and a scant two and a half months later he was hurrying to join his troops at Chickamauga where he lost a leg. He should have been retired at that point or at least given rear echelon duty, but he continued in active service and was eventually given command of the Army of Tennessee. He rode to the sound of battle strapped onto his horse. His pain and suffering must have been great and his judgment must have been clouded by alcohol, drugs, and pain killers. No amount of chemicals, however, can explain or excuse his utter disregard for his men when he wasted their lives in suicidal attacks against hopeless odds as he did at Franklin. Gettysburg is visited by more tourists and Pickett's charge better remembered in literature, but for sheer grit, determination, and bloodletting, Franklin surpasses them. After the carnage and the destruction at Nashville, Hood had the audacity to blame his men for his failures. It would have been better for Hood's memory and for the Confederacy if a Union bullet had found its fatal mark at Gettysburg or Chickamauga. As a regimental or brigade commander, Hood had few equals, and he was a favorite of Gen. Robert E. Lee. Hood's Texans in the Army of Northern Virginia created legends in an army of legends; but, as with all tragic heroes, Hood's character contained a fatal flaw which would destory him and his army when given independent command. It is said that at poker Hood would draw to an inside straight, a rash move indeed; and the story is told that whenever Hood saw a bugler standing around idle, he would order the charge! Both tales are probably fictional, but they reveal what men thought of Hood and perhaps explain his conduct during the last days of the Army of Tennessee. Many brave men forfeited their lives for Hood's failures, and Stockdale has brought their story to life and offered the reminder that even in defeat the men of the Army of Tennessee marched into history with their honor bright.

John McGlone
Murfreesboro, Tennessee
1992

". . . The Army of Tennessee had died in front of the gap at Franklin and on the hillsides at Nashville." (*The Gallant Hood,* p. 303, John P. Dyer.)

I

Exordium

The Battle of Nashville was the last great battle in the West before the surrender. It was a decisive battle in that it decided the fate of the Western Confederacy and brought about the defeat and destruction of the Western Confederate Army of Tennessee. The Battle of Nashville, while not as sanguinary as many of the past battles, was filled with dramatic incidents. A large group of civilian spectators gathered on house tops and hills to witness the struggle. Most of them were in sympathy with the South. They hoped against hope for a Confederate victory, only to be disappointed and dejected. They were described as "A large and sullen crowd."

During the first day's battle, two young ladies on different parts of the field risked their lives while trying to rally the Confederates. After the war, one of these girls would become the wife of a brigadier fighting that day with Forrest's cavalry.

During the second act of the tragedy, on December 16th, Colonel Edward W. Rucker, commanding a Confederate cavalry brigade under Chalmers on the left flank, engaged in a desperate hand-to-hand saber fight, on horseback, with Colonel George Spalding, 12th Tenn. Cavalry (Union), and a Captain Joseph C. Boyer, same regiment. Rucker inflicted a severe blow to the head of Boyer during this encounter, and according to one official report, Boyer shot Colonel Rucker in the left arm causing him to surrender. All of this action occurred after dark on December 16th, in the cold and rain.

Also late on the second day of battle, after the salient on Compton's Hill (later known as Shy's Hill) was overrun by hordes of Bluecoats. Brigadier General Thomas Benton Smith surrendered the remaining Confederates. As he and his men were being marched back to Nashville as unarmed prisoners-of-war, Smith was approached by a Union colonel from Ohio who, without provocation, struck him over the head three times with his saber, opening the skull so that the brain oozed through the wound. Smith was expected to die, but survived and was sent North as a prisoner-of-war. Smith was twenty-six years old. (See Appendix I)

The principal actor in the second part of this great drama, who is perhaps best remembered and memorialized, was twenty-six year old Colonel William M. Shy, 20th Tennessee Regiment. On this fateful day, he commanded the diminished ranks of the consolidated 2nd, 10th, 20th, and 37th Tennessee Regiments of infantry. Compton's Hll was renamed Shy's Hill to honor his brave defense and sacrifice. The story surrounding his brief life and his untimely death unfurls and spreads out before us, even unto this day, in a tragic display. His story reveals to what an extent the story of the War for Southern Independence is still with us. The hill named in his honor is today surrounded by modern houses, some dug into its base. Colonel Shy's story is one of unselfish devotion that could well be emulated.

> I vow to thee my country . . .
> The love that never falters, the love that pays the price,
> The love that makes undaunted the final sacrifice. (I vow To Thee My Country, Sir Cecil Arthur Spring-Rice).

Colonel William Mabry Shy was born May 24, 1838 in Bourbon County, Kentucky. There were ten children in the family, and in 1861, when the war started, a brother, living in Perry County organized the Perry Guards. This brother, Dr. Louis Shy, was disabled early in the war and discharged.

Bill Shy, as he was popularly known in the regiment, enlisted as a private in Company H, Twentieth Tennessee Regiment, and was appointed one of the color guard. After the battle of Fishing Creek, Kentucky, he was elected Lieutenant in his company. In May 1862 at Corinth, he was appointed captain of Company H, and was a very popular and effective company commander. Deering J. Roberts describes Shy as "of an unusually quiet disposition, he was not much given to words, but when he did speak, it was to the purpose. He was unquestionably a man rather of deeds than words. Modest as a woman, and as gentle, kindly to all with whom he came in contact, in time of battle he was the embodiment of courage, determined and brave to a degree. In the hottest of the fight, in the dash of a charge, he was always calm and collected; with no excitement at any time, as calm and cool under the hottest fire of shot and shell as by the reminiscent campfire and indulging in reveries of home and stories of the days of peace."

Shy was promoted to major in 1863 and soon after to lieutenant colonel. After Tyler was wounded at Missionary Ridge commanding

Bate's old brigade, Thomas Benton Smith succeeded to the brigade command at that time, and Shy assumed command of the Twentieth Tennessee. Promotion to colonel came in September, 1864 when Smith was made brigadier general before Atlanta.

The Twentieth Tennessee followed Hood on the Tennessee campaign in Tyler's (Smith's) brigade, Bate's division. At Franklin Shy led the Twentieth on the left of the assault and with the right of Bate's division took the breastworks and held them until morning. Bate's division was not in the thickest of the fighting here. According to Dr. J. McMurray who wrote the history of the Twentieth, "This was the first engagement during the entire war, that the Twentieth Tennessee Regiment was engaged in, that they failed to get into the hottest part of the battle, and the boys thought they were in luck."

When Hood marched on to Nashville, the Twentieth with Bate's division was temporarily detached to Murfreesboro with Forrest until a day or two before the Battle of Nashville. On the evening of December 15, 1864, Bate's divison was transferred to the left of Hood's line, holding the angle on Compton's Hill (later renamed Shy's Hill). This hill was intended to be the strong point on the left, but due to the surrounding terrain it was an easy artillery target from three directions. Due to the angle, the hill was hit from front, flank, and rear. Coleman's Texas and North Carolina brigade had first occupied the hill and built fortifications at night too far back from the military crest. The attacking hordes would be on top of the defenders before they could fire at them. The Confederates waited under sharpshooter fire and heavy artillery pounding, and were still in possession of the hill until late afternoon of December 16th. Rain and much colder weather added to the misery of the thinly clad, and in some cases, barefooted Confederates, but they doggedly hung on. The enemy massed at the base of the hill, and at 4:00 p.m. the assault took place. For awhile there was some desperate hand to hand fighting, but the Federals came in such great numbers that the thin line was swept aside. As General Bate reported, only 65 men escaped, and these singly and not as a unit. As the regimental historian says in his account of the battle, "It was here that the brave, generous, and manly W.M. Shy of the Twentieth Tennessee Regiment was killed, and the place is now known as Shy's Hill. . . . He fell, a minnie ball piercing his brain, his hand grasped around the trigger guard of a fallen soldier's Enfield which he had just discharged at the advancing lines of blue. . . . It can be said of him, as of Bayard, he was 'le Chevalier sans peur et sans reproche.' " His name is inscribed on fame's immortal scroll. There was no hope of holding the hill. The very numbers of the enemy made the task impossible and the end a foregone conclusion.

When news of his death reached his father and mother at their home, Two Rivers near Franklin, they desired to recover the body. "When the death of this brave young officer was made known to his mother, who lived near Franklin, only a few miles away, it is said that she remarked that she would to God that she had a hundred sons to die for such a cause."[1] According to descendants of the Shy family, the family at the time of Colonel Shy's death were not permitted to go through the lines to recover his body. Dr. Daniel B. Cliffe, a friend of the family, but pro-Union, offered the services of his wife to retrieve the body. Because of his Union sympathies he was able to get his wife permission to make the trip. A family descendant (Colonel Shy was unmarried and left no direct descendants). Virginia Oliver Bell left this account:

"When word came that he (Shy) had been killed, his family was not allowed to go through the Yankee lines to claim his body. A family friend, Virginia Whitfield Cliffe, wife of Dr. Dan Cliffe, took a spring wagon with a negro man to drive and brought his body home. This privilege was accorded her because of Dr. Cliffe's connection in the North. Mrs. Cliffe found him without a stitch of clothing on, shot through the center of his forehead and impaled on a tree with a bayonet. He was buried in the family graveyard. ...." The bayonet with which his body was impaled to the tree and his canteen are still in the possession of the family descendants.[2]

Col. Shy was shot at close range, the area around the wound was powder burned. Whoever inflicted the wound intended that it be fatal. Shy was either killed first and then impaled or pinned to the tree and then killed. It seems clear that an atrocity was committed.

Emily Compton says that she was at her parent's home when the battle was fought a short distance away on Shy's (Compton's) Hill. "The hill was owned by my father Felix Compton for years and was known as Compton's Hill. It is not a part of Overton and Lea Range, but stands alone facing the hill which was also my father's, on which the

[1] W. J. McMurray, *History of The Twentieth Tennessee Regiment Volunteer Infantry* (Nashville, Publication Committee, 1904; repr., Nashville, Elders Bookstore, 1976) p.368.

[2] John T. Dowd, *The Pillaged Grave of a Civil War Hero,* (Nashville, TN: Mini-Histories, 1985), p. 6.

Yankee batteries were placed on the afternoon of Dec. 15. . . . Both the Granny White and Hillsboro pikes ran through the Compton farm."

Chalmers' headquarters had been in the Compton house for ten days, then Gen. Walthall's until the afternoon of Dec. 15. The house fronts on the Hillsboro pike.

She watched the camp fires of "our boys" all night of the 15th of Dec. "They were camped in my father's hills and in the hills of my great uncle, Harry Compton. . . . There were 150 dead and wounded in our home at one time. My mother and I were permitted to give water to the Confederates and some bread and milk, for that was all we had for three days, except what an old black mammy stole and begged from the Yankees for us. For 17 days the house was a hospital. In the first three days Lt. Giles of Franklin, Tenn., and Lt. John Chambers of Tuscaloosa, Ala., died in the house. We buried Mr. Chambers in the garden. After the war his father came for the body. Lt. Giles family buried him at his home."[3]

Some of the dead were laid out on the front gallery. Emily Compton, tells about seeing the young colonel among the dead:

"Colonel Shy fell on the afternoon of December 16. His body, with many others of both armies, was laid upon the front gallery of our home. Shortly afterwards a Federal guard called my attention to Colonel Shy. Then turning back from the face a gray blanket which some kind friend had placed over the body, I saw him as he lay so peacefully there with that cruel hole in his brow."

The body of the young hero was brought home to Two Rivers Mansion near Franklin and interred in the family plot near the house. It lay there undisturbed for over a hundred years until Christmas Eve 1977.

The grave is marked by a marble headstone, but his rank of Lt. Colonel is in error, since he had been promoted to Colonel before the Battle of Nashville.

Grave robbers, apparently looking for Civil War artifacts, broke open his cast iron casket on Christmas Eve, 1977. Mrs. Mary Griffith and her husband had bought Two Rivers to restore. She was showing a

3*Confederate Veteran*, 17, 1909, pp 522-523.

visitor around the grounds of the old home when she saw that the grave had been disturbed and called the Williamson County sheriff. When the sheriff came he found a headless body half out of the casket, and thought at the time that it was a recent homicide. He thought the murderers were trying to put a recently murdered corpse into Shy's casket. The county coroner who examined the body found flesh on it and came to the conclusion that the victim had been dead not over a year. Doctors in the Metro Coroner's office examined the body more closely and detected the smell of arsenic. The arsenic and the air-proof casket had preserved Shy's body for over one hundred years. The grave robbers were not apprehended at the time, nor have they yet been.

In 1986, an advertisement was placed in a Civil War memorabilia catalog for some of Colonel Shy's belongings, but the ad did not help in finding the ghoul or ghouls. However, the person in possession of his dress weapons of sword, scabbard, and brass pistol donated them anonymously to the Carter House Museum in Franklin, Tennessee, where they and the coffin are now on display.

Dr. William M. Bass, Forensic Anthropologist, University of Tennessee made the following report as to cause of death: "Blow to the left forehead, just to the left of the midline. The entrance wound is approximately 17 x 24 millimeters in diameter. The projectile traveled in a downward path through the skull before exiting. Death would have been instantaneous. The force of the projectile was so great that the skull was fractured into seventeen pieces; both mastoid processes at the base of the skull were split." His teeth showed cavities, but no fillings which was a normal condition for this period of time according to Dr. Bass.[4]

The sheriff described the burial clothes: "It wasn't a tuxedo, but it was a flashy-looking suit of clothes." The pleated shirt appeared to be silk. The flared trousers had lace down the leg. The square-toed shoes— a century-old style which had a resurgence a few years ago—had elastic in them. The suit was apparently the same one worn by Colonel Shy when he had his last photo taken in a cut-away with tails and a white shirt.[5]

After identification of Shy's body, he was reburied in a ceremony on Monday, February 13, 1978. Six members of the Sons of Confederate Veterans acted as pall bearers, while members of the United

[4]Dowd, p. 14

[5]*Nashville Banner*

Daughters of the Confederacy carried Confederate flags and placed one on the grave. The new coffin was contributed by Franklin Memorial Chapel while the Reverend Charles Fulton, Rector of St. Paul's Episcopal Church gave the eulogy.

Words from the ancient *Aeneid* would seem to apply to Colonel Shy: "Everyone has his allotted day. Short and irrecoverable is the lifetime of all; but to extend our fame by deeds, this is the task of greatness."

Requiescat in Pace

PICTURES

Colonel William M. Shy
1838—1864
C.S.A.

Two Rivers Mansion, Col. Shy's home.

The Compton Home where Col. Shy's body was brought after the battle.

Colonel Shy's cast iron coffin.

Col. Shy's grave behind the Two Rivers Mansion.

Pictures courtesy of Mini-Histories, Nashville, 1985, from The Pillaged Grave of a Civil War Hero, by
John T. Dowd

Colonel William M. Shy
1838—1864
C.S.A.

Two Rivers Mansion, Col. Shy's home.

The Compton Home where Col. Shy's body was brought after the battle.

Colonel Shy's cast iron coffin.

Col. Shy's grave behind the Two Rivers Mansion.

II
Hood Moves on Nashville

The Confederacy had been at war for almost four years by late 1864 and the war was not going well. General Lee was under seige on the Richmond-Petersburg front. Atlanta had fallen and Sherman was marching to the sea. The Confederate army was on starvation rations but the walking skeletons still had some fight left. Desperate times called for desperate measures. The dashing but impetuous Commander of the Army of Tennessee, John Bell Hood, headed his ragged Army north from Georgia, through Alabama and into an invasion of Tennessee. It was a long shot but it might force Sherman to withdraw from Georgia. It could lead to the capture of the vast Union Supply depot at Nashville and—dream of dreams—it might carry the Army of Tennessee all the way to the banks of the Ohio and victory.

The crippled Hood strapped to his saddle led his army north, came close to cutting off a union force at Spring Hill, and in the fury at his failure to do so he launched a suicidal attack at Franklin. The Pyrrhic victory at Franklin on November 30, 1864, had reduced Hood's infantry strength to around 22,000.

The Federal dead and non-walking wounded were left behind when Schofield withdrew that same night. By noon, December 1st, all five of the Federal divisions were safely inside the Nashville fortifications. Hood at Franklin, on December 1st, had started the day with a belated artillery bombardment of 100 rounds. This firing ceased when word reached him that only Federal dead and wounded occupied the works. Forrest's cavalry had followed the retreating Schofield and harassed the column slightly, but could not really overtake the infantry as they moved hurriedly toward Nashville. The Confederate horsemen, however, "Hung close upon the Federal cavalry on that (the right) flank." Four or five miles out of Franklin, some sharp fights took place, and Buford and Jackson made several charges. Three stands of colors were taken and one-hundred prisoners.[1]

The Journal of The Army of Tennessee for December 1, states: "The army moved out from Franklin during the morning on the Franklin and Nashville pike, Lee in front, Stewart next, and Cheatham in the rear, all camping on the pike, a few miles from Franklin; army headquarters for the night just across Harpeth River from Franklin."

When the Confederate cavalry reached the vicinity of Nashville, Forrest ordered Chalmers to move to the west and guard the Hillsborough and Harding pikes. Forrest, himself, with Buford's and Jackson's divisions took position in sight of the capitol at Nashville. Buford covered the Murfreesboro pike while Jackson went into position along

---

[1] Thomas Jordan and J. P. Pryor, *The Campaigns of Lieut. Gen. N. B Forrest and of Forrest's Cavalry* (New York: n.p., 1868; repr., n.p., Morningside Bookshop, 1973), p. 629.

the Mill Creek pike. Later, the infantry relieved the cavalrymen, and Forrest began his destruction of the railroad, block-houses, and telegraph lines leading to Murfreesboro.

After the Confederate casualties at Franklin, Schofield alone had a greater troop strength than Hood could now muster. The "massive slaughter and the death knell of a once mighty army" has aptly described the results of the Battle of Franklin for the Confederate Army of Tennessee. Hood had lost about 7,000 men of which 1,750 had been killed, 4,500 wounded, and 702 captured. This was over a period of only about five hours. Sixty-six officers above the rank of captain were casualties as follows: 18 killed, 38 wounded, 8 missing and 1 captured. The command structure in The Army of Tennessee had been shattered. Brigades were now commanded by field officers in rank, from colonel to major. Captain Edward T. Broughton, commanded Granbury's Texas brigade after Franklin. Twelve general officers were either killed, wounded or captured, (5 killed; 6 wounded—1 mortally; and 1 captured). Field officers killed outright were as follows: colonels (6), lieutenant colonels (2), majors (3). Wounded field officers: colonels (15), lieutenant colonels (9), majors (6), while colonels (2), and majors (2) were reported missing.[2] Inexperience of most of the officers at higher command, and unfamiliarity with the troops would further weaken confidence in leadership. Consolidation of regiments would contribute to a weakening of the *esprit de corps* and morale of The Army of Tennessee which had depended upon "the strong individuality of the units of the column." Soldiers in the Confederate army at the company level had been recruited from the same locale for the most part. They could depend upon each other, and due to battle experience a special closeness had developed. This gave The Army of Tennessee a specal elan which filtered upward through the regimental and brigade echelons of command. After the Franklin slaughter much of this spirit had been diluted, especially in the decimated ranks of Cheatham's and Stewart's corps.

A comparison of Federal and Confederate casualties at Franklin show a ratio of about one to eight. On the afternoon of December 1st, a congratulatory order from Hood was read at the head of each of the

---

[2]James Lee McDonough and Thomas L. Connelly, *Five Tragic Hours: The Battle of Franklin* (Knoxville: University of Tennessee Press, 1983), p. 179; U. S. War Department, *War of the Rebellion: A Compilation of the Official Records of the Union and Confederate Armies,* 128 vols. (Washington, D.C.: Government Printing Office, 1882), Ser. I, Vol. 45, Part 1, pp. 684-86 (hereafter cited as *OR*).

depleted Confederate regiments: "... While we lament the fall of many gallant officers and brave men we have shown to our countrymen that we can carry any position occupied by our enemy." Perhaps this was Hood's way of acknowledging he had been wrong when he had implied that The Army of Tennessee would not charge breastworks.

Hood now faced a hopeless, no-win situation, but he decided to press on to Nashville. He had expressed some thought to Beauregard that perhaps, E. Kirby Smith, commanding the Trans-Mississippi Department, could send reenforcements. Beuregard had approached President Davis on the matter, asking: "Cannot I send E. Kirby Smith, to reenforce General Hood in Middle Tennessee? His assistance is absolutely necessary at this time."[3] Davis replied that "There is no objection to his being called on, but he has failed to respond to like necessities, and no plans should be based on his compliance."[4] After Hood's defeat and subsequent retreat across the Tennessee River to Tupelo, Mississippi, Kirby Smith sent his reply. Smith said that troop movement would be impossible that time of year due to high water and the devastated condition of the country. His letter to Beuregard was dated January 6, 1865. General Beauregard forwarded the letter with an endorsement which suggested crossing the Mississippi in canoes.[5]

After the fighting around Atlanta, with the acquiescence of President Davis, Hood proposed to hit Sherman's line of communication around Resaca and Dalton, and draw him back for battle along the railroad.

Davis had intended that if Sherman moved south of Atlanta Hood would return and engage him. Beauregard, the department commander, had set up a supply depot at Jacksonville, Alabama for Hood about the middle of October, and had expected to find him near that place, but Hood had moved on to Gadsden, twenty-seven miles west. Since his last meeting with Beauregard "the erratic Hood had decided upon a new plan. After maneuvering on the railroad, he concluded that he would not be able to bring Sherman to battle on ground favorable to the Confederates. He then fixed upon the bold expedient of an offensive into

---

[3] *OR,* Series I, Vol. 45, Part 2, p. 636.

[4] *Ibid.*

[5] *Ibid., p. 766.*

3

Tennessee."[6] Hood's exact plans were nebulous. He changed some details, and his description of what he had in mind at the time and then after the war are at odds. In general the plan was thus: At first, he planned to cross the Tennessee River at Guntersville and head for Nashville. Part of Shermen's army under Thomas had been sent back to Tennessee. After Thomas had been defeated, Hood planned to move on to Kentucky, but if Sherman moved north from Atlanta the Confederates would engage him in Tennessee. If Sherman stayed in Atlanta and moved south, then The Army of Tennessee would go to Virginia and join Lee against Grant.[7] Such it seems, were Hood's plans.

After much delay in the Tuscumbia-Florence area, which would later prove to be a factor in Hood's defeat, Stephen D. Lee's corps, the first of Hood's troops, finally crossed the Tennessee on a pontoon bridge on November 2, 1864. Due to heavy rains, rising river, and partially submerged pontoons, the crossing of the entire army was not completed by all the troops until November 15th. Finally on November 19th, Forrest's cavalry moved out. This offensive movement put the men in high spirits—especially the Tennesseans who would be returning to their home state. The thought of being on familiar soil bolstered the morale of the hungry and ragged men. The Chaplain of the 3rd Tennessee Regiment reported seeing the captain commanding the regiment as barefoot. Again on November 8th, at Florence after crossing the river, he reported as follows: "It has been a long, weary march of nearly 500 miles, still the soldiers have stood it nobly. Many of them are barefoot, both officers and men. Where we go next is uncertain, and great is the anxiety. Every eye is turned toward Tennessee. Oh, may she soon be free. God of hosts be with us and give us success." One soldier in the 16th Tennessee Infantry noted that "many of the men were barefooted and destitute of many other articles of clothing." This was before the army had crossed the Tennessee river to begin the campaign. On November 3rd, another soldier in the same regiment noted in his diary that "Many barefooted and have no pants."[8]

---

[6]T. Harry Williams, *P.G.T. Beauregard—Napoleon in Gray* (Baton Rouge, LA: Louisiana University Press, 1954), p. 243.

[7]Thomas Robson Hay, *Hood's Tennessee Campaign* (New York: Walter Neale, 1929; repr., n.p. Morningside Bookshop, 1976), pp. 54-55.

[8]Bob Womack, *Call Forth the Mighty Men* (Bessemer, AL: Colonial Press, 1987), p. 446.

Travellers' Rest, built in 1799. Home of John Overton on the Franklin Pike, six miles from Nashville. Hood's headquarters upon reaching Nashville. This old home is open to the public for daily guided tours.

Short of supplies, short of manpower, and with no clear cut plan of action, Hood launched his ill-advised, ill-fated Tennessee Campaign which has been described as "the desperate venture of a desperate man." Among the rank and file "there was no faint-heartedness, but on the contrary, an evident desire to go forward and fight it out."[9]

Hood realized the poor condition of his army and knew he could not attack Thomas at fortified Nashville with any hope of success. He also knew there was little hope of reenforcements from the Trans-Mississippi Department. Without a victory he could not expect a flow of recruits from Tennessee or Kentucky.[10] He rationalized "Our army was in that condition which rendered it more judicious the men should face a decisive issue rather than retreat. . . . I therefore determined to move upon Nashville, to entrench, to accept the chances of reenforcements from Texas, and even at the risk of an attack, in the meantime by overwhelming numbers, to adopt the only feasible means of defeating the enemy with my reduced numbers, viz., to await his attack, and if favored by success, to follow him into his works."[11]

Hood now moved on to Nashville from Franklin. Lee's corps led the march, followed by Stewart on December 1st, while the pitiful remnant of Cheatham's corps remained at Franklin "burying the dead, caring for the wounded, and reorganizing the remains of our corps." Cheatham's corps moved out on Friday, December 2nd, "and bivouacked within five miles of the city on Mr. Regan's place."[12]

Chaplain James H. McNeilly of Walthall's Division, Quarles Brigade, had rejoined the troops around Travellers' Rest. He had been helping to care for the wounded and bury the dead at Franklin and was thus separated from the men he knew. When reunited with them he rolled up in his blanket, feeling secure, after five days of very little rest. He says: "Very soon I was with the little handful of my boys sleeping my first undisturbed sleep for nearly a week. I have mentioned before the sense of security I felt when surrounded by the men with whom I had been so long associated, a security I never felt when away from them on some errand in the country. When men have shared common dangers

---

[9]Jordan and Pryor, p. 609.

[10]John P. Dyer, *The Gallant Hood* (New York: Bobbs-Merrill Company, 1950), p. 296.

[11]John B. Hood, *Advance and Retreat: Personal Experiences in the United States and Confederate Armies* (New Orleans: privately printed by Hood Orphan Memorial Fund, 1880). pp. 299-300.

[12]*OR,* Series I, Vol. 45, Part 1, p. 731.

and hardships they get to have a confidence in each other, which is one of the strongest elements of their efficiency in battle."[13]

The plan now was to partially invest the heavily fortified city on the southeast with his Franklin decimated army, and await Thomas' attack. Thomas was still assembling and refitting his command, and did not think he could successfully launch an offensive until additional troops arrived.

He particularly wanted to remount, equip, and arm the cavalry command of Major General James H. Wilson. Wilson was an energetic, young, new-breed, Federal cavalry commander, who had revitalized that arm of the service by seeing to it that they were armed with the Spencer carbine. Now here at Nashville, Wilson would have 9,000 mounted men and 3,000 dismounted of three divisions and one brigade. The mounted troops would be armed with the new seven-shot, deadly, repeating Spencer carbine, which would give them a tremendously greater fire power over the Confederates.

By December 2, Hood had his army before Nashville near the Brentwood Hills. He had established his command post at John Overton's home, Travellers' Rest, six miles from Nashville on the Franklin pike. Here he issued his order for deployment of The Army of Tennessee before Nashville. He knew that a direct assault on the heavily fortified city would be more disastrous than Franklin. In a ten mile arc, taking advantage of the elevations, and about three miles from the capitol building, the Federal fortifications extended northeast and northwest from above and below an omega shaped bend in the river.

Lee's corps established their line of battle first, then Stewart's corps formed on Lee's left while Cheatham's moved in on Lee's right.[14] This formation would change by the second day of battle. From Travellers' Rest Hood had issued the orders for the above alignment of the army before Nashville:

"General Lee will form his corps with his center upon the Franklin pike: General Stewart will form on General Lee's left; and General Cheatham on General Lee's right. The entire line of the army will curve forward from General Lee's center so that General Cheatham's right

---

[13] *Confederate Veteran*, 26, (June 1918), p. 251.

[14] Dyer, p. 297.

may come as near the Cumberland as possible above Nashville, and General Stewart's left as near the Cumberland as possible below Nashville. Each position will be strengthened as soon as taken, and extended as fast as strengthened. Artillery will be placed in all favorable positions. All engineer officers will be constantly engaged in examining the position of the enemy and looking to all his weak points. Corps commanders will give all necessary assistance. Not a cartridge of any kind will be burned until further orders, unless the enemy should advance on us."[15]

The pitifuly thin main line of resistance was formed which more resembled a skirmish line. Even with troops dispersed so thinly, the left flank of the army on the west was still about four miles from the Cumberland, and Cheatham's right flank over a mile from the river on the east. The total length of Hood's battle line was only four miles, while they faced Federal entrenchments of ten miles in length. Eight turnpikes converged on Nashville like the spokes of a wheel and crossed the river on a single bridge. Only light Confederate cavalry patrols covered the two turnpikes on the right and left respectively.[16]

The danger of a turning movement on either flank was evident early in the confrontation. The right flank was on the Nashville and Chattanooga railroad between the Nolensville and Murfreesboro pikes while the left flank rested on the Hillsboro pike. Initially, Forrest's cavalry divisions of Buford's and Jackson's was on Cheatham's right nearest the river while Chalmer's division was assigned the impossible task of protecting the army's left flank and covering the four mile interval to the Cumberland.

Shortly after arrival before Nashville, Hood's forces were further weakened when he ordered Forrest's cavalry, less Chalmer's division, together with Bate's infantry division, to proceed in the direction of Murfreesboro. Orders were to wreck track, bridges, and blockhouses down the Chattanooga railroad. Bate's infantry division had suffered least of the seven divisions engaged at Franklin. This dispersal of his cavalry force has been called "a masterpiece of suicidal folly."[17] On the

---

[15] *OR*, Series I, Vol. 45, Part 2, pp. 640-41.

[16] Shelby Foote, *The Civil War: A Narrative*, 3 vols. (New York: Vintage Books, 1974), 3:676-77.

[17] Stanley F. Horn, *The Decisive Battle of Nashville* (Baton Rouge: Louisiana University Press, 1956), p. 36.

other hand it has been pointed out that Forrest kept approximatley 9,000 to 11,000 Federals bottled up in Fort Rosecrans at Murfreesboro and unable to reenforce Thomas at Nashville. The use of the cavalry by Hood in this manner is questionable. Their presence would be greatly needed during the approaching engagement and the resultant rout.

On the morning of December 2, the infantry division of Major General William B. Bate was ordered to proceed toward Murfreesboro and destroy the blockhouses and bridges between that place and Nashville. This division consisted of the three small brigades of Brigadier Generals T.B. Smith, H.R. Jackson, and Finley's brigade commanded by Colonel Robert Bullock, in all 1600 men including Siccum's artillery battery. Bate went by way of Triune to Nolensville. When some seven miles from Murfreesboro he learned that the town had not been evacuated as thought, but instead was held by a force of 6,000 to 10,000 men under Major General Rousseau. Bate reported this intelligence to Hood at his headquarters on the Franklin pike, and received the following order:

Headquarters, Overton House, Dec. 2, 1864

Major General Bate:—

General Hood directs me to say that citizens reported some 5,000 Yankees at Murfreesboro. General Forrest will send some of his cavalry to assist you. You must act according to your judgment, under the circumstances, keeping in view the object of your expedition, viz., to destroy the railroad. This report is sent you for what it is worth.

> A.P. Mason
> Colonel and A.A. General[18]

Bate would face nearer 11,000 at Murfreesboro rather than the 5,000 Hood thought were there. Union General Granger had been recalled from near Athens, Alabama and reenforced Rousseau's 5,000 about the time Hood left Florence. It was thirty miles from Nashville to Murfreesboro, and Hood wanted to either defeat this force or, at any rate, destroy the railroad between the two place.

Forrest's cavalry consisting of Buford's and Jackson's divisions, joined Bate on Dec. 5, ten miles north of their objective where he assumed command of the combined operation of cavalry and infantry. In all, Forrest had less than 6,000 troops. He decided against an assault on Fort Rosecrans, and hoped to lure the Federals out into the open and

---

[18]*OR,* Series I, Vol. 45, Part 1, p. 744.

defeat them there. On December 7, about 3500 Federals came out of Fort Rosecrans, and Forrest deployed his infantry to meet them. He planned to use his cavalry against the flanks, but Bate's troops, except Smith's brigade, for some unknown reason, broke and fled before the oncoming Yankees, and Forrest's plans came to nought. He rode among the fleeing troops, and tried to rally them to no avail. Perhaps the remembrance of Franklin, eight days previously, was a factor in the panic, however the performance of this division at Franklin has been described as lackluster.[19] When the Confederate infantry, except Smith's brigade, failed to meet the charge, two pieces of artillery were lost with hardly a fight. Forrest grabbed the colors of one of the fleeing regiments and tried to rally the men. He was assisted by Bate and other officers in trying to stem the rout. "No appeal or personal example could restore the spirits of these troops, veterans though they were of every hard fought field in the west, and the peers in repute for shining conduct on all previous occasions of any of that army."[20] Forrest used the staff of the seized colors as an ineffective deterrent against the retreating troops, but finally, in a disgusted manner, he flung the staff and flag from him. Ross' Texas Cavalry brigade and Armstrong's Cavalry brigade forced the enemy to fall back.

On December 9th, Bate's division was recalled to Nashville. On the trip to Nashville from Murfreesboro, H.R. Jackson's brigade of Bate's division stopped at the Tennessee Insane Asylum and cut eight or ten cords of firewood for that institution. The Superintendent had reported to General Jackson that they were without wood for heating and no means to haul any.

After his brigade arrived at Nashville, General Jackson had a close call when a Federal shell exploded directly under his horse killing the animal. He was unhurt. He was in front of Fort Negley with other officers observing the enemy lines when this incident occured.[21]

Forrest made a personal reconnaissance of the Murfreesboro vicinity with 150 men of Pinson's Mississippi regiment, and again made

[19]W. J. McMurray in his *History of the Twentieth Tennessee Regiment Volunteer Infantry* (Nashville, TN: Publication Committee, 1904; repr., Nashville, TN: Elder's Bookstore, 1976) failed to mention this panic, although Smith's brigade, of which the 20th was a part had stood firm.

[20]Jordan and Pryor, pp. 632-33.

[21]*Confederate Veteran,* 17 (January 1909), 11-12.

a complete circuit to the Murfreesboro pike. He rightly concluded that the works around Murfreesboro "were really impregnable to the force at his disposition."[22]

On the evening of December 6th, Forrest had been slightly reenforced by two small brigades of infantry, Sears Mississippians and Palmer's Arkansas.

Several brushes with the Federals took place in and around Murfreesboro. On one occasion, Forrest's bugler, Gaus, was alongside his commander blowing the charge which drew fire from a nearby enemy regiment. It was reported that he had another bugle spoiled—this one, as once before, riddled with bullets. In another action, Forrest's chief of artillery, young Captain John W. Morton, fought his guns right into the heart of the town near the courthouse. Here, most of the horses of one gun were killed, and the gun was saved when carried off by hand. This was an action under command of the intrepid Buford. On the tenth of December, Buford was ordered to take post in the vicinity of the Hermitage. His orders were to picket the Cumberland between Huntsville and the mouth of Stones river. His force did not exceed 300 men, but he performed his duties most efficiently. On the 15th, Ross's brigade, captured a train loaded with supplies and subsistence intended for the Federal toops at Murfreesboro. Adjutant George L. Griscom, 9th Texas Cavalry Regiment tells of this capture:

> December 15—Pickets fire into a train coming up RR from Stevenson and tear up RR in front and rear of it—2 regts move out at midnight to surround it—9th held as train and battery guard til night when we move with battery to RR and find them skirmishing—9th ordered to opposite and 4th side of train battery getting into position and firing on it at 400 yards—Col J(ones) slips up with the 9th on foot pouring a volley into them with a yell they break and run—9th remounts & a charge is sounded by Brig Bugler & we go at them capturing the train & guard of Lt Col & 146 men the 9th getting 100 of them & running some under cover of a block house only a mile off—Train consists of 14 boxes heavy laden with rations especially sugar, coffee and crackers etc. etc.—after plundering the train and carrying off all possible especially coffee the train was fired and we retired to the pike with our booty and prisoners just in time to meet an advance of Genl Milroy again coming to the rescue of the 200,000 rations of sugar, coffee & hardtack intended for the starving garrison at Murfreesboro—fought him back 2 miles—when his anger cooling a little he fell back to Murfreesboro and our brigade to camp . . . Our brigade brought off more than six months rations of coffee some carrying 2 & 3 bushesl—a rich harvest of overcoats

[22]Jordan and Pryor, pp. 632-33.

here fell into our hands. . . . Camp with the train—Hood fights hard at N(ashville) all day. . . ."[23]

Another small diversionary movement was a raid into Tennessee and Kentucky from December 6 until after Hood's retreat out of Tennessee. This expedition was commanded by Brigadier General Hylan B. Lyon who was the commander of the Department of Western Kentucky. His force consisted of new recruits, poorly organized and equipped, and armed for the first time only the day before crossing the Tennessee river at Danville, Tennessee, the raid started out from Paris, Tennessee with 800 men, none of whom had been in the service, exceeding four months, and a majority of them only a few days. One hundred were dismounted, but few had blankets or overcoats, and many were without shoes or clothing to make a suitable appearance.

The weather was extremely cold, and many of the men were alrady frost-bitten. It was difficult to move the men when fires were built along the roads.

Lyon was a West Point graduate 1856 and an enterprising officer who had proved himself more than once in combat. He had opened and fought the first hour of the Battle of Brice's Crossroads for Forrest six months before. Near Elizabethtown, Kentucky while on the raid, his command learned of General Hood's defeat and retreat from Tennessee. This had a most demoralizing effect upon his command, "and within two days after it was ascertained that the Confederate army had left Tennessee 500 of my men deserted and returned to their homes. . . ." Results of this raid were as follows: "Captured three steamers; burned eight fortified courthouses, several important railroad bridges, depots, stockades, and blockhouses; captured and paroled 250 prisoners; and caused to be withdrawn from Nashville McCook's entire division of cavalry, consisting of 3,000 veteran soldiers, and detained at and near Louisville Wilder's brigade of cavalry, about 1500 strong thus causing a diversion in favor of General Hood in his retreat from Nashville of 4,500 men."[24]

Meanwhile, at Nashville, on December 8, the temperature dropped to about 12° F. Rain turned the whole country around

[23] George L. Griscom, *Fighting with Ross' Texas Cavalry Brigade, CSA,* edited by Homer L. Kerr (Hillsboro, TX: Hill Junior College Press, 1976).

[24] *OR,* pp. 803-806.

Nashville into a sheet of ice, and the frozen ground was covered with sleet or fine snow. Work on the unfinished fortifications stopped. Entrenching tools could not pierce the frozen earth. Barefoot, ragged, and thinly clad Confederates huddled together under a paucity of blankets and overcoats. Men could not walk, nor animals move on the glossy surface, and "sans tents, sans overcoats, sans shoes and in many instances almost sans clothing, the Confederates were in a sorry plight to endure such exposure."[25]

Chaplain McNeilly, Quarles' Brigade, reported food and clothing were scarce, and his shoes consisted of uppers and lowers tied together with string. To supplement their food they had to supplement their rations with parched corn. He says: "One evening about dusk a Yankee soldier raised his head above their works and impudently called out, 'Hello, Johnnie, have you parched your supper yet?' Instantly a dozen guns were leveled at him, and with a profane expletive the answer came: 'Duck you infernal Yank, or we will parch you.' "

At one time McNeilly went to the top of Compton's Hill (later Shy's Hill) and got his first view of Nashville since he had left it in 1862. He says: "When I left, the range of hills immediately south of the city was covered with large trees, many of them poplars four and five feet in diameter.

Now the hills were bare of trees and were crowned with heavy forts. The Capitol stood out clear and distant with fortifications around it."[26] The trees had been cut for use in the fortifications and for firewood.

The right flank of Hood's attenuated line was anchored at a deep cut on the Nashville and Chattanooga railroad. A redoubt had been built "on a high hill commanding the Murfreesboro pike and protecting the right of the Confederate position."[27] Forrest initially was on Cheatham's right before being sent to the Murfreesboro area. In advance of the railroad cut, the 300 survivors of Granbury's brigade occupied a small lunette. This brigade lost so heavily in officers at Franklin, including their beloved commander, Brig. Gen. Hiram B. Granbury, who was killed, that it was now commanded by Captain Edward T. Broughton. One of these survivors was Captain Samuel T. Foster, Company H,

---

[25] Dyer, p. 298.

[26] *Confederte Veteran,* 26 (June 1918), 251.

[27] Horn, *Decisive Battle,* p. 35.

24th Texas cavalry (dismounted), a typical company commander in the Army of Tennessee during Hood's Tennessee campaign. An excerpt from his diary follows:

> Dec. 9—cold weather. Commenced sleeting at 8 o'clock this morning and kept it up all day. Everything white with sleet and ice. Very cold. No firewood. No trees nearer than a mile.
>
> Dec. 11—Still froze up, all quiet on the picket line. I have dug out a fireplace in the side of the ditch, and burn cedar rails. Dec. 12—Still froze up. We are suffering more for shoes than anything else, and there is no chance to get new ones. At Brigade Headquarters there has been established a shoe shop, not to make shoes, for there is no leather, but they take an old worn out pair of shoes and sew moccasins over them of green cowhide with the hair side in. The shoe is put on and kept there, and as the hide dries it draws closer and closer to the old shoe. I am wearing just such covering now, and they are about as pleasant to the foot and about as comfortable as any I ever had. Dec. 13—I am on picket today as Brigade officer of the day . . . About one o'clock they sent a skirmish line out to fight us. About 4 o'clock I am wounded in my right leg about 6 inches above the knee, the ball going in, in the front side of my leg, passing out the back side to the right of the bone without touching it.
>
> I walk to where the doctors are, and they take me into a little house where there is a family, rip my pants open to examine the wound, sticks his finger in the bullet hole as far as he can, then he sticks his finger in the other hole where the bullet come out, then he put the forefinger of the other hand in the other, and then he jabs them in and out, and the woman of the house looked at the operation until she had to run out of the house to keep from fainting—They dress my wound and send me in ambulance to the Brigade Hospital which is at an old farmer's house in his kitchen. I am put in this kitchen which is about 16 ft. square, and as full of men as can lie down in it. We lay in tiers or rows and on the hardest floor imaginable. They gave me a[28] dose of morphine after dressing my leg, and I go to sleep.

On the 14th, Captain Foster was evacuated by ambulance, with three other wounded to Franklin. It was torture riding in the ambulance over the rough roads for 18 miles. At Franklin he was made fairly comfortable, given food, more morphine—then sleep. The town was full of wounded from the Battle of Franklin, and later after the retreat the non-ambulatory would fall into Federal hands; Captain Foster, who, at the beginning of the war had been a prisoner of war, was determined not to be taken with the wounded as we shall later see. The treatment of the wounded Confederate prisoners of war at the hands of the Federal Com-

---

[28] Samuel T. Foster, *One of Cleburne's Command,* ed. Norman D. Brown (Austin: University of Texas Press, 1980), p. 153.

missary General of Prisoners did not meet the approval of the Federal Surgeon George E. Cooper, Medical Director, Department of the Cumberland: "In Franklin, Columbia, and Pulaski a large number of rebel wounded were found who had been left by their army. A sufficient number of medical officers had been left with them to give them proper attention. These wounded were, as soon as practicable, transferred in hospital cars to Nashville, where they were placed in one large hospital. The medical officer in charge was directed, to furnish them all necessaries and such luxuries as the condition of their wounds required. This was done until the arrival of the Commissary General of Prisoners, who directed that the wounded rebels should be confined to prison hospital rations. I do not think that it is the intention of the Government to deprive wounded men, rebels though they be, of everything needful for their treatment. Prison hospitals being at a distance from the front, it was not expected that wounded men would be brought there till sufficiently well to travel, where diet would be but a matter of minor import. No surgeon can give good results if he be not allowed to use every article called for by sinking nature and to treat disease untrammelled by orders from nonprofessional men."[29]

The Spencer carbine was the most widely used carbine in the service toward the end of the war. By large scale issuance of this weapon to Federal cavalry, it gave them a tremendous advantage over the Confederates. Although, the Confederates were able to capture many of these carbines, they were unable to supply the necessary ammunition. The Spencer brought to a halt the use of the single shot muzzle loader and completely changed strategy and tactics. There were objections to the weapon, originally, because it was claimed that there was a waste of ammunition. This complaint was countered that it was "far easier to carry extra bullets than a stretcher." The Winchester was the heir to the Spencer.

Here is how the Spencer operated: "The Carbine was loaded by a tubular magazine that passed through the butt of the stock and held seven copper rimfire .52 caliber cartridges. A spring fed the cartridges toward the breech. The weapon was operated by pulling downward on the trigger guard lever, as with the Sharps. This dropped the breech

---

[29] *OR*, Vol. 45, Pt. 1, p. 110

block and extracted the fired shell. Closing the lever pushed a live cartridge into the chamber. The hammer was then cocked manually in a separate motion of the thumb. Ten extra magazines could be carried in a special box, giving the soldier 70 rounds for rapid fire. The carbine weighed 8¼ pounds and had a total length of 39 inches."[30]

On the Federal side, the cavalry was remounting and being supplied with arms and equipment, including the deadly Spencer repeating carbine, under the direction of Thomas' chief of cavalry, Major General James Harrison Wilson.[31] Intelligence received indicated a large increase in Thomas' cavalry, but Hood failed to order Forrest to return until too late.[32] Thomas had telegraphed Halleck on Dec. 1st "After General Schofield's fight of yesterday (Franklin), feeling convinced that the enemy very far outnumbered him, both in infantry and cavalry, I determined to retire to the fortifications around Nshville, until General Wilson can get his cavalry equipped. He now has about one-fourth the number of the enemy, and consequently is no match for him . . . I therefore think it best to wait here until Wilson can equip all his cavalry. If Hood attacks me here, he will be more seriously damaged than he was yesterday; if he remains until Wilson gets equipped, I can whip him and will move against him at once. . . ."[33]

The nagging and carping from Washington and City Point, where Grant's headquarters was located, would now begin after receipt of the above message. After this dispatch passed through the hands of the Federal Secretary of War Stanton, he contacted Grant on December 2nd, as follows:

"The President feels solicitous about the disposition of General Thomas to lay in fortifications for an indefinite period 'until Wilson gets equipment.' This looks like the McClellan and Rosecrans strategy of do nothing and let the rebels raid the country. The President wishes you to consider the matter."

This apparently was all Grant needed for him to be goaded into

---

[30]Boatner, p. 782; Faust, pp. 708-709.

[31]Wilson was a Major General five years after graduation from West Point. He was the last surviving member of his 1860 West Point graduating class at the time of his death in 1925.

[32]Hay, p. 141.

[33]*OR*, Series I, Vol. 45, Part 2, p. 3.

starting a series of dispatches to Thomas that would have exasperated any other general of less solid character. The above reference to Rosecrans was less than complimentary as indicated by a message from Grant to Stanton the same date: ". . . Rosecrans will do less harm doing nothing than on duty. I know no department or army commander deserving such punishment as the infliction of Rosecrans upon them. . . ."

At 11 a.m. December 2, Grant wired Thomas from City Point, Va.—"If Hood is permitted to remain quietly about Nashville, you will lose all the road back to Chattanooga, and possibly have to abandon the line of the Tennessee. Should he attack you it is all well, but if he does not you should attack him before he fortifies. Arm and put in the trenches your quartermaster employees, citizens, etc."[34]

Then at 1:30 p.m., same date Grant continued his harangue—"With your citizen employees armed, you can move out of Nashville with all your army and force the enemy to retire or fight upon ground of your choosing. After the repulse of Hood at Franklin, it looks to me that instead of falling back to Nashville, we should have taken the offensive against the enemy where he was. At this distance, however, I may err as to the best method of dealing with the enemy. You will now suffer incalculable injury upon your railroads, if Hood is not speedily disposed of. Put forth therefore, every possible exertion to attain this end. Should you get him to retreating, give him no peace."[35]

Thomas answered the above two telegrams at 10 p.m. the same day as received, December 2. He could have replied as did the Duke of Wellington during his Peninsular Campaign to the effect that he could not fight a war because of the necessity of replying to all of the correspondence emanating from the War Office and assorted politicians. But, the forbearing Thomas dutifully replied:

Your two telegrams of 11 a.m. and 1:30 p.m. today are received. At the time that Hood was whipped at Franklin, I had at this place but about 5,000 men of General Smith's command, which added to the force under General Schofield would not have given me more than 25,000 men; besides, General Schofield felt convinced that he could not hold the enemy at Franklin until the 5,000 could reach him. As General Wilson's cavalry force also numbered only about one-fourth that of Forrest's, I thought it best to draw the troops back to Nashville and wait the arrival of the remain-

[34] *Ibid.*, p. 17.

[35] *Ibid.*

der of General Smith's force, and also a force of about 5,000 commanded by Major General Steedman, which I had ordered up from Chattanooga. The division of General Smith arrived yesterday morning, and General Steedman's troops arrived last night. I now have infantry enough to assume the offensive, if I had more cavalry, and will take the field anyhow as soon as the remainder of General McCook's division of cavalry reaches here, which I hope it will do in two or three days. We can neither get re-enforcements or equipments at this great distance from the North very easily; and it must be remembered that my command was made up of the two weakest corps of General Sherman's army and all the dismounted cavalry except one brigade, and the task of reorganizing and re-equipping has met with many delays, which have enabled Hood to take advantage of my crippled condition. I earnestly hope, however, that in a few more days I shall be able to give him a fight.[36]

Thomas on the same day sent a telegram to General Halleck, who had been named to the new position of Chief of Staff when Grant had been made supreme commander. "Old Brains," as Halleck was called, was another echelon of irritation for Thomas. In his message of December 2, the same day Hood was moving into position before Nashville, Thomas described the situation before him:

I have succeeded in concentrating a force of infantry about equal to that of the enemy's, and as soon as I can get the remaining brigade of General McCook's division of cavalry here I will move against the enemy, although my cavalry force will not be more than half of that of the enemy. I have labored under many disadvantages since assuming the direction of affairs here, not the least of which was the reorganizing, remounting, and equipping of a cavalry force sufficient to contend with Forrest. The signal officers and reconnoitering parties report this afternoon that the enemy are moving to our right and going into position southwest of the city, or below. That would be by far the most advantageous position he could take for us, as his line of communication would be more exposed with him in that position than in any other. The iron-clads and gun-boats are so disposed as to prevent Hood from crossing the river, and Captain Fitch assures me that he can safely convoy steamers up and down the river. I have also taken measures to have the river patrolled as high up as Carthage.[37]

Thomas mentions in the above message McCook's remaining brigade of cavalry. The diversionary raid of Brigadier General Hylan B. Lyon, CSA, into Kentucky would deprive him of the Second and Third

[36]*Ibid.*, pp. 17-18.

[37]*Ibid.*, p. 18

brigades of that division as well as the services of the division commander, Brigadier General E.M. McCook.

On November 30, Thomas had wired Admiral S.P. Lee, Commander of the Mississippi Squadron asking him to patrol the Cumberland and convoy transports up and down. He received an agreeable reply from Lee, a cousin of the Confederate General Robert E. Lee, but a complaint that "your dispatch of 30th communicated an order instead of a request." Inter-service rivalry? Anyway the patient Thomas apologized in a telegram to the petty Federal admiral on Dec. 3 when he said, "I regret much that my telegram of the 30th implied an order to you, which was not intended."[38]

Another problem for the Federal cavalry around Nashville was a scarcity of "long forage." In a message to Quartermaster General Meigs, Brigadier General Robert Allen, Chief Quartermaster at Louisville reported that "There was no scarcity of hay at Nashville until after the burning of Johnsonville, (by Forrest on 3 Nov. 1864) since which time it has simply been impossible to keep up the supply . . . All that was possible to ship has been sent, and no-one who understands the circumstances will complain. General Thomas is satisfied."[39]

"Forrest's absence from the army was unnecessary and in the end calamitous. Cheatham repeatedly informed Hood that his observations indicated a large increase in Thomas' effective cavalry, but Hood failed to order Forrest to return until too late."[40] The cavalry build-up, arming, equipping, and remounting continued. Securing suitable and sufficient mounts would be the biggest problem for General Wilson. The Secretary of War had authorized Thomas to seize and impress horses and property especially in Tennessee and Kentucky. "Receipts may be given for the property by the seizing officer, designating the property and its value."[41] Thomas accordingly gave the order for the impressment of horses on the night of Dec. 2, and informed Halleck he hoped to have 10,000 cavalry ready in less than a week.[42]

---

[38] *Ibid.*, pp. 19, 30.

[39] *Ibid.*, p. 20.

[40] Hay, p. 141.

[41] *OR*, p. 18.

[42] *Ibid.*, p. 29

18

Wilson's cavalry showed the effects of having been in combat against Forrest's troopers. They had been outfought and badly mauled around Spring Hill on Nov. 29. As previously mentioned Thomas' plan was to remain on the defensive until Wilson was ready. This plan was questioned in Washington and at Grant's headquarters at City Point, Virginia. Thomas was well-known for his careful, plodding, methodical, unhurried manner. He had served as a major in Colonel Albert Sidney Johnston's old Second Cavalry and he knew that horses required care and maintenance to continue serviceable. In the pre-Civil War army Thomas had acquired a series of nicknames. As a West Point Cadet he was "old Tom;" "Slow Trot" as an instructor at the Academy and in the Second Cavalry, and "Pap Thomas" by his men in The Army of the Cumberland. When he held the left wing against tremendous odds at Chickamauga he won the title "Rock of Chickamauga," his most famous appelation. A personal description shows him to have been "six feet in height and weighing about 200 pounds . . . (he was) studious in his habits, deliberate but decided in action, and fastidious to the point of exasperation."[43] On December 2, Wilson was ordered across the Cumberland to Edgefield to get his men rearmed, equipped and clothed, the horses shod, and to secure remounts. Rearming included issuance of the deadly Spencer carbine. This weapon was said to have "fully doubled the efficiency of the (Federal) cavalry against ours (the Confederate) with only muzzle loaders."[44] Thomas' need for a stronger cavalry force was "a cavalry force sufficient to contend with Forrest" who has "at least 12,000" veteran horsemen. This was twice Forrest's strength and six times as many cavalry as Hood actually had at Nashville.[45] It seems that the Federals, throughout the war, over-estimated the strength of Forrest's meager forces. Perhaps it was, as the Federal General Wilson said, because "a master mind was at the helm" when Forrest was in command which made the numbers seem greater.

Pursuant to the authority given by the Federal Secretary of War, General Wilson issued orders sending detachments through certain parts of Tennessee and Kentucky to seize horses to mount his cavalry. He issued such orders on December 2, and laid out districts of the surrounding country for each of his divisions. Receipts were given and pay-

---

[43] Boatner, p. 836.

[44] E. P. Alexander, *Military Memoirs of a Confederate* (New York: n.p., 1912; Bloomington, IN: Indiana University Press, 1962).

[45] Foote, 3:681.

ment obtained later by voucher through the quartermaster. Andrew Johnson, the vice president elect and future president, had two fine carriage horses impressed for cavalry service. A traveling circus and the municipal street car company in Nashville were deprived of their animals.

Meanwhile, back at City Point, Grant, on December 5 telegraphed Thomas again as follows: "Is there no danger of Forrest moving down the Cumberland to where he can cross it? It seems to me whilst you should be getting up your cavalry as rapidly as possible to look after Forrest, Hood should be attacked where he is. Time strengthens him, in all probability, as much as it does you."[46] Grant's assumption that "time strengthens him" (Hood) was probably in error. Very few supplies were reaching the Southerners. A very tenuous line of supply from Decatur, Alabama furnished little of what the troops so badly needed. Certainly he was not strengthened by reenforcements. Also on the 5th of December, Thomas wired Halleck: "I have been along my entire line today. The enemy has not advanced at all since the 3rd instant. If I can perfect my arrangements I shall move against the advanced position of the enemy on the 7th instant." . . . Thomas went on to suggest that an expedition be sent out from Memphis against the Mobile and Ohio railroad to disrupt Hood's means of supply.[47] Thomas' message to Halleck, instead of satisfying Grant seemed to have made him even more impatient. He sent a forthright telegram ordering the beleaguered Thomas: "Attack Hood at once, and wait no longer for a remount of your cavalry. There is great danger of delay resulting in a campaign back to the Ohio River."[48] Before receiving this last message, Thomas, who was spending considerable valuable time reading and replying to telegrams, had telegraphed Grant:

> Your telegram of 6:30 p.m. December 5 is just received. As soon as I can get up a respectable force of cavalry I will march against Hood. General Wilson has parties out now pressing horses, and I hope to have some 6,000 or 8,000 cavalry mounted in three days from this time. General Wilson has just left me, having received instructions to hurry the cavalry remount as rapidly as possible. I do not think it prudent to attack Hood with less than 6,000 cavalry to cover my flanks, because he has, under Forrest, at least 12,000. I have no doubt Forrest will attempt to cross the river, but I am in hopes the gun-boats will be able to prevent him. The enemy has made no new developments today. Breckinridge is reported at Lebanon, Tenn., with 6,000 men, but I cannot believe it possible.[49]

---

46 *OR*, p.55

47 *Ibid.*

48 *Ibid.*, p. 70

49 *Ibid.*

20

Finally, no doubt feeling trapped by the circumstances of military and civilian authority, Thomas sent the following to City Point: "Your telegram of 4 p.m. this day just received. (Received at 11:25 a.m., 7th). I will make the necessary dispositions and attack Hood at once, agreeably to your order, though I believe it will be hazardous with the small force of cavalry now at my service."[50]

Hood had 1,200 cavalry at his disposal after detaching Forrest, one-tenth the number estimated in the previously quoted telegram to Grant, and a total of about half the 12,000 mentioned.

An hour before his message to Grant, Thomas had sent a message to Halleck that he would be able to mount 6,000 to 7,000 men within three days, and that he would attack as soon as General Wilson could get together a sufficient cavalry force to protect his flanks.

On December 7, Stanton added fuel to the fire, by telling Grant: "Thomas seems unwilling to attack because it is hazardous, as if all war was anything but hazardous. If he waits for Wilson to get ready, Gabriel will be blowing his last horn."[51]

Grant answered Stanton: "You probably saw my order to Thomas to attack. If he does not do it promptly, I would recommend superseding him by Schofield, leaving Thomas subordinate. . . ."[52]

Again on December 8th to Halleck, Grant said, ". . . If Thomas has not struck yet, he ought to be ordered to hand over his command to Schofield. There is no better man to repel an attack than Thomas, but I fear he is too cautious to ever take the initiative." In reply Halleck seems to have had a change of heart after originally helping to foment the harrassment of Thomas. His reply at 9 p.m., December 8th to Grant: "If you wish General Thomas relieved from command, give the order. No one here will, I think, interfere. The responsiblity, however, will be yours, as no one here, so far as I am informed, wishes General Thomas' removal."

Grant to Halleck at 10 p.m., same date: ". . . I want General Thomas reminded of the importance of immediate action. I sent him a

[50]*Ibid.*, p. 70

[51]*Ibid.*, p. 84.

[52]*Ibid.*

dispatch this evening which will probably urge him on. I would not say relieve him until I hear further from him."[53]

A telegram from Grant to Thomas at 8:30 p.m., December 8th seems to indicate that Grant had received some misinformation or misconstrued Thomas' message of the 7th. "It looks to me evident the enemy are trying to cross the Cumberland River and are scattered. Why not attack at once? By all means avoid the contingency of a foot race to see which you, or Hood, can beat to the Ohio."

The same date at 9:30 p.m., Thomas informed Halleck of the true situation to the effect that "No material change has been discovered in the enemy's position today."[54] Again on the 9th, he informed Halleck "There is no perceptible change in the appearance of the enemy's lines today. Have heard from Cumberland River, between Harpeth and Clarksville, and there are no indications of any preparations on the part of the enemy to cross. The storm continues."[55] These two messages should have calmed Grant's fears that Hood would cross the river, but the barrage of advice and threats continued. Perhaps Grant did receive information as indicated in his message of 8:30 p.m., on the 8th, but there is no record extant as such.

On the 9th the following War Department, unnumbered General Orders, dated December 9, 1864, appears in the Official Records presumably a draft to be used when directed by Grant: "Please telegraph order relieving him (General Thomas) at once and placing Schofield in command. Thomas should be directed to turn over all dispatches received since the Battle of Franklin to Schofield.

The President orders:

I. That Maj. Gen. J.M. Schofield assume command of all troops in the Departments of the Cumberland, the Ohio and the Tennessee.

II. That Maj. Gen. George H. Thomas report to General Schofield for duty and turn over to him all orders and dispatches received by him, as specified above."[56]

A further exchange between Halleck and Thomas took place on the 9th: "December 9, 1864—10:30 a.m. General Grant expresses much dissatisfaction at your delay in attacking the enemy. If you wait

---

[53] *Ibid.*, p. 96.

[54] *Ibid.*, p. 114.

[55] *Ibid.*, 1 p. 97.

[56] *Ibid.*, p. 114.

till General Wilson mounts all his cavalry, you will wait till doomsday for the waste equals the supply. Moreover, you will soon be in the same condition that Rosecrans was last year — with so many animals that you cannot feed them. Reports already come in of a scarcity of forage."

Thomas to Halleck, same date 2 p.m.:

... I regret that General Grant should feel dissatisfaction at my delay in attacking the enemy. I feel conscious, that I had done everything in my power to prepare, and that the troops could not have been gotten ready before this, and if he should order me to be relieved I will submit without a murmur. A terrible storm of freezing rain has come on since daylight, which will render an attack impossible until it breaks.[57]

Now it seemed that the elements were in the conspiracy against the badgered Thomas. Both armies were immobilized by the sheet of ice that covered the Nashville area. Thomas informed Grant of conditions at 1 p.m. on the 9th:

I had nearly completed my preparations to attack the enemy tomorrow morning, but a terrible storm of freezing rain has come on today, which will make it impossible for our men to fight to any advantage. I am therefore compelled to wait for the storm to break and make the attack immediately after. Major General Halleck informs me that you are very much dissatisfied with my delay in attacking. I can only say I have done all in my power to prepare, and if you should deem it necessary to relieve me I shall submit without a murmur.

Grant replied:

I have as much confidence in your conducting a battle rightly as I have in any other officer; but it has seemed to me that you have been slow, and I have had no explanation of affairs to convince me otherwise. I telegraphed to suspend the order relieving you until we should hear further. I hope most sincerely that there will be no necessity of repeating the orders, and that the facts will show you have been right all the time.[58]

At 11:30 p.m., December 9th, Thomas again tried to explain to Grant the situation at Nashville: "I can only say in further explanation why I have not attacked Hood that I could not concentrate my troops and get their transportation in order in shorter time than it has been done, and am satisfied I have made every effort that was possible to complete the task."

---

[57]*Ibid.*

[58]*Ibid.*

Grant, however, at 11 a.m., same date as above had wired Halleck as follows: "Dispatch of 8 p.m. last evening from Nashville shows the enemy scattered for more than seventy miles down the river, and no attack yet made by Thomas. Please telegraph orders relieving him at once and place Schofield in command. Thomas should be directed to turn over all orders and dispatches received since the Battle of Franklin to Schofield."

Again Halleck seems to have put on the brakes. Instead of issuing orders as the telegram directed, he wired Grant at 4:10 p.m, December 9th: "Orders relieving General Thomas had been made out when his telegram of this p.m. was received. If you still wish these orders telegraphed to Nashville they will be forwarded."

Grant wired Halleck from City Point at 5:30 p.m.: "General Thomas has been urged in every way possible to attack the enemy, even to the giving (of) the positive order. He did say he thought he would be able to attack on the 7th, but didn't do so, nor has he given a reason for not doing it. I am very unwilling to do injustice to an officer who has done as much good service as General Thomas has, however, and will, therefore suspend the order relieving him until it is seen whether he will do anything."[59]

There is no indication in the Official Records that Thomas knew of the order having been issued that would relieve him of command, but Grant, in the above message, seems to imply that Thomas was aware of such an order. How Grant could presume to judge of events 500 miles away in Nashville seems to indicate that at this stage of his successful career, he had come to look upon himself as the only officer in the Union Army capable of fighting a battle. He, at the time, was stalemated at Petersburg. This campaign, in its initial stages was marked by confusion and tactical failure of Federal subordinates. "The ten month operation was marked by: Lack of Union leadership and resolution; decrease in Union offensive ability; slow extension of the opposing lines to the west; and the brilliance of Lee's defense."[60] Yet, he could take the time to direct and criticize Thomas!

With Grant assuming to know so much as regarded the situation at Nashville, an informer was suspected. The General-in-Chief's

[59]*Ibid.,* pp. 115-116.

[60]Boatner, p. 646.

exasperation and impatience was fed by misinformation through some-one's subterfuge. Thomas should have been, in fact, praised for the speed with which he had assembled and organized such disparate groups as composed his army. The logistics alone was a tremendous undertaking. Brigadier General William D. Whipple had been with Thomas as Chief-of-Staff since July 1863, and had served his general through Missionary Ridge, all the battles of the Atlanta Campaign, and now at Nashville. He would be with Thomas after the war, also until Thomas' death in San Francisco in 1870 while commanding the Division of the Pacific. This faithful subordinate suspected someone was using the telegraph to "Undermine his commander." Andrew Johnson, Military Governor of Tennessee, was at first suspected, but the governor was too forthright to stoop to such tactics. Thomas conferred with Steedman on the matter, and Steedman assigned an officer, Captain Marshall Davis, to make an investigation of outgoing messages at the telegraph office. He returned with a copy of a message from General Schofield to Grant which read: "Many officers here are of the opinion that General Thomas is certainly too slow in his movements." Thomas was given the message to read, then asked, "Steedman, can it be possible that Schofield would send such a telegram?" Steedman, the only major commander under Thomas who was not a graduate of the military academy suggested that Thomas should be familiar with Schofield's handwriting. Thomas, after donning his eyeglasses, examined the handwritten message carefully, then said, "Why does he send such telegrams?" Steedman says that he smiled and replied to the trusting commander, "General Thomas, who is next in command to you and would succeed you in case of removal?" "Oh, I see," he replied sadly.[61]

The weather now brought to a halt any offensive plans Thomas may have had. "On the morning of Dec. 9, there began a terrible storm of freezing rain, and by evening had covered the whole countryside with a sheet of ice."[62] On the 10th, Thomas informed Halleck "... there is no apparent change in the enemy's position today. The sleet and inclement weather still continue, rendering offensive operations extremely hazardous, if not impossible."[63]

---

[61] Horn, *Decisive Battle,* pp. 53-54; Foote, p. 683.

[62] Henry, p. 406.

[63] *OR,* p. 130

Weather conditions were again reported to Halleck at 9:30 p.m. on the 11th.

> The weather continues very cold and the hills are covered with ice. As soon as we have a thaw, I will attack Hood.

In the meantime, at 4 p.m., same date, Grant sent the following order to Thomas:

> If you delay attack longer the mortifying spectacle will be witnessed of a rebel army moving for the Ohio River, and you will be forced to act, accepting such weather as you find. Let there be no further delay. Hood cannot stand even a drawn battle so far from his supplies of ordnance stores. If he retreats and you follow, he must lose his material and much of his army. I am in hopes of receiving a dispatch from you today announcing that you have moved. Delay no longer for weather or reenforcements.

Thomas dutifully replied:

> Your dispatch of 4 p.m. this date is just received. (10:30 p.m.) I will obey the order as promptly as possible, however much I may regret it, as the attack will have to be made under every disadvantage. The whole country is covered with a perfect sheet of ice and sleet, and it is with difficulty the troops are able to move about on level ground. It was my intention to attack Hood as soon as the ice melted, and would have done so yesterday had it not been for the storm.[64]

On December 11 before receiving Grant's "Delay no longer for weather..." message, Thomas had sent instructions to each of his four subordinate commanders as follows:

Have your command put in readiness tomorrow for operations. I wish to see you at my headquarters at 3 p.m. tomorrow. Acknowledge receipt.

Also on December 11, orders were sent to Major General Wilson by Thomas' Asst. AG to "commence the crossing of your command over the river tomorrow morning, as positive orders have been received by him (Thomas) to at once attack the enemy. They will go into positions as has already been designated." Wilson then issued special Field Orders No. 1 for the movement of his command at 8:30 a.m. "Brigadier General Hatch's Fifth Division and Brigadier General Johnson's Sixth Division would cross on the pontoon bridge; Briagadier General Croxton's First Division and Brigadier General Knipe's Seventh Division would cross on the floored railroad bridge. Every man, mounted and dismounted would cross and carry three days

---

[64]*Ibid.,* p.143.

rations."[65] This was a hazardous undertaking. Many of the horses slipped and fell on the icy bridges and streets. In some cases both horses and riders were injured. 9,000 of Wilson's troopers were mounted, and about a fifth of these did not have good mounts.

On December 12 at 10:30 p.m. Thomas sent Halleck the following message:

> I have the troops ready to make the attack on the enemy as soon as the sleet which now covers the ground has melted sufficiently to enable the men to march. As the whole country is now covered with a sheet of ice so hard and slippery it is utterly impossible for troops to ascend the slopes, or even move over level ground in anything like order. It has taken the entire day to place my cavalry in position, and it has only been finally effected with imminent risk and many serious accidents, resulting from the number of horses falling with their riders on the roads. Under these circumstances I believe an attack at this time would only result in a useless sacrifice of life.[66]

Schofield reported to Thomas that the enemy had withdrawn from their advance works and left only a picket line. He recommended patrolling the river, but didn't think Hood could move at that time. On the 12th commanders were ordered to supply the men with such clothing as needed. The troops were to have three day's rations in their haversacks and to be issued sixty rounds of ammunition. Supply trains were to be loaded, including forage and artillery and horses rough shod, effective the next morning.[67]

On the 11th there was the usual activity in preparation for an offensive move. Guards were placed around the camps to prevent straggling, yet Wilson informed his command that it was not expected to move the next day, presumably because of the weather. Thomas waited for a break in the icy condition. At City Point Grant had lost his patience and dispatched General John A. Logan on December 13, to Nashville to replace Thomas and assume command. Then on December 15, Grant would leave his lines around Petersburg and prepare to go to Nashville himself.[68] Thomas reported indications of a favorable weather change to Halleck on the night of the 13th, and that everything was ready for an

---

[65] *Ibid.,* pp. 148-49.

[66] *Ibid.,* p. 155.

[67] *Ibid.,* pp. 156-58.

[68] Thomas L. Connelly, *Civil War Tennessee—Battles and Leaders* (Knoxville: University of Tennessee Press, 1979). p. 94

offensive.[69] On the afternoon of the 14th, Steedman's command made a reconnaissance in force against the Confederate right. Captain Foster, Co H, twenty-fourth Texas Cavalry (dismounted), CSA, with Granbury's brigade on the extreme Confederate right, made the following entry in his diary for the 13th: "... The Yanks have been fighting our picket line with negroes, for nearly a week, and we have killed several so close that they can't get them. So they remain where they fell froze as hard as a log. About one o'clock they send a skirmish line out to fight us....."[70]

The troops of Thomas' command stood ready to move for two days, then on the morning of December 14th there was a noticeable change in the weather.

General John A. Logan, had temporarily commanded the Army of the Tennessee after the death of General McPherson in the fighting around Atlanta, and had hoped to receive permanent command. He was in command of that unit for only five days when Sherman replaced him with General Oliver O. Howard, a West Pointer. Thomas had had a part in denying Logan this assignment, and now Logan, on December 13th, was proceeding to Nashville to replace Thomas. He was to go by rail by way of Washington and Louisville.

When he had reached Louisville, if Thomas had attacked by that time, he was instructed to get in touch with Grant by telegraph for further instructions. If Thomas had not attacked by that time Logan was to proceed to Nashville and assume command as directed in his orders.

After Logan had left City Point Grant's impatience reached the point where he decided to go to Nashville himself. He left General Meade a note in which he said, "I am unexpectedly called away." Grant caught a fast packet to Washington where he went to the Willard Hotel before leaving for the west. He reached Washington on December 15.[71]

On December 14, there was another exchange of messages between Halleck and Thomas. At 12:30 p.m. Halleck sent the following:

It has been seriously apprehended that while Hood, with a part of his forces, held you in check near Nashville, he would have time to operate

---

[69]*OR*, p. 168

[70]Foster, 153.

[71]Foote, 3:684-85.

against other important points left only partially protected. Hence General Grant was anxious that you should attack the rebel force in your front, and expressed great dissatisfaction that his orders had not been carried out. Moreover, so long as Hood occupies a threatening position in Tennessee, General Canby is obliged to keep large forces upon the Mississippi river, to protect its navigation and to hold Memphis, Vicksburg, etc., although General Grant had directed a part of these forces to co-operate with General Sherman. Every day's delay on your part, therefore, seriously interferes with General Grant's plans.

Thomas, brushing off the additional issues Halleck had concocted, sent this brief reply: "Your telegram of 12:30 p.m. today is received. The ice having melted away today, the enemy will be attacked tomorrow morning. Much as I regret the apparent delay in attacking the enemy, it could not have been done before with any reasonable hope of success."[72]

When Grant arrived in Washington on the afternoon of December 15, he learned that there had been an interruption in wire service to Nashville for the past 24 hours with no word from Thomas. Grant's anxiety mounted. He feared a footrace between Hood and Thomas to see who could "beat to the Ohio." Also he was concerned about the whereabouts and intentions of Forrest. He was well aware of the capabilities and prowess of that great cavalryman. Grant conferred with Lincoln, Stanton, and Halleck, and told of his intention to go, in person, to Nashville. In the meantime he issued an order placing Schofield in command until Grant's arrival on the scene. This order was given to a Major Thomas T. Eckert for dispatch. This officer delayed in sending the message until after word was received from Nashville. Around midnight, Thomas' message of 8 p.m., December 14th came over the wires stating "the enemy will be attacked tomorrow morning."[73] Colonel Henry Stone of Thomas' staff recalled later: "From the 2nd of December until the battle was fought on the 15th, the general-in-chief did not cease, day or night, to send him (Thomas) from the headquarters at City Point, Va., most urgent and often most uncalled for orders in regard to his operations, culminating in an order on the 9th relieving him, and directing him to turn over his command to General Schofield, who was assigned to his place—an order which had it not been revoked, the great captain would have obeyed with loyal single-heartedness."

Thomas had built up a strong force numerically, but it was under-organized and inexperienced except for Schofield's command and three

[72]*OR,* p. 150.

[73]Horn, *Decisive Battle,* p. 61.

divisions of veterans under General Smith who had arrived from Missouri on the same day as Schofield. The remainder of the infantry was made up of new recruits, garrison troops and convalescents. Time was needed to organize and equip these men, especially the cavalry, and Thomas had done a superb job in a short period of time. Wilson, the cavalry commander described the arms of the cavalry he had inherited as a "museum on horseback." In the short time before action, Wilson organized, uniformly armed, and mounted most of his men. The cavalry corps "was prepared to act as an independent, mobile striking force—the decisive force in the impending battle."[74]

After Thomas' message of 8 p.m., December 14, the deluge of bothersome telegrams from City Point and Washington would not abate. If they had ruffled the stoic Thomas, he had not given any outward indication of it. Grant would take a parting shot after receiving word of Thomas' advance and initial success, but by then most messages would be congratulatory.

On the afternoon of December 14th at 3 p.m., Thomas convened a council of war at his headquarters in Nashville at the St. Cloud Hotel. He went over his plan of battle with his generals again, which was the same as that planned for the tenth but called off due to the ice storm. At the conference each commander was asked for opinions or suggestions. Special Field Orders No. 342, dated December 14, clearly indicated what each of the commanders was expected to do, as follows:

> As soon as the weather will admit of offensive operations the troops will move against the enemy's position in the following order:
>
> **First.** Major General A.J. Smith, commanding Detachment of the Army of the Tennessee, after forming his troops on and near the Hardin (*sic*) pike, in front of his present position, will make a vigorous assault on the enemy's left.
>
> **Second.** Bvt. Maj. Gen. J.H. Wilson, commanding the Cavalry Corps, Military Division of the Mississippi, with three divisions, will move on and support General Smith's right, assist as far as possible in carrying the left of the enemy's position, and be in readiness to throw his force upon the enemy the moment a favorable opportunity occurs. Major General Wilson will also send one division on the Charlotte pike to clear that road of the enemy and observe in the direction of Bell's landing, to protect our right rear until the enemy's position is fairly turned, when it will join the main force.
>
> **Third.** Brig. Gen. Th. J. Wood, commanding Fourth Army Corps, after leaving a strong skirmish line in his works from Lauren's Hill to his extreme

---

[74]Curt Johnson and Mark McLaughlin, *Civil War Battles* (New York: Fairfax Press, 1977), p. 141.

right, will form the remainder of the Fourth Corps on the Hillsborough pike to support General Smith's left and operate on the left and rear of the enemy's advanced position on the Montgomery Hill.

Fourth. Maj. Gen. John M. Schofield, commanding Twenty-third Army Corps, will replace Brigadier-General Kimball's division, of the Fourth Corps, with his troops and occupy the trenches from Fort Negley to Lauren's Hill with a strong skirmish line. He will mass the remainder of his force in front of the works and co-operate with General Wood, protecting the latter's left flank against an attack by the enemy.

Fifth. Maj. Gen. James B. Steedman, commanding District of the Etowah, will occupy the interior line in rear of his present position, stretching from the reservoir on the Cumberland River to Fort Negley, with a strong skirmish line, and mass the remainder of his force in his present position, to act according to the exigencies of the service during these operations.

Sixth. Brig. Gen. J.F. Miller, with the troops forming the garrison of Nashville, will occupy the interior line from the battery on Hill 210 to the extreme right, including the inclosed work on the Hyde's Ferry road.

Seventh. The quartermaster's troops, under command of Bvt. Brig. Gen. J.L. Donaldson, will, if necessary, be posted on the interior line from Fort Morton to the battery on Hill 210.

The troops occupying the interior line will be under the direction of Major-General Steedman, who is charged with the immediate defense of Nashville during the operations around the city.

Should the weather permit the troops will be formed in time to commence operations at 6 a.m., or as soon thereafter as practicable.[75]

Thomas had notified Halleck that "the enemy will be attacked tomorrow morning." On the 15th, Grant remained in Washington. News of the initial success of the Federal attack reached Washington, and Grant is said to have remarked, "Well, I guess we won't go to Nashville." He did send Thomas another message, half-instructive, half-congratulatory on the 15th at 11:30 p.m.:

I was just on my way to Nashville, but receiving a dispatch from Van Duzer, detailing your splendid success today, I shall go no further. Push the enemy now, and give him no rest until he is entirely destroyed. Your army will cheerfully suffer many privations to break up Hood's army and render it useless for future operations. Do not stop for trains or supplies, but take them from the country, as the enemy have done. Much is now expected.[76]

---

[75] *OR,* pp. 183-84.

[76] *Ibid.,* p. 195.

Is it any wonder that Thomas later asked Wilson "Why was I treated like a school boy?" The message also shows the General-in-Chief's lack of knowledge of the availability of supplies in a country that had been crossed and recrossed by contending armies and denuded of most material things needed by an army.

In addition to the administration of his immediate command at Nashville, Thomas kept in close touch by telegraph with naval authorities in command of gunboats on the Cumberland. These messages had to do with patrol of the river, convoy of transports and supply vessels, and reconoitering positions along the river where enemy crossings were reported or likely. Shoals prevented deep draft, larger boats, such as the iron-clads along an extent of seventeen miles.[77] On the 13th. Thomas requested Lt. Commander Fitch to patrol the Cumberland as far up river as Carthage to detect any enemy movement. Fitch, in turn, promised cooperation, and to engage all Confederate batteries brought against him.

Earlier on the 3rd of December, Colonel Kelly, of Forrest's command, was detached with 300 men of Rucker's brigade and a section of artillery to blockade the Cumberland 12 miles below Nashville. Here he captured two transports loaded with horses and mules. He took 56 prisoners and 197 horses and mules, then tried to burn the transports. Unfortunately, for the Confederates, they ran out of ammunition, and the two transports were recaptured by four gunboats.[78] Admiral Lee enumerated the difficulties along the Cumberland in a message to Thomas on December 14th: ". . . I cannot pronounce transports perfectly safe on a long shoal, crooked and narrow river, with high banks and hills, where a mounted enemy with artillery occupying the country is ready to attack them suddenly in different localities. . . ."[79] Light draft vessels, called "tin clads" were used on the shallow rivers such as the Cumberland with success. These steamers had a draft of 2-3 feet, and were protected by iron plates ½ x ¾ inch thick attached to their sides up to 11 feet above the water line. This was enough to protect them from medium to light artillery fire.[80]

---

[77]*Ibid.*, p. 101.

[78]Jordan and Pryor, p. 636.

[79]*OR*, p. 181.

[80]Faust, p. 757.

On the 14th, Lt. Commander Fitch was informed by Thomas' headquarters of the impending attack scheduled for the following day: "I have the honor to inform you that the enemy will be attacked at an early hour in the morning. If you can drop down the river and engage their batteries on the river bank, it will be excellent cooperation, for which the major-general commanding will be much obliged. It is very probable that these river batteries of the enemy will be attacked in the rear by our forces, and it is very desirable and necessary that your fire does not injure the attacking force, and to this end it is advisable you should be informed of the proposed attack."[81]

December 2 to 7 was fair and mild. On the night of the 7th, according to Adjutant Griscom, 9th Texas Cavalry, Ross' Brigade, around Murfreesboro, "It suddenly turns bitter cold." On the night of the 8th there was a cold rain mixed with snow and the temperature dropped. By the morning of the 9th, the ground was frozen and covered with snow and sleet.[82]

The Confederate infantry suffered greatly as they huddled in their shallow, unfinished works. Many were thinly clad and barefooted. Shoes, hats, blankets, overcoats, and clothing in general were in short supply. Blankets and oilcloths were spread among the troops and shared.[83] Henry George, Co. A, 7th Kentucky mounted infantry, CSA, says: ". . . the weather was extremely cold. Numbers of the infantry were barefooted and clad in old tattered clothing. Their suffering must have been terrible. The infantry of Hood's army must have possessed the highest order of patriotism, or they would not have undergone the hardships and suffering they did that winter."[84] The Tennessee natives around Nashville remarked that "The Yankees brought their weather as well as their army with them." An aide to Thomas reported that "Thomas would sometimes sit by the window for an hour or more, not speaking a word, gazing steadily out upon the forbidding prospect, as if he were trying to will the storm away."[85]

Rain began falling on Dec. 13, which melted the sleet and ice. On the same date Hood sent a message to Gen. Beauregard, the Department Commander, asking: "Can Baker's brigade, of this army, now at Mobile, be returned? All the troops we can get are needed here. . . ." A

---

[81] *OR,* Series I, Vol. 14, p. 182.

[82] Griscom, p. 194.

[83] Henry, p. 406.

[84] Henry George, *History of the 3rd, 7th, 8th, and 12th Kentucky CSA* (N.p., n.d.), pp. 134-35.

[85] Foote, 3:687.

report from the Provost Marshal General's office, Army of Tennessee on the 13th showed that only 164 recruits had been received since entering the State of Tennessee. It was also reported that 296 dismounted cavalry had been assigned to Johnson's division, but all had deserted except 42.[86] Cavalrymen objected to being converted to infantrymen, although some of the best troops in the army were the dismounted Texas cavalrymen in Granbury's brigade.

Hood had earlier tried to make a prisoner exchange with Thomas and received the following reply:

> General: I have the honor to acknowledge the receipt of your communication of this date, (Dec 5) making proposition for the exchange of prisoners of the Army of the United States now in your possession for a like number of Confederate prisoners belonging to your army in my hands. In reply, I have to state that, although I have had quite a large number of prisoners from your army, they have all been sent North, and consequently are now beyond my control. I am therefore unable to make the exchange proposed by you.[87]

The disparity in numbers between the Federal forces under Thomas and Hood's ravaged army must have been well known to the Confederate commander. He was indeed "scraping the bottom of the barrel" in his search for replacements. Later, Hood would claim that he beseiged Nashville, entrenched, and accepted "the chances of reinforcements from Texas." On the 6th, he had ordered Roddey's small cavalry force at Decatur, Alabama to join the army at once, and "As you march to join the army destroy as much as you can of the railroad...."[88] Apparently Roddey spent considerable time destroying track because he didn't arrive at Nashville. Also on the 6th, the Confederate commander sent the following recommendation to Secretary of War Seddon in Richmond: "I respectfully recommend that Major General Breckinridge with his forces, either be ordered into Kentucky or to join this army."[89] On the 5th he had directed the Assistant Inspector General at Corinth, Miss. to "send foward at once all men belonging to this army in proper detachments, with officers to preserve discipline and prevent straggling

---

[86] *OR,* Series I, Vol. 45, Part 2, p. 685.

[87] *Ibid.,* pp. 56-57.

[88] *Ibid.,* p. 655.

[89] *Ibid.,* p. 653.

on the march."[90] The additional men received as a result of this directive amounted to very few.

With a preponderance of Confederate sympathizers in and around Nashville, Hood certainly had a reliable intelligence network. He was certain to know of the continuing troop buildup taking place behind the Federal fortifications, because ". . . his spies sifted freely into and out of the city."[91]

Colonel James F. Rusling, Chief of Staff to Federal Quartermaster General Donaldson at Nashville in a letter written Dec. 11, 1864 describes the situation at that time:

> Our line of defense is a semi-circle, drawn around the city, from the Cumberland around to the Cumberland again, with the enemy's line one-half or three-quarters of a mile distant.
>
> Our line is immensely strong, crowned with forts and bristling with cannon; and both ends of it covered by gunboats. The Rebs might as well butt their brains against the Rocky Mountains as attempt to take it. Besides, our force is quite as numerous as theirs, if not more so; and if they don't "skedaddle" soon, we shall have one of the biggest fights you ever did see.
>
> Just now, both armies are doing their best to keep warm. For three days we have had bitterly cold winter weather; diversified with rain, hail, sleet and snow. The troops on both sides must have suffered terribly. As a consequence, the beautiful woods and groves that surround Nashville on all sides, and made it one of the most lovely towns I ever saw, are all going remorselessly down before the axes of the soldiers. We are getting in wood by rail and river for the hospitals here; but the army beyond has to take care of itself. . . .
>
> Of course the Rebs must have wood too; and away it goes by the thousands of cord daily. If the Rebs coop us up here another fortnight, there won't be a tree left within five miles of Nashville.[92]

On Hood's left flank, Rucker's undermanned cavalry brigade, together with Ector's infantry brigade of only 100 men, covered the excessive interval to the Cumberland. Rucker's Brigade, at the most, had about 1500 men which consisted of the 12th Tennessee, Colonel

---

[90] *Ibid.*, p. 655.

[91] Stanley F. Horn, *Tennessee's War 1861-1865* (Nashville, TN: Civil War Centennial Commission, 1965), p. 322.

[92] *Ibid.*, p. 323.

U.M. Green, the 14th Tennessee under Colonel Rolla White, the 15th Tennessee under Colonel F.M. Stewart, and the 7th Tennessee under Colonel W.H. Taylor. During the upcoming battle these veteran cavalrymen would face 15,475 mounted and unmounted enemy cavalry armed with Spencer repeating carbines. Private John Johnston was a member of the 14th Tennessee Cavalry, and later recalled the part his unit had in the two day's battle. His memory does not serve him well in some cases, because he says in his account of the battle that "The morning of the 15th dawned clear and bright and balmy."[93] In fact, a curtain of fog hung over the city of Nashville and environs. One Wisconsin soldier reported that "Men got lost while groping about their own camps" and "soldiers, sentinels, banners loomed up in mammoth proportions" and "music of unseen bands filled the air."[94]

A curtain of fog would lift to begin the two day drama. It would end when the curtain of night on the 16th fell upon the field of battle—triumph for the Blue—defeat for the Gray.

---

[93] John Johnston, "Reminiscences of the Battle of Nashville," edited by Tim Burgess, *Journal of Confederate History,* 1 (Summer 1988), 155.

[94] *Ibid.,* p. 120.

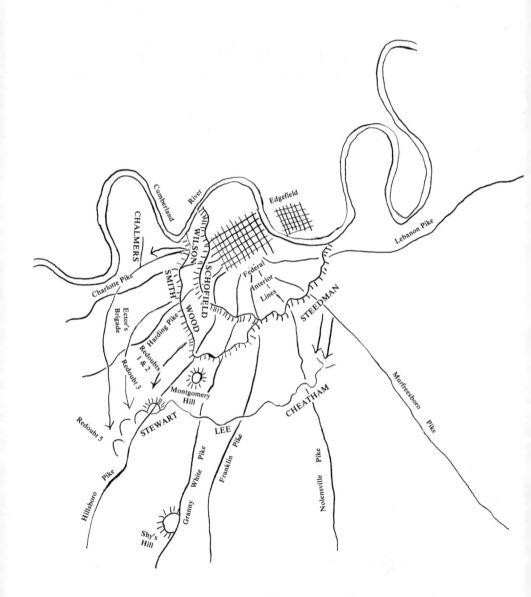

BATTLE OF NASHVILLE
FIRST DAY
DECEMBER 15, 1864

Cumberland River

Edgefield

CHALMERS

WILSON

SCHOFIELD

Lebanon Pike

Charlotte Pike

SMITH

WOOD

Federal
Interior
Lines

STEEDMAN

Ector's
Brigade

Harding Pike

Redoubts
1 & 2

Redoubt 3

Montgomery
Hill

CHEATHAM

Murfreesboro Pike

Redoubt 5

STEWART

LEE

Hillsboro Pike

Granny White Pike

Franklin Pike

Nolensville Pike

Shy's
Hill

III
The First Day's Battle

On the morning of December 14th, there was a noticeable rise in the termperature, and the snow and ice had begun to melt. Hood's intelligence network had informed him of the crossing of the Cumberland by Wilson's cavalry on the 13th from Edgefield, and that they were assembling for use against the Confederate left. General Stewart was directed to move a brigade of infantry to cover the Harding pike in support of the cavalry. Chalmers was also informed on the 13th that "the enemy was crossing their cavalry all day yesterday from Edgefield to Nashville."[1]

Before the cold weather had called a halt to military operations around Nashville, Thomas had assembled 71,842 men as follows:

9,000	at Murfreesboro
9,000	(approx.) garrison troops at Nashville, Johnsonville, and Chattanooga.
54,000	armed and equipped to be used as combat troops:
12,000	A.J. Smith
10,000	Schofield
14,000	Wood (Stanley's)
6,000	Steedman
12,000	Cavalry (Wilson)

In contrast to the Federal strength, Hood had 18,702 "effective total present" infantry and approximately 6,000 cavalry scattered around the area. "With the utmost effort Hood's army did not number 25,000 effectives."[2] If the numbers had been reversed Hood would have had difficulty breaching the defenses of the most strongly fortified city in America. As it was, there was not a ghost of a chance of success.

Captain Griscom with Ross' Texas Cavalry Brigade at Murfreesboro reported in his diary for December 14th, that it was "so dark foggy

---

[1] U.S. War Department, *War of the Rebellion: A Compilation of the Official Records of the Union and Confederate Armies,* 128 vols. (Washington, D.C.: Government Printing Office, 1882), Series I, Vol. 45, Part 2, p. 686 (hereafter cited as *OR*).

[2] Thomas Robson Hay, *Hood's Tennessee Campaign* (New York: Walter Neal, 1929; repr., N.p.: Morningside Bookshop, 1976), p. 139.

and cloudy cannot see a man 100 yards." This apparently was an indication of a change in the weather and of the coming thaw.

As late as December 14th, futile attempts were being made to get reinforcements for Hood. General Richard Taylor commanding the Department of East Louisiana, Mississippi and Alabama, tried to hasten troops belonging to the Army of Tennessee to their proper commands. Confusion of authority existed due to the overlapping of tactical command with that of departmental command. General Gideon J. Pillow and Marcus J. Wright commanding "Districts" were urged to organize provisional forces.[3]

At an early hour on December 15, the Federals began to assume their assignments as outlined in Thomas' plan of battle in Special Field Orders No. 342. The Quartermaster and assorted garrison troops, plus new recruits manned the shorter, inner line of defense, which was the main defensive line if the main, outer line should be breached. These defensive troops relieved the combat units of the Fourth Army Corps, commanded by Brig. Gen. Thomas J. Wood; Sixteenth Army Corps commanded by Major Gen. Andrew J. Smith; Twenty-third Army Corps, commanded by Major Gen. John M. Schofield; The Provisional Detachment, commanded by Major Gen. James B. Steedman; and, the Cavalry Corps, commanded by Major Gen. James H. Wilson.

Reveille sounded at 4:00 a.m. Troops were to move out at 6 o'clock. Ambulances and ordnance trains were to move out first. The heavy fog concealed the preparations and movements of the Federals, but would contribute to the delay in deployment. General Steedman originally was to make a feint against the Confederate right, but then was ordered to make a full-scale attack if he thought it would be successful. The main attack was to be against the Confederate left, and Steedman's attack was primarily to prevent Hood from moving troops from his right flank to reinforce the left. The Federal commanders had verbally rehearsed the planned attack which was a "grand left wheel" with Wood's position as the pivot.

Steedman's three brigades moved out two hours late, due to the fog, against Cheatham's corps on the Confederate right. Each of these Federal brigades was about the size of a Confederate division, and two

---

[3]*Ibid,* pp. 688-90.

of them were composed of Negro troops. This was the first use of Negroes in offensive action in the West in twenty months—since their bloody repulse at Port Hudson.[4] Under a heavy bombardment from the forts and batteries, plus fire from the gunboats on the river, Steedman's troops crossed Brown's Creek and encountered Granbury's depleted brigade of Texans, about 300 strong. Lt. Colonel Charles H. Grosvenor commanded the Third Brigade of the Provisional Division and tells of the assault on the Confederate right as he personally led the Second Battalion, Fourteenth Army Corps along with the Eighteenth Ohio:

> . . . we had to pass over a cornfield completely covered and enfiladed by the enemy's work. Two picket fences also stood right in our path, and these we had to remove. . . . The regiment (18th Ohio) charged gallantly over the palisade defense in front of the angle of the work, and succeeded in gaining with near 100 men the interior of the work. . . . In the meantime I led the Second Battalion in person to the assault of the right and southern angle of the work. . . . But the troops were mostly new conscripts, convalescents, and bounty jumpers, and on this occasion, with but few honorable exceptions, behaved in the most cowardly and disgraceful manner. The enemy, seeing the men hesitating and wavering, fired a volley and stampeded the whole line. In vain the officers tried to rally the men; in vain the old soldiers rushed forward themselves; the line broke, and all the men fled from the field.

The whole fire of the Confederates now concentrated on the Eighteenth Ohio and drove it back.[5]

Thomas had left the St. Cloud hotel at 5:00 o'clock on the morning of the 15th and rode the three miles to the battle front and established his command post on Lawrence Hill, which was a high angle out from General Wood's sector. This position gave him a clear observation of nearly all the field once the shroud of fog had lifted. Across the way he could also see Montgomery Hill, about one-half mile away where the Confederates had a similar salient. The fog did not entirely dissipate until around noon. Thomas probably could not see Steedman's movements, yet he was satisfied with the results since in his report he says ". . . Major General Steedman had, on the evening of the 14th, received orders to make a heavy demonstration with his command

[4] Shelby Foote, *The Civil War: A Narrative,* 3 vols. (New York: Vintage Books, 1974), 3:690.

[5] *OR,* Series I, Vol. 45, Part 1, p. 527. Bounty jumpers would enlist, collect their bounty, desert, then enlist again under an alias and collect another bounty. The cycle ended only if the culprit was apprehended. He was then sent to a combat unit.

against the enemy's right, east of the Nolensville pike, which he accomplished with great success and some loss, succeeding, however, in attracting the enemy's attention to that part of his lines, and inducing him to draw re-enforcements from toward his center and left."[6] The fog concealed Steedman's attack until the troops were near the Confederate fortifications. A Federal officer who had gone on top of a hill to observe the area, leaves this account in rather flowery, but descriptive language:

Underneath this silver sea our army was creeping noiselessly, stealthily forward. This silence was dread, fearful, ominous, for we knew that it betokened coming thunderpeals. The sun at last shone faintly through the fog, which drew thin and wavering, and here and there opened to reveal the point of a battle flag, or the head of some column of men. Sometimes a hill or highland emerged like an island from the deep. The mist gradually melted away, and lo, as far as the eye could reach, the valley was filled with armed men, moving still silently.[7]

Steedman's casualties among the regiments of Negro troops in the brigades commanded by Colonels Thomas J. Morgan and Charles R. Thompson were high. The Confederate skirmish line had fallen back before the oncoming Federals, but the lunette held by Granbury's brigade and Cheatham's main line stopped the attack. Some of the Federal units retired in good order, but others, as described by Colonel William R. Shafter "was done in a rather disorderly manner." One Confederate soldier described the action in this sector as follows:

Just as the batteries commenced firing, a body of troops was observed on our right moving in the direction of the rear of our position. When first seen, the distance was too great to tell whether they were white or black; but half an hour later it was known to be a division of negro troops. . . . Seeing that their route of march would bring them across the railroad below the end of the cut, it was decided to make a trap for them, and they were allowed to come on unmolested. . . . When they had moved forward far enough for our brigade to form in their rear, one of the divisions in our works about-faced and the other did likewise and wheeled to the left. We had the negroes in our trap, and when we commenced firing on them, complete demoralization followed. Many jumped into the cut and were either killed or crippled. Not a single white man was seen among the killed. Where were their officers?[8]

---

[6]*Ibid.*, p. 38

[7]E. E. Edwards, *Diary* (Greencastle: Indiana Archives of DePauw University, n.d.), December 15, 1864; and Walter T. Durham, "The Battle of Nashville," *Journal of Confederate History,* 1 (September 1988), 124.

[8]*Confederate Veteran,* 27 (1), 11; Stanley F. Horn, *The Decisive Battle of Nashville* (Baton Rouge: Louisiana University Press, 1956), p.76.

Colonel Thomas J. Morgan, commanding the First Colored Brigade, in his after battle report dated January 16, 1865, praised Colonel William R. Shafter, Seventeenth U.S. Colored Infantry as a brave and gallant officer.[9] In the same report he also reported that Lieut. Colonel Henry C. Corbin, Fourteenth U.S. Colored Infantry "does not possess sufficient courage to command brave men." Colonel Corbin was later courtmartialed on charges of "cowardice" and "misbehavior before the enemy," but was found not guilty and "most honorably" acquitted. Colonel Morgan goes on to say that a "Captain Baker in reality commanded the Fourteenth U.S. Colored Infantry in the battle."[10]

Many civilians came out to vantage points such as hills and roof tops to watch the battle. "Citizens of Nashville, nearly all of whom were in sympathy with the Confederates, came out of the city in droves. All the hills in our rear were black with human beings watching the battle, but silent. No army on the continent ever played on any field to so large and so sullen an audience."

The other Federal commands were moving to their prearranged assignments outside the works. There was some confusion, delay, and mistakes due to the dense fog and muddy roads. With Wood's Corps as the pivot, the Federal turning movement got under way. So far as the Confederate position was concerned, the pivot point "was about where the Confederate line bent back along the Hillsboro pike."[11]

The feint by Steedman had not deceived Hood, as is the traditional view, causing him to draw troops from his unengaged left and center to reinforce Cheatham. This was in Thomas' plan, but in fact it did not happen, nor did it need to happen since there existed such a disparity in numbers between the two armies.

As Steedman's diversionary attack proceeded, Wilson's cavalry and Smith's Corps started Thomas' grand turning movement, Smith's Corps on the Federal right, supported by Wilson's cavalry, some dismounted. They experienced some delay when McArthur's division moved across Wilson's front, holding up the cavalry until the infantry

---

[9]Shafter would later command the 17,000-man army that successfully invaded Cuba during the Spanish American War.

[10]*OR,* p. 537 and footnote.

[11]James M. McCaffrey, *This Band of Heroes* (Austin, TX: Eakin Press, 1985), p. 145.

had cleared. Generals Smith and Wilson had held a conference prior to the movement, and Wilson had sent a liaison officer to each division to coordinate movement between the two commands. Wilson had been ready to move at 6 a.m. according to his report, "but owing to the foggy weather and the delay of Smith's Corps could not advance until about 10 a.m.."[12] General Smith says in his report: "The First and Second Brigades of General McArthur, which moved out by the Charlotte Pike, owing to the roads diverging widely, and the stubborn resistance of the enemy's skirmishers, he having to silence one battery, did not connect with the main line until nearly 8:30. The cavalry then passed to our right and the movement began about 10 a.m., our orders being to touch to the left and guide right."[13] Once the wheel began to turn it proceeded with purpose and efficiency. The order "to touch to the left" was a part of the plan to link with Wood's right opposite Montgomery Hill, a lightly defended salient in the Confederate line north of Redoubt 1.

Brigadier General Wood, commanding Fourth Corps since the battle of Franklin where Stanley had been wounded, was a regular army officer and a Kentuckian. He had been stationed in the center at Chickamauga when Rosecrans received a false report that a gap existed between Wood's division and that of General Reynolds. He was ordered by Rosecrans to close up on Reynolds which he did after protesting. A real gap then existed which was duly exploited by Longstreet. Now he commanded the largest corps in Thomas' force of around 15,000 men. His orders from Thomas had been ". . . to support General Smith's left, and operate on the left and rear of the enemy's advanced position on Montgomery Hill." On Dec. 14 at 7:00 p.m. Wood assembled his division commanders and delivered them the following written orders:

> I. Reveille will be sounded at 4 a.m. The troops will get their breakfast, break up their camps, pack up everything, and be prepared to move at 6 a.m.
>
> II. Brigadier General Elliott, commanding Second Division, will move out by his right, taking the small road which passes by the right of his present position, form in echelon with General A.J. Smith's left, slightly refusing his own left, and maintaining this relative position to General Smith's troops, will advance with them. When he moves out he will leave a strong line of skirmishers in his solid works.

[12] OR, p. 551

[13] Ibid., p. 433.

42

III. Brigadier-General Kimball, commanding First Division, on being relieved by General Steedman, will move his division to the Hillsborough pike, inside of our lines, and by it through the lines, and form in echelon to General Elliott's left, slightly refusing his own left. He will maintain this position and advance with General Elliott.

IV. As soon as General Kimball's division has passed out of the works, by the Hillsborough pike, General Beatty, commanding Third Division, will take up the movement, drawing out by his left, and will form in echelon to General Kimball's left. He will maintain this position and advance with General Kimball; he will also leave a strong line of skirmishers behind the solid works along his present position.

V. The pickets on post, being strengthened when in the judgment of division commanders becomes necessary, will advance as a line of skirmishers to cover the movement. The formation of the troops will be in two lines— the front line deployed, the second line in close column by division, massed opposite the interval in the front line. Each division commander will, so far as possible, hold one brigade in reserve. Five wagon-loads of ammunition, ten ambulances, and the wagons loaded with the entrenching tools, will, as nearly as possible, follow immediately after each division; the remaining ammunition wagons, will remain inside of our present lines until further orders. One rifle battery will accompany the Second Division, and one battery of light 12-pounders will accompany each of the other divisions; the rest of the artillery of the corps will maintain its present positions in the lines.

It was 12:30 before Smith's Corps had made the swing to put them "on the left and rear of the enemy's position," and "prolonged the front of the Fourth Corps." They now advanced toward the entrenched Confederate line. Wood seems to have enjoyed battle. He says at one point in his report ". . . as the shells hurled through the air and burst over the troops from the enemy's batteries, added interest to the scene and showed that he was keenly watching our operations." In more colorful praise he continues:

When the grand array of the troops began to move forward in unison the pageant was magnificently grand and imposing. Far as the eye could reach the lines and masses of blue, over which the nation's emblem flaunted proudly, moved forward in such perfect order that the heart of the patriot might easily draw from it the happy presage of the coming glorious victory. A few minutes after 12:30 p.m. I deemed the moment favorable for the attack on the left and rear of Montgomery's Hill.[14]

Unknown to the Federals, Hood had moved the bulk of the troops from Montgomery Hill back to the main line on Dec. 10, leaving only a small holding force.[15]

---

[14]*Ibid.,* pp. 127-28.

[15]Horn, *Decisive Battle,* pp. 88-89.

43

At 1:00, ncecessary arrangements for the assault on Montgomery Hill were complete and Wood gave the order. Again he waxes eloquent in his report: "At the command, as sweeps the stiff gale over the ocean, driving every object before it, so swept the brigade (Second Brigade, Third division Col. P. Sidney Post, commanding) up the wooded slope, over the enemy's entrenchments; and the hill was won. Quite a number of prisoners and small arms were captured in the assault. This was the first success of the day, and it greatly exalted the enthusiasm of the troops. Our casualties were small compared with the success."[16]

Schofield's Corps had originally been stationed in reserve to the right and rear of Wood and overlapping Smith's left rear. After the assault by Wood on Montgomery Hill, Schofield was ordered to "move his command to the right to prolong General Smith's front." This forced the cavalry further around on the Confederate left and rear creating an untenable situation for the Southerners. Schofield completed the move behind Smith and formed on his right late in the afternoon. All forces now formed a continuous battle line. The extension of the line by Schofield permitted the cavalry to move further right against the Confederate left and rear. The massive wheeling movement now began to move against the Confederate left.

Wood's command moved forward to the angle in Hood's line just south of Montgomery Hill. Here, the right angle in the Confederate line was made by Gen. Loring facing north and Gen. Walthall facing west. General Kimball, commanding Wood's First Division attacked the angle and broke through the line.

Smith had formed on Wood's right and began his advance at about 10 a.m. with Hatch's cavalry division and Croxton's brigade on his right. They were heading for Stewart's left flank with ten times the number of men "Stewart would have until reenforcements could reach him."[17] Ector's brigade, now commanded by Col. David Coleman, had earlier been sent to assist Chalmer's cavalry cover the interval between Hood's left flank and the Cumberland. This 700 man brigade, composed of North Carolinians and Texans had been driven back across Richland Creek by Smith and Wilson. About 11 a.m. as they retreated between Redoubts 4 and 5, they were appealed to by Captain Lumsden

---

[16]*OR*, p. 128.

[17]Foote, 3:693.

commanding the four guns in Redoubt No. 4 to stay and help in the defense. They replied, "It can't be done. There's a whole army in your front." They kept going and formed on Walthall's left, since they were attached to his division.[18]

The Confederate left flank was refused southward from the point where Walthall's and Loring's divisions connected. Here, Walthall's men were behind a stone wall which ran south on the west side of Hillsboro pike from the angle in the line.

A redoubt is a field-work for strengthening or fortifying a military position without flanks. There were five of these detached works on the Confederate left. Redoubt No. 1 was the main salient in the line when Hood had pulled back from the advanced position on Montgomery Hill. At Redoubt No. 1, the line turned south to another fortified work east of Hillsboro pike called Redoubt No. 2. From here the line ran south-westward across the pike to Redoubt No. 3. Another work was detached a half-mile west of Hillsboro pike known as Redoubt No. 4. Redoubt No. 5, also west of the pike, was on a high hill and further out Hillsboro.[19] Redoubts 4 and 5 were manned but barely completed before the battle due in part to the frozen condition of the ground and a shortage of entrenching tools.

The main Federal attack under A.J. Smith and Wilson's cavalry on the extreme right was along Harding pike, then moved across Harding and Hillsboro pikes on a leftward swing. This brought them against Hood's left. To oppose this massive array of infantry and cavalry was Chalmer's small cavalry brigade and Coleman's (Ector's) depleted infantry brigade. These understrength units could offer only token resistance against the 24,000 now advancing. Rucker, commanding the Confederate cavalry brigade, and Coleman, commanding Ector's brigade, each had orders to retreat to the Confederate main entrenchments when they were attacked.

Private John Johnston, 14th Tennessee Cavalry of Rucker's Brigade remembered the morning of Dec. 15: "My mess had just finished a splendid breakfast which we had eaten from a large kettle filled with a mixture of beef, potatoes, turnips and probably other things, all cooked together. When we were greeted by the boom of a canon from

---

[18]*Ibid.*

[19]Horn, *Decisive Battle*, pp. 35-36.

over toward Nashville which was immediately followed by the call of "Boots and Saddles," and we hurriedly mounted our horses and galloped over the hills for a half a mile or more. . . ." Here they became engaged with the skirmishers, then a calm followed. Next one of the troopers said, "Look!—Just look at the Yankees." He says they could see line after line of Yankees. The field in his front was black with them. The enemy then moved past the front of the 14th and "swept Ector's Brigade out of their way, and pushed it back toward the Hillsboro Pike, and some of them Yankees going down the Harding Pike ran into and captured General Chalmers Headquarters. We didn't know it then, but we were cut off from the rest of our army."[20]

These troops that swept Ector's brigade back were the dismounted cavalry brigade of Hatch's cavalry division. Most of the Confederates seeing them thought they were infantry. This dismounted brigade was supported by a mounted brigade under Colonel Datus E. Coon. After the precipitate withdrawal of Ector's brigade, Hatch's division moved down the Harding pike to "Belle Meade," home of General Harding. General Chalmers and his staff had been guests there during the cold and icy period. The Hardings were very patriotic and loyal to the South. It was near here that Chalmer's headquarters train was captured by the 12th Tenn. Cavalry (Union) under Colonel George Spalding "consisting of fourteen wagons with records, clothing, forage, and safe."[21] In Chalmer's official report he mentions that Ector's brigade "swung around to rejoin the infantry on its right without giving me any notice of their movement." He goes on to report that this left the Harding pike open and the enemy was two miles in his rear when he received the first intelligence of their presence. His headquarters train had been parked in rear of Ector's brigade at the Belle Meade racecourse for greater security. Chalmers ordered Colonel Rucker to move across to the Hillsboro pike, and to leave the 7th Alabama to hold the position on the Charlotte pike until daylight. Private Johnston of the 14th Tenn. cavalry says: "General Chalmers, it is said, had ascertained that the left wing of our infantry was in position near the Hillsboro pike, or between it and the Granny White pike, so in order to get in touch with it we moved out after dark on a long circuitous march under Colonel D.C. Kelly toward

---

[20]John Johnston, "Reminiscences of the Battle of Nashville," edited by Tim Burgess, *Journal of Confederate History,* 1 (Summer 1988), 155-56.

[21]*OR,* p. 551.

Belle Meade was headquarters of Brigadier General James A. Chalmers, Commanding cavalry on Hood's left flank. This beautiful mansion is now open to the public. A video of the history of the plantation is shown and lovely docents accompany each group.

A brief fire-fight between a Confederate cavalry company under Lt. James Dinkins and a Federal force took place at Belle Meade late on Dec. 15. Bullets clipped shrubbery and nicked the square stone pillars.

the Hillsboro pike. After the night was somewhat advanced, the sky was overcast with clouds, and a light rain began to fall, mixed with a few flakes of snow. Stopping in front of a house, a man was sent in who soon came back with the head of the family whom he had aroused from his bed to act as a guide for us. This he seemed to do very cheerfully as he mounted a horse and led us as far as the Hillsboro pike, which we reached about midnight."[22]

Chalmers and Rucker, early in the day, were engaged in a desperate fight at Davidson's Landing on the Charlotte pike, where they repulsed the Federals and drove them back to their breastworks. As they drove the enemy back they "were joined by Colonel Mark Cockrell, a civilian, mounted on a good horse. He rode in front, and called to our men to come on. The field belonged to Colonel Cockrell, and he was not less than seventy-five years of age, and had little, if any, use of his right arm. He held the reins in his mouth, and his hat in his right hand. He was a picture, and his presence and bravery inspired our men to superhuman efforts."[23] The first action of the day for Rucker's brigade was early in the morning when they were shelled by the Federal gunboats. The gunboats were driven off by artillery fire, and it was later in the morning when he was attacked by General Richard W. Johnson's cavalry division. Johnson's plan was to move out the Charlotte pike with his dismounted men leading the way, but the infantry crossing in his front had delayed his move. The movement of the dismounted men was too slow to suit Johnson, so he ordered Colonel Thomas J. Harrison's First Brigade to attack Rucker. Rucker put up a stiff fight, and had time to move his artillery to the rear. Chalmers ordered a withdrawal to a line of hills about two miles back where there was a crossroad on the pike. It was here that he ordered Rucker to move across to the Hillsboro pike.

Captain James Dinkins of Chalmers escort company was ordered ahead at 4 p.m. to find the headquarters wagons at the Belle Meade racetrack. Dinkins says that he "and the escort reached a point opposite 'Belle Meade,' and, though the ridge (Walnut Ridge) was very steep, he succeeded in crossing, the men dismounting and leading their horses. The weather was intensely cold, and snow and ice covered the ground.

---

[22]Johnston, pp. 158-159.

[23]James Dinkins, *1861-1865 By an Old Johnnie,* facsimile reprint by Morningside Bookshop, 1975, p. 246.

He reached the racetrack and found the wagons had been burned. He rode down near the pike, and saw Federal soldiers moving about in the yard of Belle Meade. Several of them had no guns, some were on foot, others were mounted. He concluded it was a good opportunity, and moved the company around and behind the barn, whence they formed for a charge. The boys went yelling and firing as they passed through the yard. The enemy, some two hundred in number, were surprised and ran. They had no idea there was a Confederate soldier in the neighborhood. He pushed through the park, but, when near the creek, found a line of infantry behind a rock fence, and fell back. The enemy opened a hot fire, and as the boys returned through the yard, the bullets were clipping the shrubbery, and striking the house. Nine of the enemy were killed or wounded, and some fifteen captured. As they rode back, Dinkins saw Miss Selene Harding[24] standing on the stone arm of the front steps waving her handkerchief. The bullets were falling thick and fast about her, but she had no fear in her heart. She looked like a goddess. She was the gamest little human being in all the crowd. Dinkins caught the handkerchief from her hand as he galloped past and urged her to go into the house, but she would not, until the boys had disappeared behind the barn.[25]

Chalmers had tried to communicate with Hood, but to no avail. All his couriers were either killed or captured before they could reach him. They made their way toward the withdrawn left flank of Hood's army by a circuitous route through woods and fields and reached it about daylight on the 16th.

Brigadier General Thomas J. Wood, in his after-battle report gives the following decription of the terrain of the scene of action of the Battle of Nashville and adjacent countryside: "The basin in which the city of Nashville stands is inclosed on the southwest, south, and southeast by the Brentwood Hills. The Franklin pike runs nearly due south from Nashville. The Brentwood Hills consist of two ranges, or branches—the branch to the west of Franklin pike runs from northwest to southeast; the branch to the east of the Franklin pike runs from northeast to southwest; the two branches unite in a depression, or gap, about nine miles from Nashville. The Franklin pike passes through this gap, and in it is situated the little hamlet of Brentwood. The most northern point of each branch is about five miles from Nashville. From this description it will be perceived that the general configuration of the Brentwood Hills is that of a

---

[24]After the war, Miss Selene Harding married one of Forrest's brigadiers, Gen. William H. Jackson, who became a nationally known breeder of thoroughbred horses at Belle Meade.

[25]Dinkins, pp. 246-47.

rudely shaped V. Nashville is north of and about opposite the center of the space included between the two branches; Brentwood is at the apex. The valley inclosed between the two branches is nearly bisected by the Franklin pike. The surface of the Nashville basin is broken by detached hills, some of which rise to an elevation of 150 ft, with abrupt sides, densely wooded. About five miles from Nashville the Franklin pike passes along the base of one of these isolated heights, which is known as the Overton Hill."[26]

After the capture of the lightly defended Montgomery Hill, Wood received orders to shift his reserves to the right as far as possible since Schofield's command had moved to prolong Smith's right. His entire line now moved forward and engaged the enemy along the whole front. The artillery pounded the Confederate line, particularly the salient where the line turned southward at Redoubt No. 1. Wood says: "Impressed with the importance of carrying this hill, as the enemy's center would be broken thereby, I ordered up two batteries and had them so placed as to bring a converging fire on the crest of the hill. . . . The enemies artillery on this hill had been annoying us seriously all day. After the two batteries had played on the enemy's line for half an hour... I ordered General Kimball to assault the hill . . . nobly did the division respond to the order. With the most exalted enthusiasm and with loud cheers it rushed forward up the steep ascent and over the entrenchments. The solid fruits of this magnificent assault were several pieces of artillery and stands of colors, many stand of small arms, and numerous prisoners."[27] General Elliott had been ordered at 4 p.m. to make the assault on Redoubt No. 1, but Wood then ordered Kimball's First Division to make the attack when he felt Elliott had not properly responded to the order.

The claim for the honor of reaching the salient first was between Wood's troops and those of Smith's Sixteenth Corps, namely Third Brigade, First Division, commanded by Colonel Sylvester G. Hill. They claimed the honor of reaching the Angle first. At the time of the struggle for this salient the Confederates were already falling back to a new position along the Granny White pike.[28] At the end of Wood's first day of battle he had carried the entire front line of the enemy facing him

---

[26] *OR*, pp. 131-32.

[27] *Ibid.*, p. 129

[28] Horn, *Decisive Battle*, pp. 101-102.

and had captured eight pieces of artillery, five caissons, several hundred small arms, and about five hundred prisoners. He pursued the Confederates and tried to reach the Franklin pike, but the short December day and darkness precluded further action.[29]

Redoubt No. 1, at the angle in the Confederate line, fell to the combined assaults of Smith's and Wood's corps. Redoubts 4 and 5 were manned by men from Walthall's division. When Stewart perceived that he was to bear the brunt of the Federal onslaught, he placed Walthall in the refused line behind a stone wall facing west along Hillsboro pike. Walthall, in turn placed a company of infantry and a battery of artillery in each of Redoubt's No. 4 and No. 5. Remember that these redoubts were unfinished at the time of the battle. Sears Brigade held the salient which covered Redoubts No. 1 and 2. The line was not long enough to cover Redoubt No. 5 which was detached and unsupported on the Confederate left.

The Confederates were driven from the area west of Hillsboro pike. Wilson's cavalry swung left and overlapped Stewart's left flank threatening Redoubt No. 5. Smith's infantry pivoted on his own left, and connected with Wood's right, the hub of the movement.

The dismounted cavalry brigade of Colonel Datus E. Coon was joined by the First Brigade of McArthur's infantry division, plus a battery of artillery, and moved to the attack on Redoubt No. 5, after an hour long artillery exchange. General Smith's report describes the action:

> Pressing forward we come to the first works of the enemy . . . a small earthwork on the top of a hill, in which were four 11 pounder brass guns, the fort covered by another on the hill about 400 yards west, in which were two 12 pounder brass guns. Four batteries opened on the first fort, soon silencing their guns, and General McArthur was directed to take two brigades and carry the works by assault. Placing the First Brigade, Colonel W.L. McMillen, in advance, supported by the Second, Colonel L.F. Hubbard, commanding, the work was carried at a run. The cavalry on our right, at the same time charging directly under the guns of the rear fort on the hill, entered the first fort simultaneously with our skirmishers. The guns in the fort were all captured and about 150 prisoners. The cavalry claimed the guns as their capture, and more for their gallant charge than because they were entitled to the pieces, were conceded to them. The First and Second Brigades of McArthur's division, obliquing to the right without stopping,

---

[29]William Swinton, *Decisive Battles of the Civil War* (New York: Promontory Press, 1986), p. 459.

carried the second fort, capturing the two guns and about 200 prisoners."[30]

Colonel Datus E. Coon, commanding the cavalry brigade that overran Redoubt No. 5, says in his report:

General Hatch ordered me to charge and take the nearest redoubt. The enemy discovering the movement, changed their little messengers of shell to grape and canister, accompanied by heavy musketry from the infantry support behind their works. As I rode along the line I found each regiment competing with the others to reach the redoubt. The evidence, carefully examined, awards Second Lieut. George W. Budd, of Company G, Second Iowa Cavalry and his company, the honor of being first to scale the rebel works and take possession of the rebel cannon, which were four in number—Napoleons. On reaching the inside of the works he drew his saber upon the cannoneers and forced them to discharge the last load intended for the Federals on their own friends, then in plain view on the east side of the fort, not 500 yards distant. As the command took possession of this point a rebel battery opened from another redoubt, 600 yards distant, situated upon th top of a bluff some 200 feet high and protected by strong earthworks. General Hatch ordered me to charge the hill without delay. This order was promptly obeyed by all my command, officers and men. The "charge" was sounded, and in twenty minutes the colors of the Second Iowa Cavalry were planted on the works. During the charge the enemy kept up a brisk cannonading accompanied by heavy musketry firing from the infantry within the redoubt.[51]

The brigade commander mentions the state of exhaustion of his cavalrymen when they headed for and took Redoubt No. 4. Perhaps if these dismounted troopers had not been required to have their cumbersome cavalry sabers strapped to their waists, their state of exhaustion would have been mitigated.

Colonel Coon also reports that "the enemy kept up a brisk cannonading" in Redoubt No. 4. These artillery pieces consisting of four smooth-bore Napoleons were manned by forty-eight men under Captain Charles L. Lumsden, a VMI graduate. He had been commandant of cadets at the University of Alabama when the war began. The muster roll of his battery was said to have read like a "Who's Who" of Tuscaloosa society.[32] Assisting in the defense of Redoubt No. 4 was Captain Foster, Twenty-ninth Alabama, in shallow trenches extending from

---

[30]*OR*, Series I, Vol. 45, Part 2, pp. 433-34.

[31]*Ibid.,* p. 590.

[32]Captain Lumsden survived the war, but was killed in an accident three years afterward (Larry J. Daniel, *Cannoneers in Gray* [Tuscaloosa, AL: University of Alabama Press, 1984], note, p. 223).

both sides of the redoubt.[33] When Redoubt No. 4 was overrun after a three hour miraculous defense and display of valor, Sergeant James R. Maxwell tells of the final minutes as they were overwhelmed by the enemy:

> When the charging Federals passed my gun on the left of the redoubt, Lieutenant Hargrove ordered us to leave it. I ran towards Captain Lumsden's section, where Sergeant Jim Jones had turned No. 2 to fire canister at the Federals who were near gun No. 4. He called to me "look out, Jim." I dropped on my hands and knees whilst he fired that cannister right over my head. I took my place between his gun, and he gave the double cannister charge again. Captain Lumsden was standing with another charge of cannister in his hands. The command had been given to fire, but the man with the friction primers had run. I called out, "Captain he's gone with the friction primers." Says Captain Lumsden, "Take care of yourselves, boys." As he said that, down by my side between gun and embrasure dropped a Federal soldier with his rifle. I left him right there and lit out down the hill. As I got about halfway to the creek at the bottom of the hill, I ran over an infantryman's Enfield rifle. Noticing that it was cocked, with the cap shining on its nipple, I grabbed it up and fired at a Federal soldier who was waving his hat at the guns I had just left." Sergeant Maxwell says further: "I went down past Mr. Castleman's house, in front of which Captain Lumsden was reporting to General Stewart, who was congraulating Captain Lumsden for detaining the advance of the Federals so long. Hiller L. Rosser, one of our gunners had had part of his head shot away. That night as I was pouring some water for Lumsden to wash, he was picking something out of his beard and said: 'Maxwell, that is part of Rosser's brains.' "[34]

After the fall of Redoubts 4 and 5, the Federals heavily shelled Walthall's position along the stone wall. No direct assault was made, but his left was threatened by an overlapping force. He detached Reynold's brigade from his right to meet this force, but had to extend the other two brigades. Walthall notified General Stewart of the situation, and asked for more troops to assist Reynolds. He says: "Troops came, but the enemy were not checked. Reynolds, bravely resisting, was forced back, and it was with difficulty I withdrew my other two brigades to prevent their capture by the large force he had been opposing, which moved up in the rear."[35]

The fall of Redoubts 1 and 2 has already been mentioned, although the actual fall of these miniature fortifications was in reverse order to their numbered identification. Redoubt 3 followed the fall of No. 4. Brigadier General John McArthur's Third Brigade, commanded by

---

[33]Horn, *Decisive Battle,* p. 94.

[34]*Ibid.,* pp. 95-96; Daniel, p. 176.

[35]*OR,* Series I, Vol. 45, Part 1, p. 723.

Colonel Sylvester G. Hill advanced upon and captured Redoubt No. 3. Colonel Hill was killed in the the assault. Redoubt No. 2 opened fire on the victorious captors of No. 3, who then stormed the adjacent Redoubt No. 2 and entered it as the Confederates left. They turned the captured guns on Redoubt No. 1 which was then being assaulted by Wood's divisions.

The troops that Walthall received to assist on the left were Manigault's and Deas' brigades of Johnson's division, Lee's corps from the right. Later, General Stewart received the other two brigades of Johnson's division, Brantley's and Sharp's. Manigault had gone into the line opposite Redoubt No. 4 parallel to the Hillsboro pike. Deas' brigade was placed on Manigault's right to connect with Walthall's line. After the fall of Redoubt Nos. 4 and 5, and upon the advance of the Federals these two brigades put up but feeble resistance and fled. This enabled the enemy to outflank Walthall's position. Manigault's and Deas' brigades were rallied to protect a battery of guns which had been redrawn from Redoubt No. 1. The battery was placed on a hill east of Hillsboro pike. General Stewart says: "They again fled, however, on the approach of the enemy, abandoning the battery, which was captured. By this time the other brigades of Johnson's division had come up, but were unable to check the progress of the enemy, who had passed the Hillsboro pike a full half mile, completely turning our flank and gaining the rear of both Walthall and Loring, whose situation was becoming perilous in the extreme."[36]

Colonel W. D. Gale, Assistant Adjutant General of Stewart's Corps and signal officer tells of this incident that happened as Manigault's and Deas brigades fell back from the fighting along the Hillsboro pike: "As our men fell back before the advancing Yankees, Mary Bradford ran out under heavy fire and did all she could to induce the men to stop and fight, appealing to them, but in vain—Deas' brigade was there. General Hood told me yesterday that he intended to mention her courageous conduct in his report, which will immortalize her. The men seemed utterly lethargic and without interest in the battle. I never witnessed such want of enthusiasm and began to fear for tomorrow, hoping that General Hood would retreat during the night."[37]

When Manigault's and Deas' brigades bolted, Ector's brigade on the extreme left was cut off from Walthall's division, but made their way

---

[36]*Ibid.*, p. 709.

[37]Bromfield L. Ridley, *Battles and Sketches of the Army of Tennessee* (Mexico, MO: Missouri Printing and Publishing Company, 1906; repr., Morningside Bookshop, 1978), p. 413.

back without capture. Walthall seeing his left flank exposed, ordered his men to retire, which made it necessary for Loring to do likewise. This disengagement by these two fine divisions was done skillfully without panic. In the angle, Sears had managed to get most of the men in his brigade on the move in order to avoid capture.

All of Stewart's Corps was ordered to retire to a position between Granny White pike and Franklin pike in a southward prolongation of Lee's left. Schofield's corps, which had seen but little action so far had moved to Smith's left, and was on hand to pour through the gap left by Manigault's and Deas' brigades. Led by Major General Darius N. Couch's division, they secured high ground overlooking the Granny White pike, one of Hood's two lines of retreat.[38]

Bate's division had been with Forrest around Murfreesboro, but had rejoined Cheatham's Corps from this detached service on December 9th, together with Sears brigade. When Stewart's front began to crumble, Bate's division had been transferred from the right to shore up the left. Now the only Confederates west of the Granny White pike offering any resistance was this unit of Cheatham's corps that had made the long trek from the Confederate right on the Nolensville pike. Bate contested Couch's fresh division of Schofield's corps in a short, brisk firefight in the winter dusk, but was driven from the position he had just been assigned. Here are Bate's words: "I remained here (on the right flank) in the intrenched line, with the men uncomfortable from the extreme cold and the scarcity of wood, until the evening of the 15th, when I was ordered by General Cheatham to move to the left, where the fighting was going on, and should he not be there to report to General Hood. When I passed the Franklin turnpike streams of stragglers, and artillerists, and horses, without guns or caissons, the sure indicia of defeat, came hurriedly from the left. I formed my division for battle at once, its right resting near the turnpike, and communicated the situation to General Cheatham, who meantime had come up. It was nearly dark."[39]

---

[38]Curt Johnson and Mark McLaughlin, *Civil War Battles* (New York: Fairfax Press, 1977), p. 144.

[39]*OR,* Series I, Vol. 45, Part 2, p. 747.

Couch says he " . . . received the attack of a rebel column, which he completely repulsed in thirty minutes. . . . My line was fortified after dark. . . ."[40]

Ector's small, but all-purpose, brigade had been cut off when the brigades of Manigault and Deas had suddenly retreated eastward. General Hood had left his headquarters at Lealand in the morning, and moved to a hill southeast of the Compton house where he could better observe the action on his left. This hill, after the battle was known as Shy's Hill, named for the young colonel commanding the illustrious 20th Tennessee, famed in an army of famous regiments. The gallant Colonel Shy would fall the next day defending this strong point along with two-thirds of his regiment which were "either killed, wounded, captured on this fatal field nearly annihilating their glorious band, who had faced the storms of war for four long and eventful years."[41]

As Ector's (Coleman's) brigade passed this hill after being isolated by the retreat of Manigault's and Deas' brigades, General Hood stopped them and said: "Texans, I want you to hold this hill regardless of what transpires around you." They replied, "We'll do it, General." They formed on this hill which would be the center of the most dramatic and herotic action of the battle on the morrow, and in the dark began entrenching.

Bate's division, after being driven off the hill it had occupied, was put in "line of battle from the apex of the hill occupied by Ector's brigade in the direction of Mrs. Bradford's house on the Granny White turnpike, so that a prolongation of the same would strike the line then occupied by General Stewart. We went together and found General Sharp's brigade on the left of that corps, in the rear of Mrs. Bradford's house, somewhat parallel to the turnpike, its right resting near the woods. . . . A fire was kindled, by General Cheatham's order, to indicate the direction of my line from the given point on the left. I moved my command in the position indicated, but with much delay, attributable to the darkness of the night and marshy fields through which I had to pass. The artillery was unable to get up. . . . The earth had thawed, and the cultivated low ground was an obstruction through which even the ambulances could not pass with success; hence the artillery was left in the rear."

[40]*Ibid.*, p.370.

[41]W. J. McMurray, *History of the Twentieth Tennessee Regiment Volunteer Infantry* (Nashville, TN: Publication Committee, 1904, repr., Nashville, TN: Elder's Bookstore, 1976), p. 348.

Bate says: "Nearly one-fourth of the men were still barefooted, yet plodded 'their weary way' under these adverse circumstances (many with bleeding feet). . . ." While at Murfreesboro he had "pressed every pair of shoes which could be found for them, and in many instances the citizens gave them secondhand shoes."[42]

Bate's division spent the remainder of the night of December 15-16 digging in and making defenses with such tools as they had. A sleepless night together with hard work, and a scarcity of rations did not bode well for the coming day. The brief twilight encounter between Couch's Federals and Bate's division ended the fighting for the day.

The short December day and early darkness precluded Thomas' hopes of interdicting the last two avenues of escape for Hood. The Federal troops bivouacked where they were when the fighting for the day ended. In the darkness the lines of both armies ran in confused tangles. Lee's corps, which had seen very little action, except for the poor showing of Manigault's and Deas' brigades of General Edward Johnson's division, retired to Overton Hill, two miles down Franklin pike and established the right flank anchor with the line refused to the south. Hood's left flank was on the salient, later known as Shy's Hill, also refused southward around its western side in the shape of a fish hook.[43] The most severe fighting the next day would be centered around this salient. The entire corps of General Cheatham was transferred from the right to the left, leaving Lee on the right and Stewart in the center. It seems that Steedman, who had faced Cheatham on the 15th, was unaware that he had withdrawn from his front. Thomas reported that:

> Our line at night-fall was readjusted, running parallel to and east of the Hillsboro pike—Schofield's command on the right, Smith's in the center, and Wood's on the left, with the cavalry on the right of Schofield; Steedman holding the position he had gained early in the morning.
> The total result of the day's operations was the capture of sixteen pieces of artillery and 1,200 prisoners, besides several hundred stands of small arms and about forty wagons. The enemy had been forced back at all points, with heavy loss; our casualties were unusually light.[44]

Thomas returned to his headquarters in Nashville and got the following telegram off to General Halleck in Washington at 9 p.m.: "I attacked the enemy's left this morning and drove it from the river, below

---

[42] OR, Series I, Vol. 45, Part 1, pp. 747-48.

[43] Stanley F. Horn, *Tennessee's War, 1861—1865* (Nashville, TN: Civil War Centennial Commission, 1965), p. 337.

[44] OR, Series I, Vol. 45, Part 2, p. 39.

the city, very nearly to the Franklin pike, a distance of about eight miles. Have captured General Chalmers' headquarters and train, and a second train of about 20 wagons, with between 800 and 1,000 prisoners and 16 pieces of artillery. The troops behaved splendidly, all taking their share in assaulting and carrying the enemy's breastworks. I shall attack the enemy again tomorrow, if he stands to fight, and, if he retreats during the night, will pursue him, throwing a heavy cavalry force in his rear, to destroy his trains, if possible."

Thomas would now receive telegrams of a different cast from the ones he had received prior to the battle. Secretary of War Stanton wired him at 12 midnight: "I rejoice in tendering to you and the gallant officers and soldiers of your command the thanks of this department for the brilliant achievements of this day, and hope that it is the harbinger of a decisive victory, that will crown you and your army with honor and do much toward closing the war. We shall give you a hundred guns in the morning."

Grant also sent congratulations, but could not refrain from giving his competent underling the benefit of his sage advice.

Two telegrams were sent, one at 11:30 and another fifteen minutes later. "I was just on my way to Nashville, but receiving a dispatch from Van Duzer, detailing your splendid success of today, I shall go no further. Push the enemy now, and give him no rest until he is entirely destroyed. Your army will cheerfully suffer many privations to break up Hood's army and render it useless for future operations. Do not stop for trains or supplies, but take them from the country, as the enemy have done. Much is now expected."

Fifteen minutes later, Grant seems to have thought that congratulations on his part was due. "Your dispatch of this evening just received. I congratulate you and the army under your command for today's operations, and feel a conviction that tomorrow will add more fruits to your victory."

Grant then notified his Chief of Staff, Briagdier General John A. Rawlins at City Point that he would not go to Nashville in view of Thomas' message to Halleck.

Thomas also sent a telegram to his wife in New York: "We have whipped the enemy, taken many prisoners and considerable artillery."[45]

---

[45] *Ibid.*, pp. 194-95.

The entry in the Journal of the Confederate Army of Tennessee for December 15 states: "The enemy attacked both our flanks this morning about the same time, and was repulsed with heavy loss on our right, but toward evening he succeeded in driving in our outposts on the left."[46]

Thus ended the first day's battle.

---

[46]*Ibid.,* Series I, Vol. 45, Part 1, p. 672.

BATTLE OF NASHVILLE
SECOND DAY
DECEMBER 16, 1864

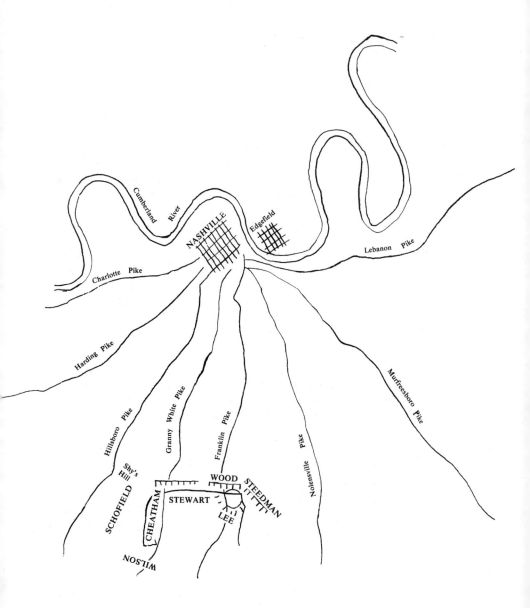

IV
THE SECOND DAY'S BATTLE

The futility of further resistance on the part of Hood never seemed to have entered his mind. It has been said that it "did not appear that he had the moral courage to acknowledge the utter hopelessness of his situation and to return to the line of the Tennessee." Thomas had some thought or hope that Hood would retreat in the night, but instead he had done as Schofield, his old West Point roommate, had predicted, "be right there, ready to fight . . . in the morning." Hood prepared for the coming day's battle as best he could. During the night his men worked frantically to strengthen their new position. Some units of Cheatham's corps had to bivouack on their way from right to left because of the darkness, and did not get into position until the next morning. The new line was shorter than that of the previous day, and covered only two of the eight spoke-like turnpikes coming into Nashville, namely Franklin and Granny White. With his flanks anchored on Overton's Hill (Peach Orchard) on the right, and Shy's Hill (Compton's Hill) on the left, his new line was shorter, more compact, and man-saving. It was in rear of yesterday's defensive front, and about three and a half miles in length compared with six miles the previous day.

Although Hood intended to stand and fight there seems to have been a lingering doubt in his mind as to his chances of success. He sent his wagon trains south to Franklin the afternoon of the 15th. Captain Samuel T. Foster, (Co. H, 24th Texas Cavalry (dismounted), who had been wounded on December 13th, and evacuated to Franklin by ambulance, wrote in his diary for December 15-16:

> Last night the wole town was in an uproar of excitment.
>
> The army trains commenced passing about midnight and kept passing until daylight. The report is that our army has been defeated, and are in full retreat, but before an hour by sun the excitement has subsided. It appears this morning that there has been a fight of some sort, but our army is still in front of Nashville.
>
> Later, the rumor is that the Yanks massed their forces in front of Stewart's Corpse (*sic*) and broke his line, but was reinforced by Cheatham, and retook the line again.[1]

Futher indiciation of uneasiness on the part of Hood is this message sent to Stewart at 8 a.m. on the 16th from his headquarters at Lea's house:

---

[1] Samuel T. Foster, *One of Cleburne's Command,* ed. Norman C. Brown. Austin, TX: University of Texas Press, 1980.

Should any disaster happen to us today, General Hood directs that you will retire by the Franklin pike, and Lee is directed to hold it in front of this large ridge, that you may pass to his rear. After passing Brentwood you would again form your corps in the best position you can find, and let the whole army pass through you. There are some narrow gorges beyond Brentwood toward Franklin. At all times the road must be left open for artillery and wagons, the men marching through the fields and woods.

A. P. Mason
Colonel and Asst Adjt. General

Cheatham would move by the Granny White pike.

A.P.M.

There is no written record that the other two corps commanders received this order. They may have received it also, and in the ensuing confusion of battle and retreat it was not preserved. Or, the order may have been passed verbally.

Stewart, in turn, pursuant to the above order, sent the following order to Walthall: "Should Bate fall back, keep your left connected with him, falling back from your left toward right and forming a new flank line extending to hill in rear."[2]

When the new defensive line was formed by Hood, Lee's corps fell back two miles along the Franklin Pike with his right, and the right of the army, on Overton's Hill, (Peach Orchard Hill). His divisions were posted with Clayton's on the right, Stevenson's in the center, and Johnson's on the left. Johnson's division had rejoined the corps after its poor showing in the fighting on the left on the 15th. The right of the line on Overton's Hill was refused southward with Gibson's and Stovall's brigades occupying this portion. Brantley's brigade of Johnson's division, was on the extreme right to further strengthen this flank.

The divisions of Stevenson and Clayton had seen very little action the previous day, and had not been engaged at Franklin at all. Johnson's division had seen limited action at Franklin when it was committed an hour after dark, yet their total casualties had been 587.

Why did Hood not place Lee's corps on the left to meet the main Federal thrust instead of the jaded, Franklin decimated units of Cheat-

---

[2]U. S. War Department, *War of the Rebellion: A Compilation of the Official Records of the Union and Confederate Armies,* 128 vols. (Washington, D.C.: Government Printing Office, 1882), Series I, Vol. 45, Part 2, p. 696 (hereafter referred to as *OR*).

ham's and Stewart's Corps? Perhaps because of the same lethargy and poor control evidenced at Spring Hill, where command and staff breakdown were so evident. Hood, himself, symbolized the army he now commanded, as well as the Confederacy itself, at this stage of the war. Later, on the retreat, one ragged Tennessean was heard to say, "Ain't we in a hell of a fix: a one-eyed President, a one-legged General, and a one horse Confederacy."[3]

After Chickamauga, Hood should have been retired for physical disability instead of being given field command. Sam Watkins of the First Tennessee Regiment describes his commanding general's physical condition at the time: "I remember when passing by Hood, how feeble and decrepit he looked, with an arm in a sling, and a crutch in the other hand, and trying to guide and control his horse. . . . I prayed in my heart that day for General Hood. Poor fellow, I loved him, not as a general but as a good man. . . . Every impulse of his nature was but to do good, and to serve his country as best he could."

At the end of the first day's fighting Cheatham's Corps was transferred from the right wing to the left. Watkins describes the situation from the private soldier's viewpoint: "We were continually moving to our left. We would build little temporary breastworks, then we would be moved to another place. Our lines kept on widening out, and stretching further and further apart, until it was not more than a skeleton of a skirmish line from one end to the other. We started at a run. We cared for nothing. Not more than a thousand yards off, we could see the Yankee cavalry, artillery, and infantry, marching apparently still further to our left. We could see regiments advancing at double-quick across the fields, while, with our army, everything seemed confused. The private soldier could not see into things. It seemed to be somewhat like a flock of wild geese when they have lost their leader. We were willing to go anywhere, or to follow anyone who would lead us. We were anxious to flee, fight, or fortify. I have never seen an army so demoralized. The whole thing seemed to be tottering and trembling."[4]

Earlier Watkins had mentioned the state of Cheatham's Corps after Franklin. "We can see our ragged soldiers, with sunken cheeks and

---

[3] Shelby Foote, *The Civil War: A Narrative,* 3 vols. (New York: Vintage Books, 1974), 3:709.

[4] Sam Watkins, *Co. Aytch,* (New York: Macmillan, 1962), p. 238.

famine-glistening eyes. Where were our generals? Alas! There were none. Not one single general out of Cheatham's division was left—not one. . . . Nearly all our captains and colonels were gone. Companies mingled with companies, regiments with regiments, and brigades with brigades. A few raw-boned horses stood shivering under the ice-covered trees, nibbling the short scanty grass. . . . We were not allowed to have fires at night, and our thin and ragged blankets were but poor protection against the cold, raw blasts of December weather. . . ."[5]

Watkins regiment, the grand old First Tennessee, was consolidated with its sister regiment, the 27th Tennessee, under the command of Lieut. Col. John L. House. Only six months ago, these two regiments, as part of Maney's brigade, helped to hold the Dead Angle on the Kennesaw line. A Georgia Colonel who had observed the action at this salient, had described these regiments as follows: "Words cannot picture the gallantry of those Tennesseans! It was grand—glorious! It was the sublimity of manhood!" But now, they "continued marching toward our left, our battle line getting thinner and thinner." The effective total present in the nine regiments of Maney's brigade as of December 13th was 654, or an average strength per regiment of only 73 men.[6] The fighting around Atlanta, and the Franklin slaughter had taken their toll, and now these regiments, smaller than original companies, were further extended to the left.

After moving to the left flank of the army, Cheatham's field headquarters was at the residence of Wesley Greenfield on the Franklin pike, while Hood's headquarters was near the Lea home. Bate's line connected on his left with Ector's (Coleman's) brigade while his right "in the cornfield, advanced toward Nashville, hence not quite at right angles with the turnpike." He went to Cheatham and warned him of the angle in the line where he connected with Coleman, and the fact that his right was not connected with anyone. Cheatham informed him that he was not authorized to change it, and that General Stewart was to connect with his right. Bate reported that the men "worked with alacrity the balance of the night (nearly all under my immediate supervision), and constructed works along my entire front impervious to ordinary shots."[7]

---

[5] *Ibid.,* p. 236-37.

[6] *OR,* Series I, Vol. 45, Part 1, p. 680.

[7] *Ibid.,* p. 748.

Bate's line was formed with H.R. Jackson's brigade on the right, connecting with Walthall's division, then Finley's and Tyler's. Finley's brigade (Finley had been badly wounded at Jonesborough, Georgia, Aug. 31—Sept. 1, 1864, and incapacitated) was now commanded by Major Jacob A. Lash. All his regimental commanders were captains. Tyler's brigade (Tyler had lost a leg in the fighting around Missionary Ridge) was commanded by Brigadier General Thomas Benton Smith and would be in the storm center of the fighting on Shy's Hill. Ector's brigade, which had been posted on this hill personally by Hood, as mentioned before, was on Smith's left occupying the west side of the angle. The line was then prolonged southward by Brown's old brigade of Alabama and Mississippi troops, now commanded by Brig. General Mark P. Lowrey. Lowrey was a Baptist minister with very little formal education, but a capable leader. Major General John C. Brown had been badly wounded at Franklin where he and his men had penetrated deepest into the Union defenses. His losses at Franklin had been terrible, and he himself so badly mangled in the three-way crossfire that his active career was ended. Lowrey's brigade now occupied a ravine and stretched to a hill south of Shy's Hill. On his left was Cleburne's old division, now commanded by Brig. General James A. Smith. This Smith was a West Pointer, Class of 1853, and he had proved himself in every battle of the Army of Tennessee since Shiloh. He was wounded at Atlanta, returned to duty, and participated in Hood's Tennessee campaign. Cleburne, the popular division commander had died along with five other general officers in the tragic slaughter at Franklin.

Upon assuming command of Cleburne's casualty riddled division, General Smith says: "Being the senior officer present with the division after the death of General Cleburne, I took command of it on my arrival. I found it much reduced in numbers, especially in officers, many having been killed and wounded in the Battle of Franklin on the 30th of November; nor was the tone and morale such as was desirable, owing to the fearful loss sustained in that battle. The division was at this time (Dec. 6) in line of battle on the extreme right of the army. . . ."[8] Smith's left covered the hill south of Shy's Hill and was refused eastward for a short distance. Bate describes the terrain on this part of the battlefield and the enemy artillery disposition:

---

[8]*Ibid.*, p. 739.

The hill on which my left rested was confronted by a similar one within 400 yards and an open field in the intervening valley. On this hill the enemy had planted several rifle pieces during the night. There was a deflection on the left of this, and then a series of hills occupied by the enemy extending to its left and culminating opposite Lowrey's left in an irregular range and greater altitude than those held by us, surmounted here and there by a commanding peak. The range of hills, from the point where Lowrey's left rested, extended at right angles across the Granny White turnpike, almost parallel to and in rear of my line of battle, a distance of not more than 600 yards, with open fields between.

At daylight I found a road skirting the inner border of the hills on my left over which artillery could pass, but not without difficulty. I ordered Captain Beauregard to send a section of Howitzers and place them upon a small plateau making out from the declivity of the hill just in rear of Finley's brigade, from which they could sweep the front of my right and the entire line of General Walthall. A desultory fire by sharpshooters was kept up during the night and morning until about 8 o'clock, when the enemy began to deploy additional masses, advanced his lines into the woods held by Stewart's corps the night previous, where he soon planted batteries."[9]

Stewart fell back to the new line and, his corps was now the Confederate center. He says in his after battle report: "During the night of the 15th the army was placed in position to receive the attack expected at an early hour next morning. . . the position of this corps, it being in the center, Lee's corps on the right, Cheatham's on the left, extending from the hill (Shy's Hill) occupied by Bate's division, Cheatham's corps, along the range of hills on the west side of the Granny White pike. The line of this corps extended from the side of the hill occupied by Bate across the pike, along a stone fence on the east side of the pike. In rear of the line and some half mile or more distant a high ridge lies in a general east and west direction, through the gaps of which runs the Franklin, Granny White, and other pikes."[10]

About 2 a.m., the corps engineer officer indicated the position in the new line where Walthall's division would be posted. Brigadier General Sears' 150 man brigade of French's division, which was attached to Walthall's command, had lost a portion of its strength in the fight for the critical angle at Redoubt No. 1 the day before. General Sears had lost a leg when a solid shot passed through his horse and struck

---

[9]*Ibid.*, p. 748.

[10]*Ibid.*, p. 710.

him just below the knee. He pulled most of his remaining men out after being assaulted from two directions. As they were retreating, he turned to survey the lost position with his field glasses, and was struck by the solid shot which crushed his right leg. At a field hospital surgeons removed his leg that night. Brigadier General Claudius W. Sears was from Massachusetts, and was a graduate of the 1841 West Point Class. He resigned from the army after one year and had gone South. He taught at Holly Springs, Miss., and at Tulane before the war. By the time the war began his sympathies lay with the South, and he entered the Confederate service as an enlisted man. He was recognized as one of the more combative leaders and was made a brigadier general in March 1864.[11]

The left of Walthall's division connected with Bate's right, Quarles' brigade, commanded by Brigadier General George D. Johnston, was on the right, and next in line was Brigadier General Charles M. Shelley, commanding Cantey's brigade, then Reynold's brigade, commanded by Brigadier General Daniel H. Reynolds, and on the left, connected to Bate's division was Sears' Mississippians now attached to Walthall's division. Ector's brigade commanded by Colonel Coleman had been withdrawn from the Angle on Shy's Hill around 8 o'clock in the morning, and was held in reserve under the cover of a hill on Walthall's left. Lines had to be further extended as a result to compensate for Coleman's withdrawal. Major Trueheart reported to Walthall with a section of artillery (four guns) and positioned them next to Captain Rene' Beauregard's guns. Later, Turner's Mississippi battery was brought up on the crest of the hill occupied by Maney's brigade. The artillery was spread so thinly that it made but feeble response to the powerful long-arm of the Federals. There were ten smoothbores in the vicinity of the salient on Shy's Hill, but they were outgunned by the "torrent of Federal fire that blasted the hill."[12]

Due to a serious eye infection Major General Samuel G. French had been given medical leave, and his division had been attached to Walthall's. This had included the small brigades of Ector and Sears. The other brigade was Cockrell's 1st Missouri. Brigadier General Francis Marion Cockrell had been wounded at Franklin and Colonel Flourney

---

[11]Patricia L. Faust, ed., *Encyclopedia of the Civil War* (New York: Harper and Row, 1986), p. 664.

[12]Larry J. Daniel, *Cannoneers in Gray* (Tuscaloosa, AL: University of Alabama Press, 1984), p. 177.

now commanded this fine brigade of Missourians. Major General French was from New Jersey and a West Point graduate, class of 1843. He left the army in 1856, became a Mississippi planter, and married into a Southern family. His interests and new allegiance compelled him to follow Mississippi, and Oct. 23, 1861, he was appointed Brigadier General. He was appointed Major General Aug. 31, 1862, and in May 1864 he was assigned to the Army of Tennessee where he saw action in the Atlanta Campaign, followed by Hood's Tennessee Campaign. After Hood's retreat and the break-up of the Army of Tennessee, French was assigned to Mobile where he and his command put up a stubborn resistance until their surrender on April 12, 1865.[13]

On December 6, Cockrell's brigade had been placed on detached service and ordered to the mouth of Duck River to build a garrison and a fort. After the Battle of Nashville, the brigade was ordered to abandon its position and rejoin the army on its retreat. At Bainbridge, the 1st Missouri Brigade rejoined Stewart's corps after having marched cross-country by way of Waynesboro from the mouth of Duck River. The further weakening of his command by Hood when he detached this brigade is again questionable.[14]

Brigadier General Francis Marion Cockrell was not a career military man, but proved to be an exceptional leader. The First Missouri Brigade, under his command as brigadier general, was one of the best drilled and most effective commands in the Army of Tennessee. The "thanks of the Confederate Congress" was bestowed upon Cockrell and his troops in May 1864 for publicly renewing their "pledge of fidelity to the cause of Southern independence." When the Atlanta Campaign began, Cockrell's troops were assigned to French's division and served with distinction in that command until the end of the war. After the war, Cockrell had a distinguished political career, and served five terms as senator from Missouri. During the war he was captured three times, and wounded in five different engagements.[15]

The only remaining division in Stewart's corps was Loring's,·

---

[13]Faust, p. 292.

[14]Ephraim McD. Anderson, *First Missouri Confederate Brigade* (St. Louis: Times Printing Company, 1868; n.p.: Morningside Bookstore, 1972), p. 574.

[15]Faust, p. 148.

between Walthall's right, and the left of Lee's corps. Adam's brigade, now commanded by Colonel Robert Lowry since Adam's death at Franklin, connected with Walthall's right.

The night of December 15-16, the Federals rested on their arms where darkness had stopped their advance. During the night hours they fired random artillery rounds in the direciton of the new Confederate positions. There was no rest for the Confederates. After fighting all day, the night was spent wielding spades and entrenching tools in an attempt to throw up what field fortifications they could in the cold and darkness. At some points they were close enough to the Federals to hear their voices and see their campfires.[16] Confusion among Confederate units especially on the left, was very evident in trying to form new positions in the darkness. On the right, Lee's corps had seen very little action during the first day of battle, and locating the new right flank was not a problem. He moved back southward two miles along the Franklin pike and established his line as heretofore mentioned with Overton Hill as the anchored right flank of the army.

After Bate's men occupied the line on Shy's Hill, where Ector's Brigade had been removed, Bate found that:

> The line established by Ector's brigade had been located in the darkness of the night, and was unfortunately, placed back from the brow of the hill, not giving a view and range on the front of more than five to twenty yards, and the curvature of the hill as well as the gradual recession of the lines from the Angle, forbid any flank fire giving protection to the front of the Angle. The works were flimsy, only intended to protect against small arms, and had no abatis or other obstruction to impede the movements of an assaulting party. From the hour this became a part of my line it was impossible to remedy it. The constant fire of sharpshooters from the neighboring hills made it fatal to attempt a work in front.[17]

Ector's brigade was unable to locate the military crest of the hill in the darkness. The construction of the hasty defensive works would later prove to be a great disadvantage to the defending force. This would permit an attacking force to be immediately upon them before defensive action could be taken. The new Confederate positions, in general, were

---

[16]Walter T. Durham, "The Battle of Nashville," *Journal of Confederate History*, 1 (Summer 1988), p. 133.

[17]*OR*, pp. 748-49.

completed about midnight, but minor adjustments were made next morning when possible.

The Federal units were in disarray as night closed in on the 15th, and they bivouacked in line of battle on the ground occupied at the close of day.

The weather on Friday, December 16, 1864, was fairly mild for a winter day, but about noon a cold rain began to fall. There seems to have been no formal written orders issued by Thomas for the resumption of action on the 16th. Some verbal instructions were given the corps commanders and passed down the chain of command to regimental commanders. Some "advanced at daylight" while others mention the specific time of 6 a.m., among them Steedman. General Thomas in his official report says that after the first day's fight: "The whole command bivouacked in line of battle during the night on the ground occupied at dark, whilst preparations were made to renew the battle at an early hour on the morrow."[18]

General Thomas J. Wood, commanding the Federal Fourth Corps in his report says:

> After having provided for the safety of the corps for the night I repaired to the quarters of the commanding general to receive his orders for the operations of the morrow. These orders were to advance at daylight the following morning, the 16th, and if the enemy was still in front to attack him; but if he had retreated to pass to the eastward of the Franklin pike, to face southward, and pursue him till found.
>
> At 11:30 p.m. on the 15th instructions were distributed to the division commanders to advance at daylight and attack the enemy if found in front of their commands; but if he should not be found to cross to the eastward of the Franklin pike and move southward parallel to it. At 6 a.m. on the 16th the corps commenced to move toward Franklin pike. The movement at once developed the enemy in our front, and sharp skirmishing commenced immediately. The enemy was steadily driven back, and at 8 a.m. we gained possession of the Franklin pike.[19]

It seems that the usual ambiguous orders as to time were given for resuming the attack on the 16th, "daybreak," "sunrise," "daylight," "break of day," etc. were prevalent in the armies of that time for starting

[18]*Ibid.*, p. 39.

[19]*Ibid.*, p. 130.

a movement or action. In Virginia, prior to Second Manassas, Pope had used the poetic term "at the very earliest blush of dawn."

General Wood, commanding Fourth Corps apparently was careful that the instructions he received from General Thomas the night of the 15th for the following day's operations were disseminated down to the regimental level. Major Joseph T. Snider commanding the Thirteenth Ohio Veteran Volunteer Infantry says: "Friday morning, December 16, before daybreak, in compliance with orders received the night previous. . . . At about 7:30 a.m., the advance again commenced."[20] Brigadier General Samuel Beatty, commanding Third Division of Wood's corps gives further indication of Wood's thoroughness: "During the night I received orders from the corps commander to advance at daylight the next morning, the 16th, conforming to the movements on my right."[21]

General Schofield reports that

In the night of the 15th I waited on the major-general commanding at his headquarters, and received his orders for the pursuit of the enemy on the following day. Our operations during the 15th had swung the right and right center forward so that the general direction of the line was nearly perpendicular to that before the attack. Only the right was in contact with the enemy, and was therefore much exposed. Apprehensive that the enemy, instead of retreating during the night, would mass and attack our right in the morning. I requested that a division of infantry be sent to reinforce the right which was ordered accordingly from Major General Smith's command. In response to this order General Smith sent five regiments and a battery (about 1600 men), which were put in reserve near the right.[22]

To appease the nervous Schofield, the Third Division, Sixteenth Army Corps, commanded by Colonel Johnathon Moore was sent to the right just before daylight the 16th. Later, before the general assault on the Confederate left, Schofield would ask for an additional division from Smith. After ascertaining that these troops were not needed in that sector, Thomas refused the request after a protest from Smith. General Smith in his report does not mention having been given any field orders prior to the advance of his corps on the 16th. In his report he says:

---

[20]*Ibid.*, p. 316.

[21]*Ibid.*, p. 289.

[22]*Ibid., pp. 345-46.*

"Night coming on, the troops bivouacked in line of battle. . . . On the morning of the 16th, advancing my lines in the same order as on the previous day, the First on the right and the Second Division on the left. It was discovered that the enemy had taken position at the base of a chain of hills called the Brentwood Hills, with a front nearly perpendicular to our line, and had strongly entrenched themselves by throwing up breastworks and massing artillery in every available position."[23]

General Wilson's cavalry corps consisted of the First Brigade, McCook's Division, commanded by Brigadier General John T. Croxton. The Second and Third Brigades were absent chasing General Lyon's Confederate raiders in western Kentucky. The Fifth Division under Brigadier General Hatch had two brigades, the First and Second; the Sixth Division, commanded by Brigadier General R. Johnson with the First and Second Brigades and a battery of 4th U.S. Artillery; the Seventh Division, commanded by Brigadier General Joseph F. Knipe with First and Second Brigades and an Ohio Light Artillery battery.

General Hammond's Cavalry pickets of the First Brigade, Seventh Division, had been along Granny White pike all night, and began skirmishing early on the 16th. The hilly country was not good cavalry terrain. General Hatch was on the right of Schofield's infantry and connected with Hammond's left. He was ordered to move with Hammond, and in conjunction to drive the enemy from their entrenched positions by hitting flank and rear. The movement began at 9:30 and they soon established themselves in the enemy's rear and perpendicular to the Granny White pike. They extended from the right of Schofield's corps, "a few hundred yards from the Hillsborough pike, across the Granny White pike toward the Franklin pike. The enemy was driven steadily back from hill to hill, but particularly in front of General Hatch's left. The positions occupied were heavily wooded and very difficult ascent, but Hatch with great labor, carried his battery into position enfilading and taking in reverse the enemy's line."[24]

Croxton's Cavalry Brigade (First Division) had been held in reserve along the Hillsborough pike, but late in the day on the 15th was ordered to move beyond Hammond's right to the Granny White pike. Not a lot was accomplished due to the lateness of the day.

---

[23] *Ibid.,* pp. 434-35.

[24] *Ibid.,* p. 552.

70

On the Federal left Steedman mentions that his command "moved on the enemy's works," December 16, at 6 a.m., in obedience to orders of Major General Thomas. He found the enemy position of the 15th evacuated during the night. He says his troops drove the Confederate cavalry, apparently Biffle's brigade, consisting of the 9th and 10th Tennessee cavalry, down the Nolensville pike, and took position to the left of Wood's Fourth Corps. His right rested on the railroad, and his left refused near the pike. Brigadier General Cruft, commanding the provisional division in Steedman's command, sent Colonel John G. Mitchell's brigade forward to occupy Riddle Hill to protect ambulance and ammunition trains. One of Steedman's brigade commanders was Colonel Benjamin Harrison, a future president of the United States. Steedman's orders had been to vigorously press and harass the Confederates—not just a show of force or a limited objective type of action. As a result, in conjunction with Wood, and in obedience to orders from Thomas, he assaulted the Confederate right. At 1 p.m., the assault was made with Colonel Charles H. Grosvenor's brigade and the Second Colored Brigade under Colonel Charles R. Thompson. Steedman praised the courage and steadiness of these troops, but they were forced back by the concentrated musketry fire and canister from Clayton's division and Pettus' brigade of Stevenson's division. After a reconnaissance, Wood had recommended the attack hoping to carry Peach Orchard Hill, and turn the Confederate right. This would effectively block the Franklin pike and eliminate that avenue of retreat.

Steedman says the assaulting force was driven back with great loss. Here on the Federal left was the bloodiest fighting of the Battle of Nashville. The 13th U.S. Colored Troops of Thompson's brigade had the greatest number of casualties for a regiment on either side—221.

As the day progressed, the weather became more inclement, and a cold rain set in around noon. At 3 p.m. Wood gave the order for his troops to advance and Steedman's troops moved simultaneously. In his report Wood says:

> "The front of the assaulting force was covered with a cloud of skirmishers... for the purpose of drawing the fire of the enemy... and to annoy his artillerists, and to prevent... the working of his guns. The assaulting force was instructed to move steadily forward to within a short distance of the enemy's works, and then, by a "bold burst," ascend the steep ascent, cross the abatis, dash over the rude but strong parapet, and secure the coveted goal.

The troops were full of enthusiasm, and the splendid array in which the advance was made gave hopeful promise of success. Near the foot of the ascent the assaulting force dashed forward for the last great effort. It was welcomed with a most terrific fire of grape and cannister and musketry, but its course was onward. When near, however, the enemy's works (a few of our men, stouter of limb and steadier of movement, had already entered his line) his reserves on the slope of the hill rose and poured in a fire before which no troops could live. Unfortunately, the casualties had been particularly heavy among the officers, and more unfortunately still, when he had arrived almost at the abatis, while gallantly leading his brigade, the chivalric Post was struck down by a grapeshot and his horse killed under him. The brigade—its battalions bleeding, torn and broken—first halted and then began to retire; but there was little disorder and nothing of panic. The troops promptly halted and were readily reformed by their officers. But for the unfortunate fall of Colonel Post, the commander of the assaulting brigade, I think the attack would have succeeded. . . . Not a prisoner was captured from us—a fact almost unparalleled in an assault so fierce, so near to success, but unsuccessful; and no foot of ground previously won was lost. After the repulse our soldiers, white and colored, lay indiscriminately near the enemy's works at the outer edge of the abatis.[25]

From the defender's point of observation, General Stephen D. Lee, commanding the Confederate left corps says:

About 9 a.m. on the 16th the enemy, having placed a large number of guns in position, opened a terrible artillery fire on my line, principally on the Franklin pike. This lasted about two hours, when the enemy moved to the assault. They came up in several lines of battle. My men reserved their fire until they were within easy range, and then delivered it with terrible effect. The assault was easily repulsed. It was renewed, however, several times with spirit, but only to meet each time with a like result. They approached to within thirty yards of our line, and their loss was very severe. Their last assault was made about 3:30 p.m., when they were driven back in great disorder. . . . Too much credit cannot be awarded Major General Clayton and these gallant troops for their conspicuous and soldierly conduct.[26]

General Wood whose troops made the assault on Lee's line felt that "while the assault was not immediately successful, it paved the way for the grand and final success of the day. The reinforcements for the Overton Hill, which the enemy had drawn from his left and left center, had so much weakened that part of his line as to assure the 'success' of General Smith's attack."[27]

---

[25] *Ibid.,* pp. 133-34.

[26] *Ibid.,* p. 688.

[27] *Ibid.,* p. 134.

General Lee says:

The enemy made a considerable display of force on my extreme right during the day, evidently with the intention of attempting to turn our right flank.
He made, however, but one feeble effort to use this force, when it was
readily repulsed by Stovall's and Brantley's brigades, which had been
moved to the right. Smith's (Cleburne's) division of Cheatham's corps,
reported to me about 2 p.m. to meet any attempt of the enemy to turn our
right flank. It was put in position, but was not needed, and by order of the
commanding general, it started to Brentwood about 3:30 p.m.[28]

Wood was correct in his assertion that troops were drawn from the
Confederate left and weakened that part of the line. Smith's division was
Cleburne's old command, and had suffered heavy casualties at Franklin, but saw very limited action at Nashville. This fine division called the
"Stonewall Divsion of the West" was unsurpassed for courage, energy,
and endurance by any other in the Confederacy. After Cleburne's death,
General Hardee said: "When his (Cleburne's) division defended, no
odds broke its lines; where it attacked, no numbers resisted its onslaught, save only once, and there is the grave of Cleburne." The rifles of
this division had been heard in all the battles of the West, and now their
depleted ranks would be a part of the famous rearguard which would
soon be needed.

The horrendous casualties suffered by this gallant division may be
illustrated by the following reorganization after the campaign:

First Florida formed from six regiments

First Georgia formed from three regiments

Fifty-fourth Georgia formed from two regiments and the Fourth
Battalion Georgia Sharpshooters

Govan's brigade was formed into one regiment from ten Arkansas
regiments and the Third Confederate

Granbury's brigade was consolidated into one regiment and
assigned to Govan as follows: Four Texas infantry regiments, and four
Texas dismounted cavalry regiments.

Lowrey's brigade was broken up after the retreat and assigned part
to Stewart's corps and part to Lee's corps.

---

[28] *Ibid.*, p.689.

73

The division virtually lost its identity. It has been said that "The old Stonewall Divsion of the West 'sat at the cradle of the Confederacy and followed its hearse.' "[29]

The repulse of the Federals on their left was accompanied by severe losses for the assaulting troops. The Peach Orchard Hill near "Traveller's Rest" was covered with the bodies of the blue clad dead and wounded strewn so thick that a person could have stepped from one body to another and not touched the ground.[30]

Smith's (Cleburne's) division had been moved into position on the extreme left of the army on the morning of the 16th West of the Granny White pike. It had been in position but a short time when Smith was ordered back to the right to assist Lee. Govan's brigade, however, was left in position—on Cheatham's left. The removal of these troops by Hood was a serious mistake. By the time they reached the right at around 3:30 the attack had been repulsed, and now there was not sufficient time for them to return to the beleaguered left. At 2:00, Stewart, who knew from experience what to expect, sent the warning message to Walthall as previously mentioned.

Shy's Hill was to be the scene of the most dramatic action of the day. Five Federal Infantry divisions formed a semicircle around the base of the hill on the North and West. As mentioned before, at about 8 o'clock, Ector's brigade was taken out of the line and placed in reserve. This caused Bate to stretch his lines still more and cover additional ground. He had no reserves.

By 12 o'clock the Granny White pike was in Federal hands, and Wilson's numerous cavalry had pressed Chalmers' little band of cavalry back on the infantry. Two of Wilson's divisions were fighting dismounted. The other two were mounted and swung wide around the Confederate left, and were astride the Granny White pike south of Shy's Hill. Wilson says the order was to "drive the enemy from the hills and push them as vigorously as possible in flank and rear." This order was given about 9:30 a.m. The movement began at once, and was sustained with great steadiness throughout the balance of the day. Hatch's

---

[29] Irving A. Buck, *Cleburne and His Command*, ed. Thomas Robson Hay (Jackson, TN: N.p., 1959), pp. 305-307.

[30] Stanley F. Horn, *The Decisive Battle of Nashville* (Baton Rouge: Louisiana Univeristy Press, 1956), p. 123.

division and Hammond's brigade, Knipe's division, soon succeeded in establishing themselves firmly in the Confederate rear, on a line perpendicular to the Granny White pike, and extending from the right of the Twenty-third corps, a few hundred yards from the Hillsborough pike across the Granny White pike toward the Franklin pike.[31]

Hatch had moved out on the 15th to the attack dismounted, with the exception of one regiment in each brigade mounted. General Richard W. Johnson, commanding the Sixth Division of Wilson's cavalry mentions the slowness of the movements of the dismounted cavalry, the first day of battle, owing, "I suppose, partly to their being unused to maneuver as infantry, partly to the difficulty in crossing the creek, and partly to their sabers, which the commanding officer of the Fourteenth Illinois cavalry had, with a singular shortsightedness, permitted his men to bring with them...."[32] General Johnson does not mention if these same troops of Colonel James Biddle's brigade were still so encumbered on the 16th. By noon, Hatch's division was across Granny White and secured a line of hills along the pike. He brought a section of artillery and fired fifty rounds into the backs of the defending Confederates. Also, these Federal cavalrymen through the efforts of their commander, Gen. Wilson, were armed with the Spencer repeating carbine. This was the first successful carbine to fire the metallic cartridge, and would definitely turn the war in favor of the North. The Ordinance Department was not at first (1861) impressed with the Spencer, but a small order was given the manufacturer. The first Spencer to be used in battle was by Sgt. Francis O. Lombard of the First Massachusetts Cavalry at Cumberland, Maryland on October 16, 1862. By summer of 1863 the Spencer rifle had been used at Hoover's Gap, Tenn., and on Sept. 19, 1863 at Chickamauga. At Gettysburg, Custer's Michigan Brigade used the Spencer against Jeb Stuart's Confederate cavalry. Around 75,000 Spencer carbines and rifles were produced for the Federal Army through 1865. Also, the Blakeslee cartridge box, invented by a Colonel Erastus Blakeslee of the First Connecticut Vol. Cavalry enhanced the firepower of the weapon even more. "His cartridge box was designed to carry between 10-13 tinned tubes containing seven Spencer cartridges each. This would give the Union cavalryman an additional 70-91 cartridges at his fingertips."[33]

---

[31] *OR*, p. 552.

[32] *Ibid.*

[33] John D. McAulay, *Carbines of the Civil War* (Union City, TN: Pioneer Press, 1981), pp. 6-9.

Wilson was a new breed of Federal cavalry officer that was emerging toward the last part of the war. In 1864 at the time of the Battle of Nashville he was only 27 years old, and a Major General only five years after graduating from West Point. He had headed the Cavalry Bureau in Washington from Feb. 17—April 7, 1864 where he insisted that that branch of the service be armed with the Spencer carbine. He saw considerable active service in Virginia before coming to the Western Theater again in 1864. He commanded the Cavalry Corps for Major General Thomas at Nashville, and reorganized and re-equipped his men into a potent and effective fighting force that helped in defeating Hood and pursuing him to end the Tennessee Campaign. He was the only Union general to outmaneuver and outmarch Forrest. On May 10, 1865 his troopers added to their laurels by the capture of Jefferson Davis. Wilson left the service in 1870, but returned at the beginning of the Spanish-American war. He retired in 1901 as a brigadier general, and died Feb. 23, 1925, one of the last Federal officers and last surviving member of his West Point class. Wilson only stood about five feet, ten inches in height, though his erect military bearing made him appear a trifle taller.[34]

Along the Confederate line there was a total of eighty pieces of artillery. These guns were spread thin and some could not be placed in position due to the mud, cultivated fields, and the darkness of the night of December 15-16. Stephen D. Lee had twenty-eight guns on the right; Stewart in the center had eighteen; Cheatham on the left had thirty-four. On the morning of the sixteenth the Federal artillery commenced a heavy bombardment all along the line, but especially against the salient hills on either Confederate flank. Shy's Hill was hit by the artillery barrage from three different directions. Schofield's batteries on the south facing the refused left flank of the Confederates hit Bate's left brigade on Shy's Hill from the rear. Other artillery batteries pounded this brigade from the northeast near the Bradford house. Captain Alonzo D. Harvey of the Fifteenth Battery, Indiana Light Artillery of Couch's division reported that he alone expended 560 rounds of shell from 1 to 4 p.m. against Shy's Hill. From the ridge across Sugartree Creek other batteries pounded Cheatham's lines from the east. To reply to this array of guns, the Confederates only had ten smooth bores in the vicinity. They were clearly out-gunned. General Jacob Cox men-

---

[34]Mark M. Boatner, *Civil War Dictionary* (New York: David McKay Company, 1959), pp. 930-31; and Faust, pp. 832-33.

tioned "The superiority of the national artillery was such that the Confederate gunners were forced to reload their pieces by drawing them aside with the prolonge, to the protection of the parapet."[35]

Lt. Thomas J. Ginn, Third Battery, Indiana Light Artillery, Second Brigade, Second Division, A.J. Smith's corps, reported that during the day (16th) his battery fired 923 shell, case, and solid shot. On the Confederate right flank it was very much the same story. The guns of Wood's and Steedman's commands as well as Smith's corps, laid down a heavy barrage. General Lee, says in his report: "About 9 a.m. on the 16th the enemy having placed a large number of guns in position, opened a terrible artillery fire on my line, principally on the Franklin pike. This lasted about two hours, when the enemy moved to the assault."[36]

General Holtzclaw, commanding a brigade in Clayton's division, Lee's corps, after the fighting on the 15th reported: "At night the army dropped back to a new line one mile. I brought up the rear and gained my new position at 2 a.m., which was right across the Franklin pike, the road being my center, my left behind a stone wall. I commenced work immediately, and continued until the opening of the enemy's batteries at 7 a.m. obliged me to desist. . . . At 10 o'clock he made a desperate charge, but was driven back with loss. He then commenced a most furious shelling from three six-gun batteries . . . One battery of unusually heavy guns was brought down the pike to within 600 yards of my line. The conformation of the ground prevented me sharpshooting it sufficiently to drive it away. . . . The shelling by the enemy's batteries between 12 and 3 p.m. was the most furious I ever witnessed, while the range was so precise that scarce a shell failed to explode in the line."[37]

Lee's Chief of Artillery, Lieutenant Colonel Llewellyn Hoxton says: "Courtney's battalion opened upon the enemy's skirmishers as soon as they came in view, and in return received a terrific fire from the enemy's batteries, which killed and crippled many of their horses. Orders were received by me and given to my battalions not to fire except on lines of battle or well-defined bodies of men, and consequently my batteries did little firing after 9 o'clock, except when the enemy charged

---

[35] Daniel, p. 177.

[36] *OR*, p. 688.

[37] *Ibid.*, p. 706.

the lines. . . ." He states further: "During the whole day (of the 16th) the batteries were subjected to a terrible artillery fire, which destroyed a large number of horses in the best cover I could obtain, and exploded two limber chests."[38]

Along Stewart's front in the center of Hood's line: "At an early hour in the morning the enemy approached, placing artillery in position and opening a heavy fire, which continued almost incessantly through the day."[39]

General Stevenson, Lee's corps, noted the "artillery fire which I have never seen surpassed for heaviness, continuance, and accuracy."

Capt. John W. Lowell acting Chief of Artillery, Second Division, under Federal General A.J. Smith with a total of sixteen guns says that on the 16th: "It has never been my fortune to witness so accurate and effective artillery firing as was exhibited by our batteries from this point. The enemy had four batteries, and yet so terribly effective was our fire that the rebel cannoneers could not be induced to work their guns, and three of their four batteries remained silent most of the day. . . . The Rebel Major General (Edward) Johnson, who was captured near the five-gun battery, directly in our front, said that our artillery firing was the most scientific he ever witnessed. A sergeant of this same rebel battery (who was captured) told me that his battery lost that day twenty-seven men killed and wounded by our shells; his battery also lost twenty-three artillery horses from same cause."[40]

There was some complaint from Federal artillery commanders that during both days' battle there was a great lack in the supply of ammunition. Captain Lowell says that from two to four guns were almost constantly idle in his command. From the amount of firing into Confederate positions, the shortage of ammunition was hardly discernible from that side. The fault apparently did not lie with supply, but in its issuance and distribution. General Thomas J. Wood, commanding Fourth Corps says "Our supply of ammunition was inexhaustible and his (Hood's) limited. All the batteries of the corps on the field were brought to the front, placed in eligible positions in short range of the

---

[38]*Ibid.,* pp. 691-92.

[39]*Ibid.,* p. 710.

[40]*Ibid.,* p. 498.

enemy's works, and ordered to keep up a measured but steady fire on his artillery. The practice of the batteries was uncommonly fine. The ranges were accurately obtained, the elevations correctly given, and the ammunition being unusually good, the firing was consequently most effective. It was really entertaining to witness it. The enemy replied spiritedly with musketry and artillery, and his practice with both was good."[41]

General Wood's explanation of the accurate Federal artillery firing is no doubt correct, plus rifled cannon versus smooth bore. Colonel Isaac R. Sherwood in Second division, Schofield's corps tells that on the morning of the second day's action "Sixty-five pieces of artillery had been thundering on our line more than two hours."

Robert A. Jarmin, Company K, 27th Mississippi Infantry, Brantley's brigade, Lee's Corps, says: ". . . it seemed as if the Federals were shooting crooked cannon, for they could throw their shells right in our midst, and from killed and wounded men and horses, a small branch in our rear ran red with blood, that is, bloody water."[42]

On the Confederate right, despite heavy shelling from the Federal guns, the combined assaults by Steedman and Wood between noon and 3 o'clock, were beaten back. Brigadier General Holtzclaw in his official report says: "At 12 m. the enemy made a most determined charge on my right. Placing a negro brigade in front they gallantly dashed up to the abatis, forty feet in front, and were killed by hundreds. Pressed on by their white bretheren in the rear they continued to come up in masses to the abatis, but they came only to die. I have seen most of the battlefields of the West, but never saw dead men thicker than in front of my two right regiments; the great masses and disorder of the enemy enabling the left to rake them in flank, while the right, with a coolness unexampled, scarcely threw away a shot at their front. The enemy at last broke and fled in wild disorder."[43]

The Federal cavalry had gained the rear of Cheatham's line on the Confederate left and was faced by Ector's (Coleman's) small brigade. D.H. Reynold's brigade of Walthall's division was withdrawn from

---

[41] *Ibid.*, p. 131.

[42] *Civil War Times Illustrated,* 12, no. 2 (May 1973).

[43] *OR,* p. 705.

Stewart's left center and sent to assist Coleman in holding back the blue cavalrymen. Already the Granny White pike had been interdicted early in the morning by Hammond's cavalry and blocked as an avenue of retreat for the Confederates.

Brigadier General D.H. Reynolds was from Ohio, but after graduation from Ohio Wesleyan University he moved to Tennessee, where he attended law school. In 1858 he moved to Arkansas and set up his law practice at Lake Village. When the war began his sympathy and allegiance were with the South. He rose rapidly in rank and was made brigadier general 5 March 1864. This fine officer was conspicuous here at Nashville for his heroic efforts when the Confederate lines broke and the rout began, and later as part of the rear guard. He took part later in the Carolina campaign under Joseph E. Johnston where he lost a leg in the last battle at Bentonville. After the war he returned to Lake Village and resumed his law practice.[44]

General Wilson, commanding the Federal Cavalry Corps, had earlier in the day suggested to General Thomas, through Schofield, that the cavalry be transferred to the Federal left flank. He seemed to think the Confederate right flank would be easier to turn than the left, or that the terrain was more suitable for cavalry operations. Luckily for the Federals, Thomas overruled this suggestion, and proceeded with his original battle plans. Wilson's message at 10:10 a.m., on the 16th to Schofield, had ended by stating: "It seems to me if I was on the other flank of the army I might do more to annoy the enemy."[45]

During the morning hours and until mid-afternoon, only occasional skirmishing and some probing attacks took place on the Federal right. On the left Thomas met and conferred with Wood late in the morning. He instructed him that the battle plan was the same as the preceding day—to outflank and turn the enemy's left. Also that the enemy was to be pressed on their right and constantly harassed by fire. Wood should be on the alert for any openings.[46]

All along the line artillery continued its devastating bombardment, and made a shambles of the light and hastily constructed works on Shy's

---

[44]Faust, p. 625.

[45]*OR*, Series I, Vol. 45, Part 2, p. 216.

[46]*Ibid.*, Series I, Vol. 45, Part 1, p. 131.

Hill. Bate's men hugged the rain-soaked ground and the shallow shell-swept trenches. With the accurate and well-aimed fire from three directions, one Confederate private is said to have remarked that "The Yankee bullets were coming from all directions, passing one another in the air!" A heavy cold rain was now falling to add to the discomfort of the thinly clad Confederates.

The Federals were ready to move in with their superior numbers and arms against the Confederate left and center. Wilson's cavalrymen had gained the rear of Cheatham's Corps. General Hatch had succeeded in planting a "battery into a position enfilading and taking in reverse the enemy's line."[47] The position on Shy's Hill was now being hit by well-nigh one hundred guns. Three Federal Corps surrounded the men on the hill—front and flank by two corps of infantry, and now the cavalrymen in their rear. Why the delay? Thomas after consulting with Wood, rode westward in the rain around Smith's position to Schofield's headquarters which was located west of Shy's Hill. Schofield in his report says: ". . . ordered General Cox to advance in conjunction with the cavalry, and endeavor to carry a high wooded hill beyond the flank of the enemy's intrenched line, and overlooking the Granny White pike. The hill was occupied by the enemy in considerable force, but was not intrenched. My order was not executed with the promptness or energy which I expected." General Cox in his report does not acknowledge any such order, but says Schofield ordered him to hold his part of the line tenaciously.[48]

All of Cheatham's Confederate Corps was now caught in a hopeless dilemma. These old battle-wise veterans of Shiloh, Chickamauga, and the other great battles of the Western theater, knew when the odds were insurmountable. These men who would soon be vanquished and routed were not cowards. They had faced tremendous odds before and matched the enemy successfully or with near success on many a hard fought field. Today it was a matter of survival and escape—escape from death or one of the Northern prisons, tantamount to death in many cases.

When Wilson was in position in rear of Cheatham's corps he notified Thomas and Schofield. This was a signal for a concerted effort

---

[47]*Ibid.*, p. 552.

[48]*Ibid.*, pp. 346, 407.

on the part of the infantry and cavalry to move against the enemy. Schofield, overcautious, asked for another infantry division from Smith. When Thomas' Chief of Staff, ascertained that it was not needed, and Smith protested, Thomas revoked an original order for Smith to furnish the additional troops.

Wilson was very impatient of Schofield's delay and sent various staff officers urging him to move. Finally, after about a two hour delay, Wilson went personally to urge the attack. Thomas was there. Schofield was still "reluctant to move from fear of the loss such an assault would produce, but Thomas said: 'The battle must be fought, if men are killed.' "[49]

General Smith in his report says that "The Twenty-third Corps (Schofield's) was on my right in the intrenchments thrown up by them the night before, and nearly at right angles with my present line. Expecting that corps to take the initiative, as they were on the flank of the enemy, I held the command in its present position, keeping up a slow artillery fire at their lines without eliciting any reply." It seems that Smith waited in vain for Schofield to take the initiative. General McArthur, commanding First Division, Smith's Corps says: "I moved the division forward . . . and moved up at 9 a.m. to within charging distance of the enemy's line of works, but finding no dispositions made by the corps on my right to cooperate with me, I ordered the command to construct rifle-pits to protect them from the infantry fire of the enemy's main line, my batteries in the meantime being used with good effect on their works. Continuing in this position until 3 p.m., (a total of 6 hours), when, again consulting with Major General Couch (commanding Schofield's Second Division, Sixteenth Corps) commanding divison on my right and being informed that he had no orders to advance, and fearing that if delayed until next day the night would be employed by the enemy to our disadvantage, I determined to attack, sending word to this effect to the major general commanding corps, and no contrary orders being received I prepared for the assault."[50]

Smith in the meantime had presented to Thomas, McArthur's request to make the assault, but the salient being directly in front of Couch's division of Schofield's command, Thomas had said: "No; the

[49]Horn, *Decisive Battle*, p. 132.

[50]*OR*, p. 438.

prescribed order of attack gives the initiative to General Schofield in conjunction with the cavalry, and I desire the maintenance of this order; I will ride to General Schofield's position and hasten his attack." While Thomas and Schofield were discussing the matter: "... Thomas looked to the left and observing that McArthur was moving upon the angle in the enemy's line, said to General Schofield: 'General Smith is attacking without waiting for you; please advance your entire line.' At this time General Wilson called the attention of the commanding general to the movement of the cavalry upon the fortified hill on the extreme flank of Hood's line."[51]

Couch, commanding Second Division, Schofield's Corps in his report says his troops, other than an Ohio battery of artillery, were not seriously engaged. At one point during the day he reported to Cox, on his right, that a "heavy column of the enemy was passing partially in view across his front toward our right." These troops may have been Reynold's brigade which had been removed from Walthall's sector, east of Shy's Hill. This brigade together with Coleman's kept Wilson's cavalry west of Granny White pike to a great extent, but it was not enough. Cheatham's line on the left was bent inward to face Wilson. Hatch and Hammond worked together to exploit advantage in numbers. Their troops were extended in Hood's left rear for about a mile and a half and parallel to the Confederate main line. They were directly in back of Bate's and Walthall's divisions. Heavy artillery fire continued unabated. Cheatham's men were being surrounded except for the limited avenue through and over the hills to their immediate rear. In addition to Hammond's and Hatch's divisions, Croxton's brigade (the only unit of the First Division present) was held in reserve until nearly dark, when it was thrown across Granny White pike. The trap was closing. The decisive encounter on Shy's Hill was about to take place.

McArthur, whose troops made the assault on the angle on the hill, "ordered the First Brigade, Col. W.L. McMillen, commanding, to move by the right flank and take position in front of and to take the hill. Major General Couch sending forward a brigade to occupy and hold the intrenchments vacated by Col. McMillen, in case of an emergency, the Second and Third brigades having orders to charge as soon as the First had advanced half-way up the hill, which was the salient point of the

---

[51] Thomas B. Van Horne, *History of the Army of the Cumberland* (Cincinnati: Robert Clarke and Co., 1875), pp. 330-32.

position. The First Brigade, with fixed bayonets, without a cheer or firing a shot, but with firm resolve and without doubting their success, commenced the difficult ascent, and without a halt, although exposed to a murderous fire, which none but the bravest troops could withstand, planted their colors on the very apex of the hill. At the appointed time the Second and Third Brigades . . . moved forward on the enemy's works. Their path lay across a cornfield, traversed by stone walls and ditches, which together with softness of the ground, exposed as they were to direct fire in front, and enfiladed by batteries on the flanks, for a time held with intense interest the most experienced officers who beheld it; but onward was their motto, and their banners were planted on works defended by the choicest troops of the rebel army . . . ."[52]

Compton's Hill obtained the denomination, Shy's Hill, shortly after the battle. Some say the Yankees themselves so named it for the heroic and obstinate stand made by the young 25 year old Tennessee colonel and his brave men.

The hill was swept by a crossfire from sharpshooters and artillery. Lieutenant James Litton Cooper, a staff officer with General Thomas Benton Smith's brigade reported in his diary, Dec. 1864; "After 2 o'clock it was swept by the most searching fire of shell it had ever been our fortune to experience. Three or four batteries at short range were playing upon the few acres about the top of the hill, and if a man raised his head over the slight works he was very apt to lose it.

About 4 o'clock, as things seemed approaching a crisis, I was ordered by General Smith to go to the left of the brigade. His adjutant, Captain Jones, was sent to the right, while he remained in the center, where we were to make report if necessary. . . .

In a few minutes what had been feared all day occurred. A large force of the enemy massed under the crest of the hill, and, by a gallant charge, dashed over the flimsy works before some of the men had time to fire a single shot. More than half the brigade was killed, wounded or captured in a hand-to-hand struggle, prominent among the killed being Colonel Shy."

---

[52]*OR*, p. 439.

84

While the lines were caving in on all sides of them, the men of Shy's regiment and Benton Smith's brigade fought on, even after their young colonel had fallen. Death seemed to be the last choice for all of them until their general waved a white handkerchief and called for a cease-fire. The wounded and corpses of their comrades lay all about them. Out in front of the shell-wracked positions of the Confederates the dead from four Minnesota regiments lay indiscriminately on the rain soaked slope. "It has been said that in the taking of Shy's Hill, Minnesota's losses were the greatest suffered by their state in any Civil War engagement—302 killed, wounded, or missing, from the Fifth, Seventh, Ninth and Tenth Minnesota Regiments."[53]

When the death of Colonel Shy "was made known to his mother, who lived near Franklin, only a few miles away . . . she remarked that she would to God that she had a hundred sons to die for such a cause. . . . The death of the gallant Shy and the capture and wounding of General Thomas Benton Smith, who was so long the Colonel of the Twentieth Tennessee Regiment, with two-thirds of its number either killed, wounded, or captured on this fatal field, nearly annihilating this glorious band, who had faced the storms of war for four long and eventful years."[54]

Men who have known combat can imagine the conditions under which these battered Confederates fought on this beleaguered hill. They were surrounded on three sides by thousands of Federals. It was raining, and they were tired, cold, hungry, wet, and without sleep or rest, but still they held on. The term "shell shock" had not yet entered the military lexicon, but the cumulative strain of their experience must surely have affected some of them at least. They were thinly clad—some barefoot. Sam Watkins, Co. H, First Tennessee Regiment wrote: "It is a singular fanaticism, and curious fact, that enters the mind of a soldier, that it is a grand and glorious death to die on a victorious battlefield."[55] Perhaps the same feeling is prevalent in a forlorn hope such as here on the crest of Shy's Hill. *Dulce et decorum est pro patria mori.*

Bate had called for reinforcements, but there were none to be had. In his after-battle report he writes: "About this time the brigade on

---

[53] John T. Dowd, *The Pillaged Grave of a Civil War Hero* (Nashville, TN: Mini-Histories, 1985), p. 20.

[54] W. J. McMurray, *History of the Twentieth Tennesee Regiment Volunteer Infantry* (Nashville: Publication Committee, 1904; repr., Nashville, TN: Elder's Bookstore, 1976), p. 348.

[55] Watkins, p. 163.

the extreme left of our infantry line of battle was driven back, down the hill into the field in my rear, and the balls of the enemy were fired into the backs of (killing and wounding) my men. (Note: The brigade mentioned was Govan's of Cleburne's division now covering a division front since the shifting of the rest of the division to the right flank.) The lines on the left (as you go into Nashville) of the Granny White pike at this juncture were the three sides of a square, the enemy shooting across the two parallel lines. My men were falling fast. I saw and fully appreciated the emergency, and passed in person along the trenches in the angle built by Ector's brigade, where I had placed troops who I knew to be unsurpassed for gallantry and endurance, and encouraged them to maintain their places."[56] Bate ordered Captain Rene' Beauregard who commanded his artillery, to move his battalion back to the Franklin pike, since Granny White pike was blocked by the enemy. Bate goes on to say:

> About 4 p.m. the enemy with a heavy force assaulted the line near the angle, and carried it at that point where Ector's brigade had built the light works, which were back from the brow of the hill and without obstructions; not, however, until the gallant and obstinate Colonel Shy and nearly half of his brave men had fallen, together with the largest part of the three right companies of the Thirty-seventh Georgia, which regiment constituted my extreme left. When the breach was made, this command, the consolidated fragments of the Second, Tenth, Fifteenth, Twentieth, Thirtieth, and Thirty-seventh Tennessee Regiments—still contested the ground, under Major Lucas, and, finally, when overwhelming numbers pressed them back, only sixty-five of the command escaped, and not as a command, but individuals. The command was nearly annihilated, as the official reports of casualties show. Whether the yielding of gallant and well-tried toops to such pressure is reprehensible or not, is for a brave and generous country to decide. The breach, once made, the lines lifted from either side as far as I could see, almost instantly and fled in confusion.[57]

General A. J. Smith commanding the Federal corps, of which McArthur's division was a part, reported that no sooner had the First Brigade begun the ascent "than the Second Brigade, Col. L.F. Hubbard commanding, eager in emulation, also took up the attack, immediately followed Third Brigade, and lastly, the Second Division. The enemy opened with a fierce storm of shell, cannister, and musketry, sadly decimating the ranks of many regiments, but nothing save annihilation

---

[56]*OR,* p. 749.

[57]*Ibid.,* p. 750.

could stop the onward progress of that line. Sweeping forward, the right of the line up the hill and the left through mud and over walls, they gained the enemy's works, calling forth the remark from one of their general officers that "powder and lead were inadequate to reisst such a charge." The enemy were whipped, broken, and demoralized. Prisoners were taken by the regiment, and artillery by batteries.[58] Bate tried to rally the men, but to no avail. Sam Watkins says "General Frank Cheatham and General Loring tried to form a line at Brentwood, but the line they formed was like trying to stop the current of Duck River with a fish net. I believe the army would have rallied, had there been any colors to rally to. I saw a wagon and team abandoned, and I unhitched one of the horses and rode on horseback to Franklin, where a surgeon tied up my broken finger, and bandaged up my bleeding thigh. My boot was full of blood, and my clothing saturated with it. I was at General Hood's headquarters. He was much agitated and affected, pulling his hair with his one hand (he had but one), and crying like his heart would break."[59]

Bate goes on to say: "The men then, one by one, climbed over the rugged hills in our rear and passed down a short valley which debouched into the Franklin pike. The whole army on this thoroughfare seemed to be one heterogeneous mass, and moving back without organization or government. Strenuous efforts were made by officers of all grades to rally and form line of battle, but in vain. The disorganized masses swept in confusion down the Franklin turnpike, amid the approaching darkness and drenching rain, until beyond Brentwood, when the fragments of command were, in some measure, united and bivouacked in groups for the night."[60]

Over on the Confederate right flank General Stephen D. Lee reported: "The troops of my entire line were in fine spirits and confident of success—so much so that the men could scarcely be prevented from leaving their trenches to follow the enemy on the Franklin pike; but suddenly all eyes were turned to the center of our line of battle near the Granny White pike, where it was evident the enemy had made an entrance, although but little firing had been heard in that direction. Our men were flying to the rear in the wildest confusion, and the enemy following with enthusiastic cheers. The enemy at once closed toward

---

[58]*Ibid.*, pp. 435-36.

[59]Watkins, pp. 240-41.

[60]*OR*, p. 750.

the gap in our line and commenced charging on the left division (Johnson's) of my corps, but were handsomely driven back. The enemy soon gained our rear, and was moving on my left flank, when my line gradually gave way. My troops left their line in some disorder, but were soon rallied and presented a good front to the enemy."[61]

Lee's personal bravery and gallantry at the time of the crisis was a deciding factor in rallying his troops. At the time of the break General Lee was sitting mounted, in the rear of Clayton's division. Over on the left he could see confusion, and a Federal line advancing from the rear and attacking Johnson's division on the left wing of Lee's corps. Everything else had apparently been swept before it. Clayton's division was divided by the Franklin pike. General Lee rode across the pike, taking both stone fences, followed by one of his staff and two of his escort. "He rode until he reached the rear of Stevenson's division of his corps, rode right into the midst of fugitives and in the face of the enemy who by this time had reached the rear of Pettus' brigade. General Lee seized a stand of colors from a color bearer and carried it on horseback, appealing to the men to rally. 'Rally, men, rally! For God's sake, rally! he cried.' This is the place for brave men to die!" The effect was electrical. Men gathered in little knots of four or five, and he soon had around him three or four other stands of colors. The Federals, meeting this resistance, hesitated and halted. (It was late in the evening and misty.) The rally enabled Clayton's division to form a nucleus and establish a line of battle on one of the Overton Hills to the rear, crossing the Franklin pike in the woods near Colonel Overton's house. General Lee came back from his advanced position to this line. Here he was joined by a few pieces of artillery and a little drummer boy who beat the long roll in perfect time. Gibson's brigade came up and formed a rear guard."[62]

The small force of Confederate cavalry on the left under Chalmers was kept busy. Chalmers had tried unsuccessfully to communicate with Hood on the 15th but his couriers were either killed or captured. Early on the 16th, he received an order to hold the Hillsborough pike and get in contact with Hood's left wing. Rucker's brigade was placed at the point

---

[61] *Ibid.,* p. 689.

[62] *Confederate Veteran,* 12, no. 7, p. 750.

where the road coming from Brentwood intersects Hillsborough pike. Soon he was skirmishing with the Federal cavalry. In Chalmer's words:

> The force opposed to me was Hatch's division of cavalry, and their object was evidently to move down the cross-road to Brentwood, which would have placed them entirely in rear of our army, and put them in possession of the road by which it afterward retreated. Finding some hindrance in their way on this line of march, a brigade was sent rapidly across to the Granny White pike to move down it. I moved across the latter pike with my escort and the Twenty-sixth (Forrest's) Regiment of Cavalry, and placing them in a strong position, held the enemy in check for more than three hours and saved Cheatham's ambulances. In the meantime Johnson's division of the enemy's cavalry had moved across from the Charlotte pike, following our path, and attacked Colonel Rucker in the flank, while the remainder of Hatch's divison engaged him in front. Colonel Kelley having been forced back from his position, Colonel Rucker was withdrawn from the Hillsborough pike as soon as possible to support him, and the whole brigade (excepting the Seventh Tennessee Cavalry) was formed in front of Brentwood, to protect the wagons and ambulances which were collected there. The Seventh Tennessee was sent down the Hillsborough pike (by General Hood's orders) to report at Franklin and aid in guarding the wagon trains at that place. About 4:30 p.m. I received an order from General Hood directing me to "hold Granny White pike at all hazards," and Rucker's brigade was moved back and placed in position in rear of that from which Colonel Kelley had been driven. It was attacked at once, front and flank, by Hatch's and Johnson's divisions, and, after a sharp struggle, was forced back in some disorder. By this time it was so dark that it was impossible to reform the men, or indeed to distinguish friend from foe, so closely were they mingled together, but an irregular firing was kept up for some time until we were compelled to retreat toward the Franklin pike.[63]

It was about 4:30 p.m. when Chalmers was instructed by Hood to "hold Granny White pike at all hazards." Near where the road to Brentwood leaves Granny White, Chalmers erected a hasty barrier of fence rails, logs, and tree limbs. Private John Johnston, Fourteenth Tennessee Cavalry says:

> Thus while the Yankee cavalry with overwhelming force was moving down the road for the purpose of cutting off the retreat of our army and of striking it in the flank and rear, we were hurrying over to throw ourselves in their way.

---

[63] *Ibid.*, p. 766.

It was growing dark when we reached the pike, a part of our command—Forrest's old regiment and some others, probably the 7th Alabama Cavalry, had already taken position squarely across the turnpike where it wound up through a gorge in the hills and the firing had already begun. . . . We became immediately engaged with the Yankee cavalry who came on us in great numbers. . . . We could not have more than 1,200 men in line . . . But we sprang to our work with great alacrity and the whole line was ablaze with the light of our guns. We could see nothing in our front, but poured a stream of shot out into the darkened field and woods.

Time passes so rapidly while engaged in battle that one is not really conscious of time. I do not know how long this fight lasted but must have lasted several hours, as I learned from Colonel Kelley after the war that we had repulsed repeated attacks made by the Yankees, and Gen. Wilson in his report said the fighting was kept up until midnight.[64]

In his official report Wilson says: "Hatch was ordered to mount his division and press rapidly down the Granny White pike for the purpose of striking the enemy again at or beyond Brentwood. He had not proceeded far before he encountered Chalmers' division of cavalry, and then it was almost dark, attacked it with the greatest promptitude and vigor, driving it from a strong position behind rail breastworks. Brigadier General Rucker, commanding a brigade, a number of prisoners, and the division battle-flag were captured. The night was so dark and wet, and the men and horses so jaded, that it was not deemed practicable to push the pursuit farther."

Wilson later gave the following account of the action against Chalmers:

It had become so dark before they were well underway in pursuit that the men could scarcely see their horse's ears. It was a rainy and disagreeable night . . . Hatch's column had not gone more than two miles when its advance under Colonel Spalding encountered Chalmers' cavalry strongly posted across the road behind a fence-rail barricade. They charged it at once, and a spirited hand-to-hand melee ensued, in which many men were killed and wounded on each side. Colonel Spalding had the honor of capturing Brigadier General Rucker in a personal encounter, in which each had seized and wrested the other's saber from him and used it against its owner.

It was a scene of pandemonium, in which every challenge was answered by a saber stroke or a pistol shot, and the flash of the carbine was the only light by which the combatants could recognize each other's position. The gallant Confederates were driven in turn from every fresh position taken up

---

[64]John Johnston, "Reminiscences of the Battle of Nashville," edited by Tim Burgess, *Journal of Confederate History,* 1 (Summer 1988), 160-61.

by them, and the running fight was kept up until nearly midnight. Chalmers, however, had done the work cut out for him, gallantly and well. He was overborne and driven back, it is true, but the delay which he forced upon the Federal cavalry by the stand he had made was sufficient to enable the fleeing Confederate infantry to sweep by the danger-point that night, to improvise a rear-guard, and to make good their retreat the next day.[65]

Chalmers' small force put up a stiff fight at the battle of the fence rails, but there was no doubt as to the outcome since he was greatly outnumbered. Chalmers merely says: "It was attacked at once, front and flank, by Hatch's and Johnson's divisions, and after a sharp struggle, was forced back in some disorder."[66] A Federal writer stated: "A running fight took place, charge and countercharge following in quick procession in which the shouts of the combatants, the clang of sabers, and the rattle of pistols and rifles made the night one never to be forgotten."

Colonel Rucker had gone rearward to emplace a section of artillery and left Colonel Kelley in command. Private Johnston says: "The gallant Col. D.C. Kelley who was in command on the field rode up and down behind us saying as he passed—'pour it into them, boys, pour it into them.'" He escaped unhurt, but a ball clipped a patch out of the shoulder of his coat. Just at that instant the whole line broke and went to pieces like a rope of sand. And the break came none too soon as we afterward learned that the enemy had already passed our left and had almost reached the pike. . . . We now ran back to our horses as fast as we could, every man for himself." Johnston and a fellow soldier rode double until his friend came upon another horse. They made their way across to the Franklin pike where they came upon the infantry passing in retreat. He says:

> Just then, the clouds broke and the moon shed a brilliant light over the scene. While I sat my horse and saw this long line of infantry passing, my heart sank within me, for the first time, I felt that our cause was lost.
>
> We had been so busy since the battle began that we did not know what had happened. We had not heard any sound of battle except our own, and did not know until then that our army had been defeated. I mean of course the private soldiers and subordinate officers, but now my heart sickened at what was passing before me.

Something of interest to Johnston, unknown to him at the time, was the fact that the fight that night took place

"Within a few hundred yards of the grave of my Great Grandfather, (Major

---

[65] *OR*, p. 552.

[66] *Ibid.*, p. 766.

John Johnston) an old soldier of the Revolution who had moved out from Salisbury, N.C. in 1796, and settled at this place. . . . He owned all of this ground on both sides of the pike, and the little church, and graveyard and battleground were all on a part of his land.[67]

The Seventh Alabama Cavalry fought manfully under Rucker and Kelley that night in the desperate and costly stand on Granny White pike. They "were able, however to check the further progress of the Federal cavalry down the turnpike; and notable in their ranks for splendid courage on the occasion, as through the day, were a company of cadets from the Alabama University—mere youths—commanded by one of their number. The unconquerable tenacity, the brilliant valor of these boys, who faced and fought all odds, until their ranks were cut to pieces, excited general notice and praise." About three months later, on March 30, 1865, Wilson would issue a directive to his First Division commander, Brigadier General E.M. McCook, to destroy the University at Tuscaloosa. On April 4, 1865, the order was duly executed by Croxton. The senseless burning of the university buildings was denounced as "a savage act, unworthy of civilized war and was apparently done as retribution."[68]

General Hatch, whose command fought Chalmers at the fence rail barricade says: "About eight miles from Nashville we struck Chalmers' division. It was then nearly dark. Throwing some dismounted men upon the flanks of the road, Colonel Spaulding, of the Twelfth Tennessee (Union), charged the center, capturing the division colors and Brigadier General Rucker. The enemy were thrown into confusion, and only the darkness saved them from a thorough rout. Camped there that night."[69]

It has been reported by more than one that this cavalry fight at the barricade was one of the most desperate and fierce hand-to-hand encounters of the war, and that it probably saved Hood's Army. In fact General Wilson described it as "one of the fiercest conflicts that ever took place in the Civil War." It was in the vicinity of this melee in the dark that Colonel Rucker became involved in a personal combat with Colonel George Spaulding, Twelfth Tennessee (Federal). Each officer

[67]Johnston, pp. 167-68.

[68]Thomas Jordan and J. P. Pryor, *The Campaigns of Lieut. Gen. N. B. Forrest and of Forrest's Cavalry* (New York: n.p., 1868; repr., n.p., Morningside Bookshop, 1973), p. 643.

[69]*OR*, p. 578.

was mounted and armed with a sword or saber and entered the conflict in earnest when each recognized the other as the enemy. The weather was cold and wet. It was hard to either manage a horse or hold on to a weapon. Rucker's saber, as he struck with all his strength, missed its objective and fell from his hand. He caught the Federal officer's arm, and wrenched his saber from his grip. A grim duel ensued. Spalding had retrieved Rucker's saber. Rucker could now see that he was in the midst of a Yankee regiment, and looked around for an avenue of escape. The breastworks of rails was at his front, and at least an enemy regiment to his rear. About htis time, a Federal trooper fired a pistol shot that broke Rucker's sword arm. His horse bolted and threw him to the ground against some rails. The resultant concussion rendered him speechless, and "there was a rush upon the prone Confederate, as of so many hounds upon the dead quarry of their long pursuit. After some moments of wild, fierce clamor and rough handling, Rucker, replaced on his horse, was carried to General Hatch, a short distance off, and questioned, with the result that the Federal Commander was probably satisfied that Forrest (previously supposed to be at Murfreesboro) had come up and was covering Hood's retreat."[70]

Rucker's sword was Spalding's spoil of war. It remained in his possession for a quarter of a century. By that time, Rucker was a very successful businessman in Birmingham, Alabama, and he appreciated the gesture of reconciliation on the part of his former enemy when his sword was returned to him.

As for Rucker's immediate fate two accounts follow, one General Wilson's, the Federal cavalry commander, and Rucker's own. Here is Wilson's:

> My quartermaster having selected a house by the roadside for a hospital, I occupied it also with my staff as soon as I had given the necessary orders for the night. Rucker was among the wounded who had found shelter there, and had been assigned to a bed in my room. His arm had been so badly shattered that my staff surgeon had amputated it before I got there. Of course, every attention possible under the circumstances was extended to the gallant sufferer, who was made as comfortable as our field resources would permit. He was, however, more or less excited and wakeful, while I was compelled to receive dispatches, send out orders, and make arrangements

---

[70]Jordan and Pryor, p.642.

for the next morning. Under such circumstances neither of us slept much, but as Rucker's excitement wore away, and my business was dispatched, we both fell into silence and may have caught an hour's restful sleep. . . .[71]

The Federal officers, Generals Wilson and Hatch, and Colonel Spalding were most attentive to the brave Rucker. Rucker leaves the following report of his treatment by his captors that night:

During the night General Hatch came to me and said that he wanted to make me more comfortable, and offered me his bed. I thanked him very much, and he made a courteous reply. I was taken to a room in which there were two beds. One of these I occupied, and later in the night General Wilson came into the room, and was told that the other bed was for him. He did not retire, however, but sat up in that bed cross-legged like a tailor, all night, writing orders and receiving dispatches. I do not think either General Wilson or I slept a wink. I certainly didn't. General Hatch laid down on the floor by my side, and (God bless him) got up frequently during the night, and gave me water, and the next morning, when we left for Nashville, he provided me with a small flask of good whiskey.[72]

Private John Johnston of the 14th Tennessee Cavalry will have many who agree with his assertion "I have always felt a pride in the conduct of our cavalry at the Battle of Nashville and especially in this last stand on the Granny White pike. There seems to be no question, but that the single resistance we made at this place put a stop to the movement of the Federal cavalry, and saved the Confederate Army from destruction that night."[73]

Two infantry brigades that did yeoman's service were Reynolds' and Coleman's (Ector's) brigades when the lines broke on the left. Reynolds' brigade moved from the gap in the north of the hills, and formed on the northern side of a hill about 300 yards east of Granny White pike. Coleman's were placed south and a little west of Reynolds on a range of hills. A country road ran through the gap by which Cheatham's men retired. They were closely pursued by Wilson's troopers, but Reynolds' so deployed his brigade that he slowed down the Federal cavalry, and enabled Cheatham to get most of his corps safely through. Reynolds, only then, withdrew his Arkansas brigade to the gap and posted his men across the south end. He stayed until Cheatham's

---

[71] *Ibid.*

[72] John Allen Wyeth, *That Devil Forrest* (New York: n.p. 1959), p. 494.

[73] Johnston, p. 67.

94

men had all passed, then waited for Coleman to withdraw his small brigade from their exposed position. Reynolds then followed the retreating army as a rearguard. He halted to beat back an attack and wait for the ordinance trains to pass, but found out that they had been abandoned. He then continued his way on to Brentwood.[74]

Opposite, on the Confederate center, the enemy had planted artillery in positions at an early hour in the morning, and blasted Stewart's lines all day. His lines were also probed with the chief efforts against the flanks, for the purpose of reaching the roads in his rear. He tells of dispatching Ector's (Coleman's) and D.H. Reynolds' brigades to the left flank to oppose the enemy who had crossed to the east side of Granny White pike where they had gained the rear of the Confederate left and endangered the Franklin pike. It was well that he so deployed these two brigades.

Stewart, who had been sent for by Hood, was not present when the lines gave way. He says: "It would seem, however, that when once broken it very soon gave way everywhere, and the whole army made for the Franklin pike."

Walthall praised Coleman and Reynolds in his report and says: "These brigades, both of which did valuable service in holding the only passages through which many detachments of the army were afterward enabled to reach the Franklin pike, . . . By 4 o'clock a line (of Federal cavalry) was distinctly visible on the hills in our rear, covering much of our corps, which was the center in the army line. About this time the force in my front moved upon my position, but there was no spirit in the assault, and it was promptly repulsed without difficulty; but the hill to my left (Shy's Hill) just then was carried, and to save any part of my command an immediate withdrawal was necessary."[75]

Major General Edward Johnson commanded Lee's left division joining Stewart's right. After the attack on Shy's Hill, Smith's men hit Stewart's troops on their left. Seeing the lines on their left collapse, they "retreated in the wildest disorder." One attack was thrown back, but the Federals flanked Lee's corp, and cut off many of Edward Johnson's

---

[74]Thomas Robson Hay, *Hood's Tennessee Campaign* (New York: Walter Neale, 1929; repr., N.p.: Morningside Bookshop, 1976), pp. 163-64.

[75]*Ibid.*, pp. 711, 723, 724.

division including Johnson himself, who was made a prisoner. Johnson, had been crippled from a wound received at the Battle of McDowell, Virginia in May 1862. He was rather eccentric, in his ways, but a man of great warmth. He had a series of nicknames including "Old Allegheny," "Allegheny Ed," and "Old Clubby," the latter from a large walking stick he carried as a result of his wound. He had only been exchanged from a northern prison about two months earlier in October, after his capture at the "Bloody Angle" at Spottsylvania in May 1864. Johnson was a West Point graduate, class of 1838. After his exchange he was sent to the Army of Tennessee, as was the case of many surplus officers from the Army of Northern Virginia. At the time his lines were overrun, he was unable to make his escape. His physical condition due to his wound and imprisonment, plus the fact that he was not mounted, resulted in his capture.

All three of Bate's brigade commanders were captured. Brigadier General Thomas Benton Smith[76] and Major Jacob Lash were both captured on Shy's Hill. Major Lash assumed command of Finley's Florida Brigade as its ranking officer after Colonel Robert Bullock had been severely wounded near Murfreesboro on December 4th. All of the regimental commanders in his brigade were captains. Brigadier General Henry R. Jackson was captured when trying to make his way back to his horse from the front line. This particular Jackson was an honor graduate of Yale in the class of 1838. He was a lawyer and politician from Georgia, and a veteran of the Mexican War. From 1853-1858 he had been minister to Austria. Early in the war he had fought with Lee in Virginia, but in 1864 after the fall of Atlanta he joined Hood and took part in the Tennessee campaign. After his capture, which is described by Charles B. Martin, 1st Georgia Confederate of Jackson's brigade he spent the remainder of the war in a Yankee prison. Martin says: "a loud hurrahing was heard in our rear" and the federals were coming in from the rear of their line on their left flank. The brigade was ordered to move out to the right. Martin then tells what happened:

> Assisted by Lieutenant Colonel Gordon of my regiment, the General was walking to where his horse had been sent, but the ground was thawing and the walking was slow and tedious. At every step our feet became encumbered with two or three pounds of stiff mud. The enemy were trying to cut us off and, though at some distance, were firing at us and calling out: "Surren-

---

[76]*Ibid.*

der!" The General was becoming exhausted, and requested the Colonel and myself to leave him. Being near the pike, Colonel Gordon told him that he thought we might get away. The General's horse was in the edge of the woods just beyond, and we felt we could reach the animal. I remained with the General, however.

After crossing the pike and while getting over the stone fence, it rolled from under him and threw him into the ditch beyond. I assisted him out and persuaded him to pull his heavy boots off, as they were so loaded with mud that he could scarcely walk. He had got one off and was trying to remove the other when we heard the cry: "Surrender, damn you!" Looking up, we saw the muzzles of four guns aimed at us across the fence, not more than seventy or eighty yards distant. "They have got us, General," I said, and called out: "We surrender."

The general commenced to pull on his boot, and I turned his coat collar down to prevent our captors from discovering his rank, as I hoped we might be recaptured. The men—one corporal and three privates—sprang over the fence and came up to where we stood just as General Jackson succeeded in getting his boot on, and in pulling at it his collar assumed its natural position. The corporal walked around the General once or twice, then standing in front of him said: "You are a General." "That is my rank," was the reply. The corporal, taking off his hat, waved it around his head and cried out: "Captured a General, by God! I will carry you to Nashville myself."

At a command in German from the corporal, two men took charge of the General and with the corporal crossed the fence to the pike and started with him toward the city, leaving me in charge of the other man, who in very strong language informed me that if I tried to run he would shoot my head off. I told him not to worry; I had run as far as I could. Then he started with me toward Nashville.

We were on the edge of the ground over which Johnson's Division had fallen back, and blankets, knapsacks, etc., were scattered very liberally over it. The Dutchman told me to go to a very large knapsack, and when we reached it he proceeded to open and examine its contents. In kneeling to open it he let his gun fall into the hollow of his left arm, the muzzle almost touching my body. The temptation to knock him in the head took hold upon me; and while he was unbuckling the straps to the knapsack I jerked his gun and, whirling it, struck him back of the head. He fell across the knapsack, then I stepped over him and made off in the direction of the Franklin pike.

Just as I entered the woods I met Lieutenant Colonel Gordon with General Jackson's horse. He asked me for General Jackson and I reported his capture. "Mount his horse," said the Colonel, "We must get away from here, as the Yankee cavalry are trying to gain the pike in our rear." We rode to the Franklin pike, where we saw demoralization in the extreme. Riding down the pike about a mile, we saw General Hood with other commanding officers trying to rally the men, but in vain. I saw one man who had been stopped by General Cheatham dodge beneath the

General's horse and continue on his way while the General was trying to rally others.[77]

Most of the after action reports written by the various commanders on both sides tend to present themselves and their units in the best possible light. Wood is no exception. He painted a word picture of another brave assault on the same stoutly defended position on the Confederate right that he had failed to carry previously.

"After withdrawing and reposting the troops that had been engaged in the assault I rode toward the right to look to the condition of the First and Second Divisions. Shortly after reaching the First Division, which was on the right of the corps, an electric shout, which announced that a grand advance was being made by our right and right center, was borne from the right toward the left. I at once ordered the whole corps to advance and assault the enemy's works, but the order was scarcely necessary. All had caught the inspiration, and officers of all grades and the men, each and every one, seemed to vie with each other in a generous rivalry and in the dash with which they assaulted the enemy's works. So general, so combined an attack on all parts of the enemy's line was resistless. It rushed forward like a mighty wave, driving everything before it. The sharp fire of musketry and artillery did not cause an instant's pause. I advanced with the First Division and witnessed, with the highest satisfaction, the gallant style in which it assaulted and carried the enemy's works. The division carried every point of the works in its front and captured five pieces of artillery, several hundred prisoners, and many hundred stand of small arms. The Second Division gallantly carried the enemy's works in its front and captured many prisoners and small arms. The Third Division reassaulted the Overton Hill, carried it, and captured four pieces of artillery, a large number of prisoners and small arms, and two stand of colors. The enemy fled in the utmost confusion.[78]

By contrast Steedman merely says: "My troops, in conjunction with General Wood's immediately pursued, (after the break in the line), rapidly, taking a number of prisoners. The pursuit was continued until after dark. . . ."[79]

General Kimball, commanding Wood's First Division, carried on the idea of a successful assault at 4 o'clock. General Lee states that his lines only gave away gradually when the enemy "gained our rear" and

---

[77] *Confederate Veteran*, 17 (1), p. 11; Horn, *Decisive Battle*, pp. 142-44.

[78] *OR*, p. 134.

[79] *Ibid.*, p. 505.

was moving on his left flank. The falling domino effect from the left never quite reached Clayton on Lee's right. He had been able to withdraw from Overton Hill in good order and form in a clump of woods half a mile down Franklin pike. General Stevenson reported that the horses for Rowan's battalion could not be brought up in time. One of the guns of Corput's (Georgia) battery was lost by being driven full speed against a tree and the carriage broken.

An artilleryman living up to his name was Major Daniel Trueheart, Stewart's corps. He had been placed with his section of artillery on a hillside to the left of Walthall's division of Stewart's corps and in rear of Bate's division. "On the hillside facing east, in rear of the position held by Bate, was Major Trueheart with a section of artillery, all that remained of his battalion, in command of his gunners, cool and deliberate, directing the fire of his guns into the advancing and victorious enemy, until he was surrounded and captured and his gun turned on the retreating Confederates. Trueheart and his brave gunners, facing the enemy and intently serving his guns, his battalion colors flying while surrounded and captured, was the heroic figure on that historic field, so disastrous to Confederate arms." This according to Major D. W. Sanders of French's division.

While the heroic Major Trueheart continued to fight his guns "on the hillside facing east, in rear of the position held by Bate," his battalion trains, except his ordinance, had been moved to the rear. A youthful member of his battalion had been ordered to accompany the train, and he leaves an account in a letter written on December 16th—to his father in Mobile, Alabama. Kate Cumming, the famous Confederate nurse, knew the family and on January 12, 1865 in her journal entry says: "The late bad news from Tennessee is confirmed. A friend—one of our most influential citizens—has received a letter from his young son, which gives a graphic description of the retreat of our brave but unfortunate army from before Nashville. I give it as it is written, knowing the writer's veracity to be beyond a doubt:

Camp Wagon-Train, Trueheart's Battery
Near Franklin, Tennessee,
December 16, 1864

My Dear Father—Before this reaches you, the news of our defeat yesterday will have been received. As you will be anxious, let me say, in the first place, that I came through without a scratch.

Yesterday morning early the enemy began sharp-shooting in our front; that is, the front of Stewart's Corps, which was the extreme left of Hood's line. We soon received orders—that is our ordnance train and forage wagons, which are under command of the battalion quartermaster, Captain Spindle, with whom I am detailed as clerk—to be ready to move at any moment. This must have been about 2 o'clock, and was the first notice we received that there was any danger. No one had any idea that the enemy were then massing on our left. The firing soon became heavy, and . . . Major Trueheart being in the line, Captain Spindle dispatched a courier to him, to know whether he would move his train out or not, as the enemy's shells began to fall pretty thick. Before the courier returned, Captain Spindle decided to move all this train, except the ordnance, further to the rear, and ordered me to go with him.

I started, and got upon a high hill, where I could see the Yankees moving on our left, and preparing to charge Lumsden's battery.

And here, in order that you may understand the whole affair better, I will give you a description of our position, as far as I saw it, from the left toward the right.

It was in the form of a half circle, the center about a mile and a half from the Yankee line around Nashville. Cheatham was on the right, Lee in the center, and Stewart on the left. Walthall's division of Stewart's corps was on the extreme left of our corps. Our battalion was with Walthall's division, Lumsden's battery being on the left; one section of Tarrant's battery came next; one of our (Seldon's battery) about a half mile further to the right; the other section of Tarrant's battery came next, and the remaining two guns of our battery on the extreme right of Walthall's division.

The enemy first flanked and took Lumsden's battery, the captain and most of his men making their escape. They immediately turned our guns on us, and took Tarrant's two guns. About this time I succeeded in getting to the section of our battery to which my gun belongs. I saw the enemy advance and take Lumsden's battery. On getting to my piece, I took a blow, and then went to work. I found Major Storrs in charge of the section.

The enemy soon began to appear in two lines of battle on our immediate front, and we poured shell and solid shot on them very heavily, causing them to halt. Our ammunition getting scarce, the major ordered us to reserve our fire. Our infantry support, consisting of about one hundred men of Sayre's (Sears') brigade (the general himself in our works), continued to fire a few rounds now and then. The Yankees about this time commenced a furious cannonading, and we had to remain idle behind our works.

We received orders about this time to hitch up and save our guns, as the enemy was now seen coming up the pike, in our rear, and at the same time charging in two or three lines of battle on our front and right flank.

We got our two pieces about four hundred yards from our works, in a muddy field, where we had to abandon one of them; two of the horses being shot, leaving only four, and they were not able to pull it. Our other gun and our ammunition wagon we brought off. Just as we arrived in this field, the last brigade, either Shelly's (Cantey's old brigade) or Reynolds', being flanked, and the Yankees two hundred yards, in two lines of battle, on their left and rear, broke, General Walthall himself giving the order. From this time it was one perfect stampede for a mile. As I came out, I saw a pony rearing and pitching, and being nearly worn out, went back and got him. But after doing this I got so far behind, and the shells and minies came so thick and fast, I could not mount the pony until I reached a skirt of wood. As soon as I got on him I felt so relieved that I did not care much what came, I was so nearly worn out, that had I not got the horse I do not know what I should have done.

After falling back nearly a mile (I may not be correct in the distance, as the fatigue made it seem much longer than it really was, I suppose) we formed a second line of battle, and there I left the front, as my piece had gone on, and we had no ammunition with which to fire any longer. As I had nothing to eat, and no blanket, I started to find our wagons, which I did after walking three or four miles, en route for this place. Being tired out, I got in a wagon and remained in it til we reached our present camp, which is a mile and a half south of Franklin. We reached here about 1 or 2 o'clock in the morning; I am not certain whether this is the 15th, 16th or 17th; I think it is Friday, the 16th.

I am so tired and sleepy that I can scarcely write, and only do so because an opportunity of sending a letter tomorrow offers, and I know you will want to hear from me. I fear many of our infantry were captured. All of Trueheart's battalion of artillery was taken except Sergeant Riddle's piece (eleven out of twelve), to which I belong. I gave up hope once or twice, and felt sure that by this morning I would be on my way to some Yankee prison; but, God be thanked, I am safe and sound.

When I left the front, about 8 P.M., no one knew whether we were going to stand and form a new line, or fall back to this point. I never had such a fine view of the enemy approaching before. If we had only had some works; but even without these, had we only been reinforced, we might have done better, for it was very evident to every one that the Yankees had massed on the extreme left.

Give my sincere love to mother, sisters, and all the family, and many kisses to the little ones. God grant that we may yet be victorious, and that peace may soon spread her balmy wings over this troubled land.

I do not know how General Hood intended to protect his flank; I do not see how he could have expected to do so, but I am no general. If he does not take some stronger position than he has at present, I fear the enemy will do him more damage yet, by taking possession of the pike, and cutting him off entirely.

If anything happens, I will add before closing. With much love, etc. H.

P.S.—Two of our men have just come in from the front; they report the Yankees advancing down a pike which intersects the Nashville and Franklin pike, between our position and Franklin. I hope this is not so.

Douglas' Texas Battery, Lee's Corps lost one of its guns, as reported by one of the gunners: "Closer and closer they came. We began to give them double-shotted loads of canister direct in their faces, and our infantry turned loose its fire. . . . Just then somebody shouted, 'Look to the west!' and, turning in that direction, we saw the old fields far to the southwest covered with a mass of Confederate soldiers fleeing diagonally across our rear, in the direction of the Franklin pike, the only way open to retreat. With lightening celerity from Captain Douglas, our battery horses were brought forward, and we succeeded in escaping with the loss of two (one) of our artillery pieces."[80] Later on the 17th, on the retreat, Douglas' battery would be overrun, as reported by Lt. Colonel Hoxton, commanding Lee's artillery: "During the day the enemy's cavalry dashed into our lines on the pike, between the divisions of Generals Stevenson and Clayton, and captured the three guns of Douglas' battery. They destroyed the harness and cut down the guns, and when we recaptured them we could not carry them off and were compelled to abandon them."[81] Douglas' Texas Battery was now gone as a fighting unit, as were many others, including some of the most renowned of the "long arm" branch of the Army of Tennessee—Dent's Confederate, Stanford's Mississippi, Lumsden's Alabama, The Eufala (Alabama) Light Artillery, Selden's, Alabama, The Louisiana Washington Artillery, and Fenner's Louisiana. The roar of their guns had been heard in all of the great battles of the west. Some of the best leaders of the artillery branch were gone, too: Colonel Robert F. Beckham, dead, Captain John Rowan, dead, and Major Daniel Trueheart, captured. After the Battle of Nashville, only seven field officers were left in the artillery branch.[82]

During the morning Turner's Mississippi Battery was brought up on the crest of a hill which was held by Maney's brigade. These guns had been captured from the enemy at Perryville, Kentucky in 1862, and had "found echo in battle" in every engagement since. Private Thomas Jefferson Walker, Company C, Ninth Tennesee Infantry Regiment tells of his part in the battle: "Our brigade (Maney's, commanded by Colonel Hume R. Feild) was on the left, occupying a commanding knob, many of which surround Nashville. In our center was posted our beloved Na-

---

[80]Horn, *Decisive Battle*, p. 145; Daniel, pp. 178-79.

[81]*OR*, p. 692

[82]Daniel, pp. 180-81.

poleans. With many a moistened eye we had to leave them to fall into the possession of the enemy among whom they had created such deadly havoc in their ranks. We beat a hasty and disorderly retreat."[83]

Sam Watkins, Co. H., First Tennessee Infantry, Maney's brigade, had helped bring those four Napoleons off the night after the Perryville fight. He was a skirmisher this day at Nashville, and with Maney's brigade on the extreme left of the army. He found himself in the midst of a Yankee line of battle. After shooting one, he ran but was wounded in the hand and thigh. He describes what he saw as he ran back:

> " . . . it was one scene of confusion and rout. . . . soon the whole army had caught the infection, had broken, and was running in every direction. Such a scene I never saw. The army was panic stricken. The woods everywhere were full of running soldiers. Our officers were crying, "Halt! Halt!" and trying to rally and reform their broken ranks. The Federals would dash their cavalry in amongst us, and even their cannon joined in the charge. One piece of Yankee artillery galloped past me, right on the road, unlimbered their gun, fired a few shots, and galloped ahead again.
>
> Hood's whole army was routed and in full retreat. . . . Wagon trains, cannon, artillery, cavalry, and infantry were all blended in inextricable confusion. Broken down and jaded horses refused to pull, and the badly scared drivers looked like their eyes would pop out of their heads from fright. Wagon wheels interlocking each other, soon clogged the road, and wagons, horses, and provisions were left indiscriminately. The officers soon became infected with the demoralization of their troops, and rode on in dogged indifference. . . . And as the straggling army moves on down the road, every now and then we can hear the sullen roar of the Federal artillery booming in the distance. . . .
>
> The winter of 1864-65 was the coldest that had been known for many years. The ground was frozen and rough, and our soldiers were poorly clad, while many, yes, very many, were entirely barefooted. Our wagon trains had either gone on, we knew not whither, or had been left behind. Everything and nature, too, seemed to be working against us. Even the keen, cutting air that whistled through our tattered clothes and over our poorly covered heads, seemed to lash us in its fury. The floods of waters that had overflowed their banks, seemed to laugh at our calamity, and to mock us in our misfortunes.
>
> All along the route were weary and footsore soldiers. The citizens seems to shrink and hide from us as we approached them."[84]

Wood, commanding the Federal Fourth Corps on the left describes the Confederate rout:

---

[83]Thomas J. Walker, *Confederate Chronicles of Tennessee*, ed. E. B. Bailey (Nashville, TN: N.p., 1986).

[84]Watkins, pp. 240-41.

The enemy fled in the utmost confusion. The entire corps pushed rapidly forward, pressed the pursuit, and continued it several miles til the fast approaching darkness made it necessary to halt for the night. In the pursuit the Third Division captured five pieces of artillery. The batteries of the corps advanced with the infantry in pursuit and by timely discharges increased the confusion and hastened the flight of the enemy. The corps bivouacked eight miles from Nashville, and within a mile of the Brentwood pass, which was under our guns. By the day's operations the enemy had been driven from a strongly entrenched position by assault and forced into an indiscriminate rout. In his flight he had strewn the ground with small-arms, bayonets, cartridge boxes, blankets, and other material, all attesting to the completeness of the disorder to which he had abandoned himself. The captures of the day were 14 pieces of artillery, 980 prisoners, 2 stands of colors, and thousands of small arms.[85]

The initiative for pursuit lay with Wood who was astride the Franklin pike and with Wilson's cavalry. However, as Wood says: "The entire corps pushed rapidly forward, pressed the pursuit and continued it several miles and till the fast approaching darkness made it necessary to halt for the night." Wilson, after the fight at the barricade with Chalmers, says: "The night was so dark and wet, and the men and horses so jaded, that it was not deemed practicable to push the pursuit further."

Darkness came early. It was rainy and cloudy. December 16th was less than a week from the winter solstice—the shortest day of the year. The drenched Confederates were streaming down the Franklin pike. Lieutenant Edwin H. Reynolds, Company K, Fifth Tennessee Infantry, Strahl's Brigade, had been on picket duty on the refused left line of Cheatham's corps when the break came. He related:

The pickets to our right were driven in, and as we were thus flanked on both sides, I ordered the picket line to retire. As I mounted the breastworks and looked across the valley and noted that as far as I could see our troops were in retreat. I said to Capt. B.F. Peeples, who I met just behind the works: "If you ever expect to get out of here, it is time you were going. Look yonder," pointing to the fleeing Confederates. He glanced in the direction indicated and ordered a retreat. At the same time Lieutenant Colonel Finley's attention was called to the situation and he ordered the regiment to retire. (The regiment was the consolidated remains of the 4th, 5th, 31st, 33rd, and 38th Tennessee Regiments). And now began a race for liberty between the closing wings of the Federals. The ground was just thawing out of a smart freeze, and the sticky mud which, with the crabgrass, adhered to our shoes

[85] *OR,* p. 134.

and soon loaded us as with weights, and fast progress was impossible, and so ever and anon we had to stop and kick off these impediments. To avoid a high ridge in our rear it was necessary to take such a direction as brought us continually nearer the pursuing enemy in converging lines. Soon the foremost of our pursuers came within range of the fleeing Confederates and they kept up a desultory fire on them as they ran. Some of the bolder Confederates would occasionally stop and fire back at them and then continue their retreat. We soon came to a gap in the ridge, through which ran a road, and through this gap the demoralized Confederates poured to the rear. Lieutenant Colonel Finley took a stand in the gap, and, with pistol in hand, tried, by ordering and threatening, to induce the men to halt and make a stand, but the sound of rifles coming nearer and nearer to the line of retreat, rendered it impossible to enthuse any but the bravest, and soon it was found best to resume the retreat. The road we were traveling led into the pike at an acute angle, but upon nearing this point it was found that the rear of those troops using the pike as a line of retreat was just passing and a Federal battery was throwing shells into the fleeing fugitives, and so we had to change our direction and enter the pike further on. Night soon closed in upon us, and after marching a few miles the different commands began to halt and bivouack, the passing men continually calling out: "Where is such and such a division?" or "such and such a brigade?" By this means they were most of them able to locate their commands. Next morning as the march was resumed it was a sad sight to see how few men formed on the colors of the different regiments.[86]

Colonel W.D. Gale, Assistant Adjutant General of Stewart's corps, in a letter to his wife tells of his observations and experience in the second day's battle and rout. Mrs. Gale was the daughter of General and Bishop Leonidas Polk who was killed at Pine Mountain, Georgia June 14, 1864. He writes:

The enemy adapted their line to ours, and about 9 a.m. began the attack on Cheatham, trying all day to turn him and get in his rear. They succeeded about 2 or 3 p.m. in gaining the pike behind the gap, and in crossing, got in the rear of General Stewart's headquarters, which were on the side of the knob looking toward Nashville. We could see the whole line in our front—every move, advance, attack and retreat. It was magnificent. What a grand sight it was! I could see the capitol all day, and the churches. The Yanks had three lines of battle everywhere I could see, and the parks of artillery playing upon us and raining shot and shell for eight hours. I could see nearly every piece in our front, even the gunners at work. They made several heavy assaults upon General Lee's line near John Thompson's, and one in front of Mrs. Mullins'. At length having gained our rear, about 4 p.m. they made a vigorous assault upon the whole line right and left. Bate gave way,

[86]Edwin H. Rennolds, *A History of the Henry County Commands* (Jacksonville, FL: N.p., 1904; repr. Kennesaw, GA: Continental Book Company, 1961), pp. 111-12.

and they poured over in clouds behind Walthall, which of course, forced him to give way, and then by brigades the whole line from left to right. Lee held on bravely awhile longer than the center and left.

Here was a scene which I shall not attempt to describe, for it is impossible to give you any idea of an army frightened and routed. Some brave effort was made to rally the men and make a stand, but all control over them was gone, and they flatly refused to stop, throwing down their guns and indeed, everything that impeded their flight and every man fled for himself.

Reynold's brigade was ordered to go to the right just before the rout began, and got to where I was when I halted it and got the General to form it in line across the point of the knob just in the path of the flying mass, hoping to rally some men on this and save the rest by gaining time for all to come out of the valley. Not a man would stop! The First Tennessee came by, and its Colonel, House, was the only man who could stop with us, and finding none of his men willing to stand, he, too, went on his way. As soon as I found all was lost, and the enemy closing in around us, I sent a courier to General Stewart, who had gone to General Hood's headquarters in the rear of Lea's house, to inform him of the fact that he might save himself. This courier was mortally wounded, and left at Franklin. Finding the enemy closing in around us, and all indeed gone, I ordered the couriers and clerks who were there to follow me, and we rode as we could to where I thought General Stewart and General Hood were. They were gone and in their places the Yankees. I turned my horse's head toward the steep knobs and spurred away. It was the only chance of escape left. The first place I struck the hill was too steep for my horse to climb, and I skirted along the hills hoping to find some place easier of ascent, but none seemed to exist. Finally I reached a place not too steep, and in the midst of a thousand retreating soldiers I turned my horse's head for the ascent, resolved to try it. The bullets began to come thick and fast. I now found my saddle nearly off, and was forced to get down, but I went on foot. All alone, the poor, frightened fellows were crying out to me, "Let me hold on to your stirrup, for God's sake" "Give me your hand and help me, if you please." Some were wounded and many exhausted from anxiety and over-exertion. On I struggled until I, too, became exhausted and unable to move. By this time the enemy had gotten to the foot of the hill and were firing at us freely. What was I to do? I twisted my hands in my horse's mane and was borne to the top of the hill by the noble animal, more dead than alive. I was safe, though, and so were my men. We descended the southern slope and entered the deep valley, whose shades were darkened by approaching night. The woods were filled with our retreating men. I joined the crowd and finally made my way to the Franklin pike, where I found General Stewart, who was much relieved, for I had been reported as certainly killed or captured.[87]

---

[87]Bromfield L. Ridley, *Battles and Sketches of the Army of Tennessee* (Mexico, MO: Missouri Printing and Publishing Company, 1906; repr., N.p., Morningside Bookshop, 1978), pp. 413-15.

Chaplain James H. McNeilly was with the 49th Tennessee Regiment, Quarles' brigade, now commanded by Brigadier General George D. Johnston. Quarles had been badly wounded at Franklin and languished in a Federal prison until after the war. When the rout began, the Chaplain tells how the panic spread and how he got temporarily caught up in the hysteria of the moment. He was with the wagons and ambulances of the surgeons helping with the wounded when the route began:

> I saw our men running toward us in confusion. It was plain that our line was broken and that the enemy would soon be upon us. At once the teams were hitched to the wagons and ambulances and they moved off at a gallop. Directly the retreating soldiers were upon us, then I realized that it was a panic. I could not find out what had happened. Every man only seemed anxious to save himself. I ran with them; and as the mass of fugitives increased, the panic grew. Every man had some dreadful tale. According to these stories, the Yankee batteries would soon be in position on a rise in the road just behind us and would blow us all to smithereens, and there were at least a hundred thousand Yankees on our track. I ran as fast as I could; and the faster I ran, the worse was I scared. I could almost feel the grape and canister plugging me in the back. I had plenty of company scared as badly as I was. At length, being nearly exhausted, I had sense enough left to see that I must get out of the crowd or be run down and trampled on; so I stopped off probably twenty yards from the road. To my surprise, I became at once as calm as I ever was in my life. As soon as I got out of the panic physically I was fit mentally. I began to call men to me and directly had a squad ready to make a stand.[88]

The Federal action on the 16th in some ways was reminiscent of the earlier battle of Antietam in Sep. 1862. There the Federals under McClellan launched a series of uncoordinated attacks and Lee was able to shift troops to oppose these assaults. Here at Nashville there were piecemeal attacks, but at the last, after McArthur's assault on Shy's Hill, the entire force moved forward to success. This attack was a surprise to the other Federal units along the line. Captain Carter of McArthur's division east of Granny White pike says: "There was no intention of charging the Confederates on the 16th, as we had received orders to intrench, and our details sent for intrenching tools had nearly reached our lines when the charge took place. Besides, Colonel Marshall (William R. commanding Seventh Minnesota Infantry) told me a few days after, that he went to General Smith's headquarters and urged the General to make a charge, and that the General said: 'No,

---

[88] *Confederate Veteran,* 26 (June 1918), p. 251.

there will be no charge. We are going to intrench.' While talking he heard the noise of the charge, the increased fire, and the cheering, and he said to the General: 'They are charging now,' to which the General replied: 'No, I don't understand that there is to be a charge.' But the Colonel did not wait for any more words—he put spurs to his horse and dashed up, as I have described, and ordered the charge."[89]

With the rout of the Confederates and their disorganized retreat down Franklin pike the main battlefield became quiet except for the occasional "sullen roar of the Federal artillery booming in the distance." The pike was clogged with the fugitives of the once-proud Army of Tennessee. Lt. Colonel Isaac R. Sherwood, 111th Ohio Infantry gives an interesting account: "This charge ended the battle with the defeat and practical destruction of the last Confederate army in the West.

Just before culmination of this victorious charge I saw a sight never witnessed before on any battlefield. I saw a group of the Sisters of Charity on our line of battle, each with a decanter of wine, going from wounded comrade to wounded comrade, lifting their heads from the snow and giving wine with words of comfort and cheer. I shall never forget the spectacle."[90]

Thomas in his after action report says: "During the two days operation there were 4,462 prisoners captured, including 287 officers of all grades from that of Major General, 53 pieces of artillery, and thousands of small arms. The enemy abandoned on the field all his dead and wounded."[91]

Thomas was on Overton Hill after Lee's troops had departed and the battle ended. He could see long lines of Confederate prisoners being marched back toward Nashville. In his exuberance he lifted his hat and exclaimed, "Oh, what a grand army I have! God bless each member of it." He then came down from Overton Hill and was making his way in the gathering darkness down Granny White pike. He overtook Wilson,

---

[89]Stanley F. Horn, *Tennessee's War, 1861-1865* (Nashville, TN: Civil War Centennial Commission, 1965), pp. 347-48.

[90]*Ibid.,* p. 345.

[91]*OR,* Series I, Vol. 14, Part 1, p. 40.

and asked, "Is that you, Wilson?" The young cavalry general replied that it was. Then Thomas said in a manner suited to an old dragoon, "Dang it to hell, Wilson! Didn't I tell you we could lick 'em? "[92]

Schofield, with his caution, respected the fighting qualities of the defeated army. He said, "I doubt if any soldiers in the world ever needed so much cumulative evidence to convince them they were beaten." One Confederate officer, a prisoner, when asked when he realized the end was near said not until he had seen the army routed at Nashville.

Thomas after meeting Wilson, turned and rode back into Nashville and left the debris of the battlefield to others, perhaps remembering the words of the Duke of Wellington in a dispatch in 1815 who said: "Nothing except a battle lost can be half so depressing as a battle won."

The night of December 16-17 was almost eerie after the guns were silent. Rain continued to fall with flashes of lightning now and then. The Christian Commission was out with lights looking for wounded men lying cold and wet out in the open. It is not known whether their Christian concern extended to the wounded Confederates since they were left to suffer on the field. Nashville became one vast hospital. All churches in the city and the courthouse were used as hospitals. All day Saturday, following the battle, the dead were buried, many where they had fallen, and the wounded brought in in wagons and ambulances. Around two thousand wounded from both armies were collected. In addition eighteen hundred Federals and two thousand Confederates were moved in from Franklin. Convalescents able to travel were shipped north, but almost eight thousand remained in Nashville. Families of Southern sympathy took wounded Confederates into their homes.

Prisoners of war also flooded the city as a result of the battles at Franklin and Nashville. A total of 8,300 were said to have been taken at both places, and the Federals forwarded them on north because of a lack of facilities in the city to care for such a large number.

Cleaning up the tragic debris of the battle took at least four days, and details of soldiers with horse-drawn wagons were sent out for this purpose. With Christmas approaching, Nashville tried to return to nor-

---

[92]Horn, *Decisive Battle,* pp. 152-53.

mal. Federal authorities permitted the local people to take food and gifts to the Confederate prisoners.[93]

That long marching army—The Army of Tennessee—again was leaving its name-sake state, never to return. The troops moved out into the gloom of stormy night, and many knew in their hearts that their cause was lost, but clung to that glimmer of hope even here "in misery's darkest cavern."

The Battle of Nashville was over. Now would begin one of the longest and perhaps the most agonizing retreats in American military history. At the same time, one of the most skillful and heroic rear guard actions by American troops took place on that retreat. ". . . nothing in the annals of war exceeds in soldierly excellence the conduct of the Confederate rear guard from Columbia to Shoal Creek; and the results signally illustrated how true it is in war, as the Latin poet says:

'They can because they think they can.' "[94]

---

[93]Durham, pp. 145, 147-48.

[94]Jordan and Pryor, p. 654.

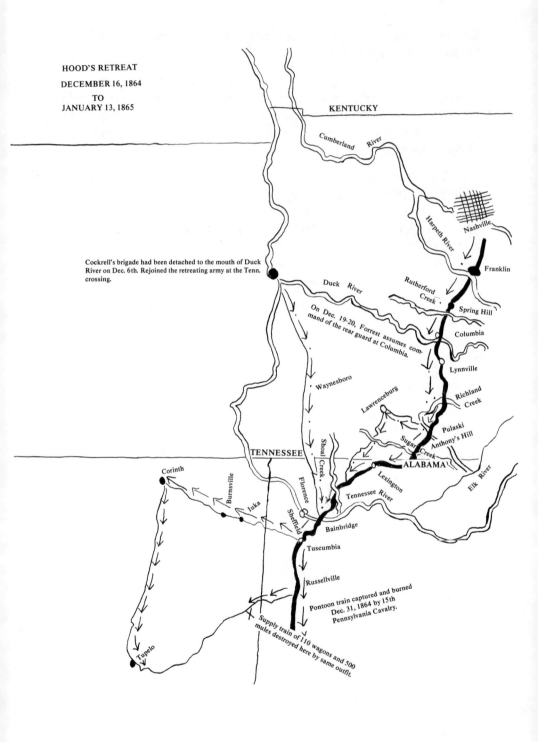

HOOD'S RETREAT
DECEMBER 16, 1864
TO
JANUARY 13, 1865

KENTUCKY

Cumberland River

Harpeth River

Nashville

Cockrell's brigade had been detached to the mouth of Duck River on Dec. 6th. Rejoined the retreating army at the Tenn. crossing.

Duck River

Franklin

Rutherford Creek

Spring Hill

On Dec. 19-20, Forrest assumes command of the rear guard at Columbia.

Columbia

Lynnville

Waynesboro

Richland Creek

Lawrenceburg

Pulaski

Anthony's Hill

TENNESSEE

Shoal Creek

Sugar Creek

ALABAMA

Corinth

Burnsville

Florence

Lexington

Elk River

Iuka

Sheffield

Tennessee River

Bainbridge

Tuscumbia

Russellville

Pontoon train captured and burned Dec. 31, 1864 by 15th Pennsylvania Cavalry.

Supply train of 110 wagons and 500 mules destroyed here by same outfit.

Tupelo

V
RETREAT AND PURSUIT

Wilson's cavalry had moved around the right wing of Schofield's Twenty-third Corps, and formed a continuous line facing north behind Cheatham's Confederate corps. This line extended on across the Granny White pike as heretofore mentioned. Here is Wilson's description of events at that time:

> The dismounted men, urged on by their gallant officers, continued their pressure and by noon had driven the skirmishers close in upon Hood's main line, and had formed a continuous line from the right of Schofield's corps to and beyond the Granny White turnpike, which passed north and south through Hood's left center. Thus it will be seen that Hood's entire left wing was enveloped front and rear, and would be obliged to give way whenever it was vigorously and simultaneously assailed from opposite sides. Riding close up to the front, and perceiving the advantageous position which my men had gained, I sent my staff officers, one after another, to Generals Schofield and Thomas with information of the success, accompanied by suggestions that the infantry should attack with vigor.
>
> It was during this stage of the battles that a dispatch from Hood to Chalmers (Forrest was still absent) was captured and brought to me, and forwarded by me at once to General Thomas. The dispatch seems to have been lost after the battle; at all events it has disappeared, but its character impressed it upon the memory of all who saw it. It ran in substance as follows: "For God's sake drive the Yankee cavalry from our left and rear, or all is lost." I found Thomas with Schofield in rear of the line, and explained to them the situation, which was fortunately made entirely clear to them by the sight of the dismounted cavalrymen in full view, skirmishing heavily with the Confederate left, and also by the fire of a section of horse artillery which had been dragged up the steep hillsides to a commanding position in rear of the Confederate works, and was pouring a heavy fire into them. Occasionally a shot would pass over the heads of the enemy and fall into our own lines. Seeing all this, Thomas turned to Schofield and indicated that the time had come for the infantry to advance.
>
> This was between half-past three and four o'clock. Schofield ordered his men forward at once, and as they charged the Confederate lines in front, Hatch's dismounted cavalrymen entered them from the rear. Pressed on all sides, and perceiving that further resistance was futile if not impossible, the Confederates broke and fled in confusion from the field. . . . .

With the break in the line on the Confederate left, the one hundred and twenty miles of misery and death known as Hood's Retreat, began at this time. Wilson says, "This was shortly after 4 p.m." Captain Henry Stone on General Thomas' staff observed the fall of Shy's Hill... and the beginning of the rout.

111

The bravest on-lookers held their breath as these gallant men steadily and silently approached the summit amid the crash of musketry and the boom of artillery. In almost the time it has taken to tell the story they gained the works, their flags were wildly waving from the parapet, and the unmistakable cheer, "The voice of the American people," as General Thomas called it, rent the air. It was an exultant moment; but this was only a part of the heroic work of that afternoon.

While McMillan's brigade was preparing for this wonderful charge, Hatch's division of cavalry, dismounted, had also pushed its way through the woods and had gained the tops of two hills that commanded the rear of the enemy's works. Here with incredible labor, they had dragged, by hand, two pieces of artillery, and just as McMillan began his charge, these opened on the hill where Bate was, up the opposite slope of which the infantry were scrambling. At the same time Coon's brigade of Hatch's division with resounding cheers charged upon the enemy and poured such volleys of musketry from their repeating-rifles as I have never heard equalled.

Thus beset on both sides, Bate's people broke out of the works and ran down the hill toward their right and rear as fast as their legs could carry them. It was more like a scene in a spectacular drama than a real incident in war. The hillside in front, still green, dotted with boys in blue swarming up the slope; the dark background of high hills beyond; the lowering clouds; the waving flags; the smoke slowly rising through the leafless treetops and drifting across the valleys; the wonderful outburst of musketry; the ecstatic cheers; the multitude racing for life down into the valley below—so exciting was it all that the on-lookers instinctively clapped their hands, as at a brilliant and successful transformation scene, as indeed it was.[1]

The following letter was written by Colonel Andrew J. Kellar, commanding Strahl's brigade, Cheatham's corps, dated December 18, 1864 (two days after the fall of Shy's Hill). It was addressed to the Assistant Adjutant General, Army of Tennessee as follows:

Sir: It is a duty I owe myself, brigade, division, to the commanding general, and to the country to state facts in regard to the panic of the army on the afternoon of the 16th. The lines were broken about 3 p.m. on a high hill west of the Granny (White) pike about half a mile, which hill was occupied by Tyler's brigade. (Tyler had lost a leg at Missionary Ridge. The brigade was commanded by Brigadier General Thomas Benton Smith) Bate's division, and given up to the enemy without a struggle. My command was on Tyler's left, and the right of Cheatham's division. The Hill, occupied by the enemy, overlooked the right of the army and the troops seeing it in the hands of the enemy, and seeing the left wing of the army running without making a stand, fled also. It was not by fighting, nor the force of arms, nor even numbers, which drove us from the field. As far as I can now learn, I did not lose more

---

[1] Stanley F. Horn, *Tennessee's War, 1861-1865* (Nashville, TN: Civil War Centennial Commission, 1965), pp. 340, 342-43.

than 30 men and about thirty-five small arms, already replaced. For the first time in this war we lost our cannon. Give us a chance and we will retake them![2]

Reducing the Shy's Hill angle did not take McArthur's men very long. There was some heavy fighting for a short time. It was not given up without a struggle as Colonel Kellar says. Ralph J. Neal, Company E, Twentieth Tennessee under Colonel Shy gives this account of the preparation for the assault, the brief fight, escape, and retreat:

> The night before the Battle of Nashville, our division (Bate's) was moved from the extreme right of the army to the left of the Granny White pike. Our company was near the top of the hill. When we took our position there were no earth works, so we at once gathered up old logs and stones such as were at hand, and placed them for protection. After awhile we borrowed some picks and shovels from the Florida Brigade, and worked with them best we could, but the ground was hard and rocky, and we had accomplished but little when we had to return the tools. We laid down to sleep; R.J. Neal, W.E. Brothers and W.W. Bakey of Company E, together with N.G. Kimbro and John Davis, unarmed recruits for our Company E. Company H was with us, and we numbered seventeen in all in both company's.

> We knew that something decisive would be done on the morrow. We had a little fire at our feet, and three blankets for the five men, but the enemy's sharp shooters began to fire at the light and we had to extinguish the fire. Next morning Kimbro and Davis being unarmed, were sent to the rear, until guns could be secured for them. The enemy was seen in our front some distance off. We at once noticed that we had built our works too far back on the hill, for we could not see the enemy after they reached the foot of the hill, until they would be close upon us, but it was too late to remedy the mistake now; for as soon as they could see, the sharp shooters commenced to entertain us, the enemy using their artillery also. We had none in position with which to reply; Finally with the exception of a few of our sharp shooters with "Witworth Rifles" (*sic*) we almost ceased to fire at them, but when the "Witworth's" were fired they were answered with shells. (Whitworth) Our sharp shooters finally used our works from which to fire. The enemy now turned their artillery on Companies E and H. The logs and stones were knocked down in a "giffy," and most of the men in the two companies were wounded. We made our way up to the next company on our left and claimed protection with them; some of the wounded climbed over the hill in search of our field hospital, but from the time our works were demolished, to the time they made a general charge on us, it was not exceeding five minutes; they came in overwhelming numbers, having

[2]U. S. War Department, *War of the Rebellion: A Compilation of the Official Records of the Union and Confederate Armies,* 128 vols. (Washington, D.C.: Government Printing Office, 1882), Series I, Vol. 45, Part 2, p. 707.

massed under the hill in our front. We could fire only one volley at them before they were upon us. We gave them that volley in "great shape," but did not check them. Seven stands of colors passed over our works. Our men, some of them, performed acts of heroism and valor, that to this day seems more like a dream than a reality, when we think of it.

The enemy poured over our works in great numbers; our men at first, with clubbed guns, but for an instant—and then they broke, Yankees and Confederates all mixed up—the Confederates trying to get away, and the Yankees trying to stop them. Both parties had fired their guns and neither had taken time to re-load. Gradually we unmixed ourselves from them. Our channel of escape would have been through the gap in which the Granny White pike passes, but the enemy were already in possession of that gap ahead of us. We bore to the left, crossed the pike, and went along the foot of the ridge until we reached the Franklin pike. Many of the men rallied in small numbers and would turn and fire on the enemy, thus checking them in a measure; but the enemy were coming up the Franklin pike, too, and many of the men who had been checking their pursuers, were either captured or compelled to climb the steep hill on the right. No general attempt was made to rally until we reached the vicinity of Brentwood. Here order was partially restored, and we commenced the retreat from Nashville.

Of the seventeen men in Companies E and H, we never knew what became of all of them. Lieutenant Brothers was not seriously wounded and escaped just before the final rush. R.J. Neal, having exhausted his ammunition (he was on skirmish line), started for more, and this doubtless saved him. W.W. Batey was severely wounded and left for dead, was made prisoner and recovered. The two recruits, Kimbro and Davis, were not seen anymore after being sent to the rear. But now we left our homes again, the cloud over the Confederacy lower and darker. The men were worn down with almost continued marching and fighting for months.

Yet true to their colors they marched away from home again on the retreat, sadly it is true, but determined to stand by St. Andrew's cross to the last man. And this they did without complaint. They blamed nor censured no-one, all believed that everyone from commander-in-chief to the private soldier had done his best and accepted the result as the fate of war.[3]

General Stephen D. Lee, whose corps was on the Confederate right, knew that his mission was to keep Franklin pike open for the routed army. This may have been Lee's finest hour. He performed his duty with skill, courage, and efficiency. On this brave, young corps commander evolved a tremendous responsibility—the safety of what was left of the Army of Tennessee. He says, "Being charged with covering the retreat of the army, I remained in rear with Stevenson's and part of

---

[3]W. J. McMurray, *History of the Twentieth Tennessee Regiment Volunteer Infantry* (Nashville: Publication Committee, 1904; repr., Nashville, TN: Elder's Bookstore, 1976), pp. 145-47.

Clayton's divisions, and halted the rear guard about seven miles north of Franklin about 10 p.m. on the 16th."[4] Lee was the youngest corps commander and lieutenant general in the Confederate army.

He does not mention the rear guard action along the Franklin pike and through the Brentwood Hills prior to 10 p.m., or his rallying Stevenson's division initially to halt the eager Federals. Gibson's brigade of Louisianans of Clayton's division formed a rear guard near Travellers' Rest on the Franklin pike and along the Little Harpeth River. Clayton's and Stevenson's divisions were enabled, through Lee's action, to fall back and form the new line. Before Lee's inspiring rally, Clayton's division had been in danger of being cut off.[5]

Hood sent an aide to tell Lee that the Federals were near Brentwood, they having come across from Granny White pike. Lee says: "As it was necessary to get beyond that point at once, everything was hastened to the rear." He abandoned his line along the Little Harpeth River and near the Overton House. As the troops passed Brentwood they could hear Chalmers' cavalry fighting Wilson's men at the Battle of the Barricades on Granny White pike. Wood halted his Federal infantry column about a mile north of Brentwood pass, toward Nashville, along the Franklin pike, and bivouacked for the night. His initial pursuit was not very aggressive, and Lee believed Wood was "too crippled to pursue us on the Franklin pike," and that "The only pursuit made at that time was by a small force coming from the Granny White pike."[6] A new rear guard line was established at Hollow Tree Gap, six or seven miles north of Franklin, and the troops bivouacked for the night. Chalmers' scattered cavalry had withdrawn from their fight on Granny White and moved over to the Franklin pike. They spent the night individually or in small groups near Lee's rear guard. There was a downpour of rain that froze as it fell. Private John Johnston of the Fourteenth Tennessee Cavalry put fence rails together on the ground and slept until daylight.

Even in the confusion of the rout, there were instances of courage and initiative. Many years after the battle, one veteran reported: "Just as I reached the Franklin pike someone with a battle flag waved it crying:

---

[4]*OR,* Series I, Vol. 45, Part 1, p. 689.

[5]Stanley F. Horn, *The Decisive Battle of Nashville* (Baton Rouge: Louisiana University Press, 1956), p. 147.

[6]*OR,* Vol. 45, Part 1, p. 689.

'Halt and rally round the flag, boys!' Soon there were several hundred of us formed in line across the pike, and we began firing at the bluecoats in the valley below. I don't think there were any officers present. It seemed to be a "private" affair though "free for all." They soon gave it up however, and fell back with the other retreating men to prevent capture.[7]

Chaplain J.H. McNeilly, 49th Tennessee Regiment, Quarles Brigade of Walthall's Division tells how disastrous the battles of Franklin and Nashville were for his regiment. He says: "Our organization ceased here. We had gotten thirty-five men by calling in details and the coming in of convalescents, who were under the command of Lt. George Elliott. Twenty-nine of these were either killed, wounded or captured. Lieut. Elliott was killed. I shall ever remember the feeling of desolation that came upon me as six of us gathered late that night (the 16th) under a big oak tree in the woods across the road from Col. John Overton's home and realized that we were all that remained of a thousand men."

This colorful chaplain, who could well be described as the ideal infantry chaplain, gave the following vivid description of his uniform about this time: "My hat was of brown jeans, quilted; my jacket of gray, with wooden buttons, had suffered sadly in the battle. I had thrown it off so as to better help a wounded comrade. As it lay on the ground a shell burst over us, and a spark fell on the middle of the back and gradually burned a round hole in the cotton fabric. My shirt of checked Osnaberg would not button at the collar. My pantaloons were scorched from standing too close to our fires and were in strings from the knees down, and my semi-stockingless feet were encased in a pair of brogans that let in air and mud through the gaping chinks."

In his after-battle report for the fighting around Atlanta July 28, 1864 at Ezra Church, Brigadier General William A. Quarles said of Chaplain McNeilly: "I cannot refrain from mentioning the conduct of the Rev. J.H. McNeilly, Chaplain of the Forty-ninth Tennessee Regiment. At all times a consistent and faithful follower of his Master, on this occasion he exhibited the qualities of the Christian soldier. Following the blood-stained path of his regiment, he was everywhere to be seen ministering to the physical and spiritual comfort of the dying and the wounded."[8]

---

[7] *Confederate Veteran,* April 1899, p. 154.

[8] *Ibid.,* Vol. 1, No. 10 (October 1893), 307; Vol. 26 (June 1918), 251; *OR,* Series I, Vol. 38, Part 3, p. 933.

Now, he and the other five men, all that was left of the 49th Tennessee Regiment, would move on to the Tennessee River on the retreat—less than a squad. Perhaps instances such as this was why Federal prisoners who marched with the retreat reported that the men marched "in squads of 6 or 8, up to 15-20 men." These "squads" may well have been what was left of regiments.

At the beginning of the rout,

A ludicrous occurrence took place between a private soldier and a staff officer. It was this: The different officers were trying to rally the men. About this stage of retreat a young staff officer, who had been on a furlough for a few days, arrived upon the scene. He rode to and fro, backward and forward across the pike, yelling at the top of his voice, "Halt here, men, halt, form line here. Halt, there is no danger down there," pointing down toward the valley, where Hood's little army had been contending against three to one all day. An old soldier who had been in the fight all day and was nearly exhausted, with powder all over his face and his garments of rags covered with mud, was trying to keep out of the way of the victorious Yankees. This young officer rode up to him and halting him in the road said, "Where are you going? Halt, and form line here, there is no danger down there." The old soldier said to the staff officer, "You go to Hell, I've been there."[9]

Brantley's brigade of Johnson's Division, Lee's Corps, did not retreat south down Franklin pike, from their extreme position on the Confederate right, but marched east from the Overton Hill area. It soon became dark. They were not hard pressed as were the troops on the pike. A guide was pressed to pilot them safely to the pike five or six miles from Franklin and behind Lee's position at Hollow Tree Gap. Robert A. Jarman, Company K, 27th Mississippi Infantry, Brantley's brigade says straggling was bad during the night, "but next morning they came up early, before we got up, for they were hungry." Later, from near Spring Hill Brantley's men were part of the rear guard until they reached Columbia.

Around Murfreesboro, Ross's Texas Cavalry Brigade had captured a supply train and guard on Dec. 15. They got large quantities of coffee, sugar and crackers. Also, "A rich harvest of overcoats here fell into our hands. Hood fights hard at Nashville all day." So reported George L. Griscom, Adjutant, 9th Texas Cavalry for his diary entry on December 15th.

---

[9]McMurray, pp. 349-50; *Civil War Times Illustrated,* Vol. 12, No. 2 (May 1973).

General Forrest was apprised of the Nashville debacle by a staff officer sent from Hood's headquarters by the name of Captain Cooper. Forrest was directed at this time to make disposition of his troops for protecting the army, and to move by way of Shelbyville and Pulaski. Upon receipt of word of Hood's defeat he had immediately dispatched orders to General Buford to fall back from his position on the Cumberland River through LaVergne to the Nashville-Murfreesboro pike to protect his (Forrest's) rear until he could move his artillery and wagon train. Buford was then to move across with his Kentuckians to the Columbia pike to help protect the rear of the retreating Army of Tennessee. Forrest's sick and baggage train was at Triune. He therefore crossed part of his train at Lillard's Mills on Duck River, but due to the heavy rains the stream became unfordable, he got only part of his train across. He then changed direction of march and went west to Columbia. He had previously ordered Armstrong's brigade to the Columbia-Nashville pike to also help protect the army. Forrest's attached infantry, under Olmstead, was mostly barefooted, and suffered greatly on the withdrawal. He was also encumberd with 400 prisoners, and several hundred head of hogs and cattle. The march was slower than he wished, but he doggedly hung on to his mobile food supply.

When Forrest marched out of the Murfreesboro area the night of the 16th it was pitch dark. Rain fell steadily, and changed to ice when it fell. It was so cold that guns froze to the fingers. On the 17th it rained all day. On the 18th, Captain Griscom, adjutant, 9th Texas Cavalry, made entry in his diary—"rains all day and night and turns very cold."

Forrest had sent forward all the troops he could spare to help cover Hood's retreating army, and reached Columbia with only one regiment and part of Morton's artillery on the evening of December 18th.

Smith's brigade of Cleburne's division had been sent to Murfreesboro under Colonel Charles H. Olmstead on Dec. 8th to replace Bate's division and Sears' and Palmer's brigades. Olmstead says the news of the disaster at Nashville reached him the night of the 16th. He started with Forrest's command for Pulaski by forced marches. "The roads were in horrible condition and the weather intensely cold, so that the sufferings of the men, who were many of them barefooted and all poorly clad, were intense. On arriving at Duck River it was found to be so much swollen by heavy rains as to be impassable. We were accordingly ordered to Columbia, which place we reached on the 18th. Here we remained for three days, receiving orders to report to Major General Walthall as a portion of the rearguard of the army." Olmstead in his casualty report, reported 70 missing, most of them men who broke down physically north of Duck River.[10]

Buford's Kentucky cavalry brigade, and a portion of Forrest's artillery (Morton's) on a forced march during the night of the 16th-17th, joined Chalmers in time to help Lee slow down the Federal pursuit before reaching the Harpeth. At Hollow Tree Gap Chalmers was almost constantly engaged during the day. The enemy followed with a strong force, but was held in check until nearly nightfall. By a series of bold charges, the Federals broke the lines of the infantry and cavalry but were driven back by the second line of infantry.

General Lee tells of the rearguard fight from Hollow Tree Gap to Franklin:

> Early on the morning of the 17th our cavalry was driven in confusion by the enemy, who at once commenced a most vigorous pursuit, his cavalry charging at every opportunity and in the most daring manner. It was apparent that they were determined to make the retreat a rout if possible. Their boldness was soon checked by many of them being killed and captured by Pettus' (Alabama) and Stovall's (Georgia) brigades and Bledsoe's (Missouri) battery, all under General Clayton. Several guidons were captured in one of their charges. I was soon compelled to withdraw rapidly toward Franklin, as the enemy was throwing a force in my rear from both the right and left of the pike on roads coming in to the pike near Franklin and five miles in my rear. This force was checked by Brigadier-General Gibson with his brigade (Louisiana) and a regiment of Buford's cavalry under Colonel Shacklett. The resistance which the enemy had met with early in the morning, and which materially checked his movement, enabled us to reach Franklin with but little difficulty. Here the enemy appeared in considerable force and exhibited great boldness, but he was repulsed, and the crossing of the Harpeth River effected.

In Franklin, Lee knew that there were many wounded, both Federal and Confederate, from the November 30th battle. He yielded the town with but little resistance. His engineer officer, Captain Coleman, destroyed the trestle bridge over the Harpeth while he and his pioneers were under a heavy fire of sharpshooters. The enemy was checked a mile and a half beyond Franklin near Winstead Hill. Lee reported:

> About 4 p.m. the enemy, having crossed a considerable force, commenced a bold and vigorous attack, charging with his cavalry on our flanks

---

[10]*OR,* Series I, Vol. 45, Part 1, pp. 740, 741, 756.

and pushing forward his lines in our front. A more persistent effort was never made to rout the rearguard of a retiring column.

The Federal assaults on the rearguard continued until after dark, but Pettus' (Alabama) and Cumming's (Georgia) brigades under Major General C.L. Stevenson repulsed every attack. Chalmers' cavalry covered the flanks. Wilson's cavalry managed to get in rear of Stevenson and attacked Clayton but were repulsed mainly by Gibson's and Stovall's brigades. Several guidons were captured from the enemy cavalry during the evening. Around 1 o'clock p.m., General Lee was wounded in the foot, but retained command until dark. He then turned the corps over to the gallant and able Stevenson who arranged and conducted the rearguard from that time until Cheatham's corp relieved him on the 18th.

Wilson was determined to make the annhilation complete. Contact on the 17th was frequent. The suffering on both sides of the conflict was indescribable, especially for the Confederates. Ice on the road gave way to mud. Rainfall froze on guns and pistols. Numbed fingers ached, and it was necessary to use both hands to cock the pistols. Fog and darkness stopped the struggle.[11]

After the rout began at Nashville, Stevenson's brigade and regimental commanders reformed their commands by "extricating them from the throng of panic-stricken stragglers from other commands who crowded the road." The line of march was then taken up for Franklin. Pettus' brigade was left at Hollow Tree Gap with part of Clayton's division to help bring up the rear. Stevenson then proceded with Cumming's brigade and bivouacked near the Franklin battlefield. He had orders to post guards upon the road to stop the stragglers of the army. Chalmers' and Buford's cavalry faced nearly five times their own number. It was nearly night and a mist or fog made it hard to distinguish friend from foe. Ten or twelve guns opened on Chalmers' men, and soon they were assaulted. It was a melee. General Buford was slashed over the shoulder by a blue trooper, who, in turn, was shot by Chalmers. The Confederate cavalry was overpowered and driven back. One participant says: "It was a dreadful night, the mud about a foot deep was frozen, but not sufficiently to bear the weight of our horses and the artillery."

---

[11] *Ibid.*, p. 690.

Next morning, the 17th, Stevenson was ordered by Lee to return to Franklin with Cumming's brigade where he rejoined his other brigade (Pettus'). In the heavy fighting along Franklin pike Pettus' brigade had captured a stand of colors. Stevenson's division was given rearguard duty upon leaving Franklin together with Chalmers' attached cavalry. He was not pressed heavily until five or six miles north of Spring Hill, then the enemy advanced rapidly attacking in front. It seems that Chalmers' cavalry retired in disorder and left Stevenson's troops all alone to their fate. Soon the Federals were on this flank and rear. Colonel Watkins, commanding Cumming's brigade (Cumming had been disabled by a wound Aug. 31, at Jonesborough, Ga.) was ordered "to prepare to retire fighting by the flank, and General Pettus to move in line of battle to the rear, with a regiment thrown at right angles to his flank, thus forming three sides of a square. Watkins drove the enemy in his front in confusion, moved, at the order which was given in the instant of success, by the flank and charged those on his flank, drove them also." He moved about a half mile back and again formed his small division with Pettus on the right, Watkins on the left, and a regiment refused on either flank. In this formation he began his retrograde movement, but was soon enveloped by the enemy front, flank, and rear. Although fighting constantly, the formation was never broken, and this gallant division drove its way through the enemy to within a short distance of Spring Hill. This was where the fight at the Beech Grove occurred. General Clayton, hearing of Stevenson's predicament, turned back to his assistance. Holtzclaw, of Clayton's division, formed on Watkins left flank and the rearguard was halted for a time. Several charges were made by the enemy, but all repulsed. It had rained all day and it was now some time after dark and still raining and very cold. After moving about a mile, the enemy attacks subsided, and the command moved to its rainy bivouack around Thompson's Station with the remainder of the corps. On that night Stevenson assumed command of the wounded Lee's corps.[12]

Carter L. Stevenson was born in Virginia in 1817. He attended West Point and graduated in 1838. He was a veteran of the Mexican Wars, and had taken part in the Mormon Expedition. Prior to the Battle of Nashville he had seen action in Kentucky, Vicksburg, Chattanooga, and the Atlanta Campaign. His division was kept under control at the time of the rout at Nashville through help from Lee the corps commander, himself, and was stalwart against great odds on the retreat.

---

[12]*Ibid,* p. 696; James Dinkins, *1861-1865 By an Old Johnnie,* facsimile reprint by Morningside Bookshop, 1975, p. 251.

Another of Lee's triumvirate was Major General Henry D. Clayton, commanding a division. He was a lawyer-politician and a graduate of Emory and Henry College. In March 1861 he was elected Colonel of the 1st Alabama, then the 39th Alabama. He took part in the Kentucky Campaign and Battle of Murfreesboro where he was severely wounded. He was made a brigadier general in April 1863. He and his brigade were in the thick of the fight at Chickamauga where he was again wounded, and his brigade losses were 45%. He was in the Atlanta Campaign and was made Major General in July 1864. His division formed part of the rearguard after the Battle of Nashville and he was commended by Hood for his "admirable coolness and courage." He later fought with General Joseph E. Johnston in North Carolina.[13]

When the rout became known to Clayton, he fell back from Peach Orchard Hill with his division in good order, for about one mile. He tried to bring out Stanford's artillery battery, but it was too disabled to move. Scarcely a whole wheel remained in its carriages from the fire of eighteen guns for seven hours. He did succeed in withdrawing the Eufala Light Artillery and assigned the 39th Georgia Regiment to it as a support. The officers and men of this battery were praised for the coolness with which they managed their guns. A line was formed near Travellers' Rest across Franklin pike by the whole division plus Pettus' brigade of Stevenson's division. Holtzclaw's brigade then relieved these troops, and became the rearguard of the rearguard. Clayton then moved his command off toward Franklin. Around 2 a.m. he halted seven miles from Franklin and bivouacked until 5 o'clock (a.m.-17th). By daylight they were in line of battle at Hollow Tree Gap. At 3 a.m. Holtzclaw had rejoined Clayton's troops. It was still raining and cold. Stovall's brigade and a section of Bledsoe's Missouri battery formed on the right of the pike and Pettus' brigade on the left. The two remaining brigades, Gibson's and Holtzclaw's, were in the rear. At 8 a.m. Wilson's cavalry drove Chalmers' cavalry through the line of infantry, "In a most shameful manner" according to Clayton. The Federals were repulsed with the loss of a stand of colors. An hour later there was another attack by the Federals, but they lost another stand of colors and about 100 men and horses captured. At 10 a.m. Clayton withdrew from the Hollow Tree

---

[13]Patricia L. Faust, ed., *Encyclopedia of the Civil War* (New York: Harper and Row, 1986), pp. 144-45, 739.

Gap position and crossed the Harpeth. Here he was relieved by Stevenson's division.[14]

Brigadier General Randall L. Gibson was born in Kentucky, but grew up on his father's plantation in Louisiana where he was educated privately and in public schools. He graduated from Yale in 1853, and was attache' in Madrid briefly. When the war began he was aide to the governor of Louisiana, then Captain in the 1st Louisiana artillery. He led the 13th Louisiana as colonel at Shiloh and commanded a brigade after General D.W. Adams was wounded. He fought at Perryville, Murfreesboro, Chickamauga, and in the Atlanta Campaign. Named brigadier general January 11, 1864, he fought under Hood at Atlanta and in the Tennessee Campaign where he was one of the pillars of strength in rearguard actions. After the Tennessee Campaign he was assigned to the defense of Mobile, where he held Spanish Fort until the last moment, then he and his troops made a thrilling night escape on March 8, 1865.

After the war this polished, aristocratic leader was Representative and Senator from Louisiana from 1872 until his death in 1892.[15]

At Hollow Tree Gap, Gibson's brigade was sent as a reserve about 600-yards in the rear. Here he was ordered to detach Colonel S.E. Hunter to picket a gap in rear of the division. These officers and men, about seventy-five, were later captured. Gibson beat back an enemy encroachment between the division and Franklin. He then moved about a thousand yards from the Harpeth into an earthworks. Here he says "our cavalry stampeded," and he was attacked by 5,000 of the enemy, charging in three columns, one in front, and one in rear upon the left flank, and one in rear upon the right flank. He says he found a section of artillery to open upon the columns, but it had no effect. He then ordered it to the rear to avoid capture. He had his regiments move to the rear, fighting as they went. He says, "The cavalry of the enemy charged all around us. Colonel Campbell broke up, by a well delivered fire, the column charging down the road, and thus gave time to the section of artillery to cross the river. The enemy came up within less than 100 yards of the section and fired his revolvers at those about it. My command fought its way to

[14]*OR,* Vol. 45, Part 1, p. 699.

[15]Faust, pp. 309-310; Mark M. Boatner, *Civil War Dictionary* (New York: David McKay Company, 1959), p. 34.

the river, entirely surrounded, with a loss of 10 killed, 25 wounded, 5 captured."[16]

Each individual commander had his own and different experience when the break occurred in the Confederate line, and the rout began. Brigadier General Holtzclaw, commanding brigade under Clayton tells his experience at the time and subsequent to the break:

About 4 p.m. I saw the left suddenly give way three or four brigades distant from me. Almost simultaneously the line crumbled away till it reached me. I had no time to give any order or make any disposition to check the disaster, when my command showed symptoms of taking care of themselves. I could only order them back, hoping to reform a new position. I had to retire under a destructive fire of eighteen guns, 600 yards distant, sweeping an almost open plain. I could not maintain order. The parallel stone walls on the pike (Franklin) separated my command in the center. I had neither staff officer nor courier mounted with me, and used my best endeavors to get my command all on the same side of the pike. I succeeded in doing this about one mile from the field, getting the greater body of the brigade together. I was directed by the major general commanding to take position as rearguard of the army across the pike. Shortly after dark I moved slowly back, driving up and hurrying stragglers forward. At 11 p.m. I halted four miles from Hollow Tree Gap, remaining until 3 a.m. (17th), when I moved inside of the Gap and halted in rear of Pettus' brigade. At daylight our cavalry stampeded, ran through the gap, and formed a mile in the rear. I sent, by direction of the major general, a regiment up the hollow to the left of the gap. The enemy passing to the right induced the withdrawal of the brigade from the gap. I was unable to communicate with a portion of the regiment sent out, the enemy dashing in in force between us. I moved in rear of the brigade in line of battle to within one mile of Franklin, where I passed the brigade of General Gibson, drawn up to support a section of artillery. I hurried across the river and formed on the southern bank, in Franklin. . . .

. . . The portion of the regiment I had detached in the morning and could not communicate with passed around the hills to the left of the pike, running five miles to get there. They came into the pike just at the position taken by General Gibson, exhausted with running around the enemy's cavalry. Without notice to myself or authority from the major general (Clayton), Brigadier General Gibson ordered this detachment of about seventy-five men to remain and cover the battery. Then withdrawing with the battery he withdrew his brigade, while my small detachment, in obedience to his orders, held the position, covered the retreat of himself and the section. As a matter of course they were overwhelmed by the enemy's cavalry, 2,000 or 3,000 of whom had surrounded them, three officers and five men only excaping. . . . I then marched back in line, halting every few hundred yards until I passed through the gap south of Franklin. Moving on with the divi—

[16]*OR*, Vol. 45, Part 1, p. 703.

sion I was ordered into line about six miles from Franklin just before dark. Just after I had formed, another of the many cavalry stampedes from Chalmers' division occurred. In trying to get them out of my line and formed on the left I received a severe contusion on the ankle, so painful as to prevent my doing anything for several hours.

Holtzclaw says he sought medical aid, and that a fight with the enemy's cavalry occurred soon after he left. It was this fight, kept up until long after dark, that Lee reported as so desperate and such a persistent effort to rout the rearguard. Holtzclaw rejoined his command the next day at Columbia.[17]

The infantry commanders were unfairly critical of the cavalry. The cavalry, up until Franklin, was a very small force under Chalmers facing tremendous odds, and they were the first troops to receive the shock of Wilson's massed charges each time. It is little wonder that the infantry commanders described their defeats as "stampedes" or "shameful withdrawals."

Captain Samuel T. Foster, Company H, 24th Texas Cavalry (dismounted), who was wounded while on picket duty at Nashville December 13th was evacuated to Franklin. On December 16th he got his papers "fixed up" for transfer to Columbia and "got on the cars by 10 o'clock a.m." He got off the train and some friend by the name of Bailly took him in their house and he was so well treated that he says "Who wouldn't be a soldier and get wounded for such fare as this."

On Sunday, December 18th he says: "Hood's army falling back! Great excitement! Particularly among the wounded. If Hood keeps falling back, there is no telling what I will do.

December 19th—Am fixing to leave and have had me a pair of crutches made so I can get about. It will nearly kill me, but I must go or be captured, so I will try.

December 20—Left Columbia last evening and came on the cars to Pulaski 30 miles. Hood's whole army were at Columbia when I left, passing through, and Forrest close behind them. The wagon trains are passing here now—and the report is, we (the army) is going from here to Tuscumbia (about 45 miles). The weather is very cold. I am in a church

---

[17]*Ibid.,* pp. 706-707.

used for a hospital and am in the altar close to the pulpit. Been raining last night and today—Roads very muddy. I can't imagine how I am to get away from here."[18] The above excerpt from this captain's diary gives an idea of the dilemma and worry on the part of the many helpless, non-walking, wounded. Most of them would soon fall into the hands of the approaching enemy. They would have to be abandoned by Hood.

When the line gave way on the afternoon of the 16th, General Stewart, commanding the center corps of the Army of Tennessee was at a conference with General Hood. He did not personally witness the break. He had a contingency plan in such an event but never had a chance to put it into efffect. Major Foster of the engineers had been sent to find a suitable location for holding the pike. Due to the disorganized state of most of his corps after the break, he received orders to move on to Franklin, and next morning to move toward Spring Hill and Columbia. Arriving at the latter place on the morning of the 18th, this corps took position on the north bank of Duck River, covered the passage of the entire army, and crossed about daylight of the 20th.[19]

General Walthall's report and experience following the break in the Confederate line parallels that of General Stewart, he being a division commander in that corps. The story of his courageous service as the infantry commander under Forrest in the rearguard after Columbia, will be told later.

After General Stephen D. Lee was wounded on the 17th, he did not return to duty until he joined Joseph E. Johnston in North Carolina. Upon leaving the corps he issued General Orders No. 67 on Dec. 18th praising his troops:

> Before taking temporary leave of this corps, I desire to express to the officers and men of my command my high appreciation of the good conduct and gallantry displayed by them at Nashville in the engagement of the 16th instant, and to assure them that they can be held in no manner responsible for the disaster of that day. I extend to them all my thanks for the manner in which they preserved their organization in the midst of temporary panic, rallying to their colors and presenting a determined front to the enemy, thus protecting the retreat of the army. I would also respectfully thank the officers and men of Holtzclaw's and Gibson's brigades, of Clayton's divi-

---

[18]Samuel T. Foster, *One of Cleburne's Command*, ed. Norman D. Brown (Austin, TX: University of Texas Press, 1980).

[19]*OR*, Vol. 45, Part 1, p. 711.

sion, and of Pettus' brigade of Stevenson's division, for the gallantry and courage which they met and repulsed repeated charges of the enemy upon their line, killing and wounding large numbers of the assailants and causing them to retreat in confusion. I desire also to tender my heartfelt thanks to Major General Stevenson and the officers and men of Pettus' and Cumming's brigades, of his division, for their skillful, brave, and determined conduct while protecting the retreat of the army from Franklin yesterday; constantly attacked in front and on either flank, these brave troops maintained an unshaken line, repulsed incessant attacks, and inflicted heavy loss upon the enemy.

In conclusion, my brave comrades, I beg to assure you that I am not only satisfied with your conduct in the recent campaign, but that I shall repose unalterable confidence in you in the future—a future which, despite the clouds which seem to lower around us, will yet be rendered bright by the patriotic deeds of our gallant army, in which none will gain prouder laurels or do more gallant deeds than the veterans whom I have the honor to command.[20]

On December 17th, Schofield sent a message to General Thomas as follows: "General: I have the honor to inform you that citizens on the road in rear of where we fought yesterday report that the universal testimony of rebels, officers and men, is that Forrest was killed certainly at Murfreesborough, where they admit their cavalry was badly whipped." This, of course, was misinformation as Forrest was making his way from Murfreesboro to Columbia at that time. General Rousseau from Murfreesboro also reported Forrest killed on the same date. However, Wilson in a communication to Thomas' headquarters on the 18th was correct: "A prisoner just taken states that Forrest, with Jackson's division of cavalry and two brigades of infantry, left Murfreesboro day before yesterday for Columbia, where he may be today." Forrest was very much alive. After leaving Columbia, Wilson said he could tell that a master mind was at the helm as the resistance to the Federal pursuit stiffened.

On December 18th Cheatham's corps relieved Lee's corps of rearguard duties, and General Frank G. Armstrong arrived with his brigade of cavalry from Forrest's command. Armstrong's career was interesting. He never attended West Point, but was a graduate of Holy Cross in Massachusetts. He had grown up in a military environment. His father was a regular army officer as was his step-father. He had

---

[20]*Ibid.,* Series I, Vol. 45, Part 2, pp. 706-707.

accepted a direct commission as 2nd Lieutenant in 1855 and had advanced to captain by 1861. When the war started he commanded a company of dragoons at First Bull Run for the Federals. His sympathies, however, lay with the South. He resigned and saw service in the Trans-Mississippi Department and in the Cherokee Nation. His remaining active service was with the Army of Tennessee in most of its great battles. He led brigades under Wheeler, Chalmers, and Forrest. It is said that he "was an accomplished professional soldier, always ready to fight." After the war he settled in the Southwest where he was U.S. Indian inspector and assistant commissioner of Indian affairs. He had been born in the Indian Territory. He died in 1909.[21]

On the 18th the rearguard moved down the turnpike from Franklin toward Columbia and crossed Rutherford Creek. The enemy did not press them and there was only slight skirmishing.

On the morning of the 19th Bate, of Cheatham's corps, reported some slight skirmishing, but retired with the remainder of Cheatham's corps across Duck River around 4 p.m. Cheatham had guarded the crossings of Rutherford Creek and thrown up temporary breastworks. He remained there until the wagons and artillery were safely across Duck River. Two attacks were made on Cheatham, but were easily repulsed. His rear and flanks were covered by the cavalry. Cheatham and Chalmers had held the Rutherford Creek line the night of the 18th. "It ws then, during the night, the redoubtable battle-flag of Major General Forrest reappeared among his men, with the rearguard. As Cheatham's available force of infantry did not now exceed 1500 men, Forrest offered to relieve him with his men, and this was sanctioned."[22]

It is interesting to note that Thomas reported the Army of Tennessee as "a disheartened and disorganized rabble of half-armed and barefooted men, who sought every opportunity to fall out by the wayside and desert their cause to put an end to their sufferings."[23] Cheatham's corps, perhaps hardest hit at Nashville and very disorganized at the time of the rout, was sufficiently recovered and reorganized to assume rear-

---

[21]Faust, pp. 23-24.

[22]Thomas Jordan and J. P. Pryor, *The Campaigns of Lieut. Gen. N. B. Forrest and of Forrest's Cavalry* (New York: n.p., 1868; repr. n.p., Morningside Bookshop, 1973), pp. 644-45.

[23]*OR*, Series I, Vol. 45, Part 1, p. 42.

guard duty on the morning of the 18th, less than two days after the rout. This battered corps was now patrolling the banks of the flooded Rutherford Creek. In 1905, Thomas J. Walker, Company C, 9th Tennessee Infantry Regiment of Cheatham's corps, says in his reminiscences "... Our companies, regiments, and brigades were reformed (that is those that had not been captured). Then in an orderly manner, we pursued our way back to the Tennessee."[24]

Major James D. Porter, later Governor of Tennessee in 1875, was Assistant Adjutant General, Cheatham's corps, and was on the retreat, says: "Immediately after the break in our line the troops sought their own organizations, reformed under their officers, and marched out of the state in perfect order.... The men with occasional exceptions, had arms in their hands. At Franklin there were several thousand stand of arms, a very large proportion captured from the enemy; and after the loss of fifty pieces of artillery, the army retired with fifty-nine field pieces and an ample supply of ammunition. The successful resistance to the assault of the Federal cavalry near Franklin by the rearguard of Lee's corps, repeated the next day by the rearguard of Cheatham's corps, does not sustain the Federal general's report that our army was a 'disorganized rabble.' "[25]

As heretofore mentioned, the pursuit by the Federals on the 16th, after the rout began was short-lived or non-existent. Wood halted about a mile from Brentwood pass and bivouacked for the night. He says, "The entire corps pushed rapidly forward, pressed the pursuit, and continued it several miles until the fast approaching darkness made it necessary to halt for the night."

Wilson bivouacked for the night after the fight with Chalmers' and Rucker's troopers at the rail barricade on Granny White pike.

Steedman, in conjunction with Wood's command, immediately pursued the fleeing Confederates and took some prisoners. "The pursuit continued until after dark, when our exhausted troops bivouacked for the night near Brentwood."

---

[24]Thomas J. Walker, *Confederate Chronicles of Tennessee,* ed. E. B. Bailey (Nashville, TN: N.p., 1986), Vol. 1, p. 71.

[25]Clement A. Evans, Ed., *Confederate Military History,* (Atlanta: Confederate Publishing Company, 1899), Vol. 10, p. 168.

The following morning Steedman covered the left of the line, and moved from Brentwood on the Wilson pike four miles past Brentwood. There he took a southwest road to Franklin. He bivouacked the night of the 17th after being unable to cross the swollen Harpeth. On the 18th, he crossed the river and went three miles beyond Franklin on the Spring Hill road. Here he was pulled out of the pursuit and ordered to Murfreesboro to proceed to Decatur which, after much delay, he reached on Dec. 27th.[26]

General Smith's Sixteenth Army Corps, after the rout began, pursued "until dark, when the troops bivouacked in line.... On the 17th, in compliance with orders, my command, the Third Division having joined that morning, moved out on the Granny White pike about four miles, and thence south to the Franklin pike, with orders to fall in the rear of the Fourth Corps. From thence we marched, via Franklin, Columbia, Pulaski, Lawrenceburg, and Waynesboro to Clifton, and from thence on transports to this place, (Eastport, Mississippi) without anything of importance occurring."[27]

Schofield's Twenty-third Army Corps, after defeat of the Confederates says: "Our troops continued the pursuit across the valley and into the Brentwood Hills, when darkness compelled them to desist, and they bivouacked for the night. . . .

The commanding general's orders for the pursuit of the enemy placed my corps in rear of the entire army and the main portion of its trains. I was, therefore, able to do no more than follow slowly in rear from the 17th until the 26th, when I was ordered to halt at Columbia, my troops not being needed in advance. On the 30th I received the order of the commanding general, announcing that the rebel army had been driven entirely across the Tennessee River, and ordering the pursuit to cease."[28]

Wood received orders from Thomas at 12:30 a.m., the 17th to move his command down the Franklin pike as early as he could in pursuit of Hood's forces. He passed this order on to division commanders at

---

[26]*OR*, Vol. 45, Part 1, pp. 505-506.

[27]*Ibid.*, p. 436.

[28]*Ibid.*, pp. 346-47.

6 a.m. It had rained in the night and the morning was dark and cloudy. By 8 a.m. the column was moving, but some delay occurred on the pike in letting the cavalry get into position. He reached Franklin at 1:20 p.m. He observed that the road to Franklin had been strewn with small arms, blankets and miscellaneous equipment left by the retreating Confederates. The bridges over the Harpeth had been destroyed, and it was necessary to rebuild them before the infantry could pass. The pontoons had not yet come up to the advancing column. Through a clerical error or a mix-up in communications the pontoon train had been sent down the Murfreesboro pike instead of the Franklin pike. It had to take cross-country roads to get to the Columbia pike, and finally caught up the night of the 21st at Duck River, five days after the retreat began. The pressure from the pursuing Federals, as a result of the misrouted pontoons, was eased much to the relief of the retreating Confederates.

A bridge was built over the Harpeth by the Ninth Indiana, and was ready for Wood's corps to cross early on the morning of the 18th. The cavalry had forded the river on the 17th and was already engaged with Lee's rearguard. Wood marched eighteen miles that day, and bivouacked a mile in advance of the cavalry. That night the rain fell in torrents and continued on the following day. Orders were received for the cavalry to pass ahead at 6 a.m., and the infantry to follow at 8 a.m. Rain continued, and all movement off the pike was curtailed. Three miles away the corps came to Rutherford Creek which was out of its banks and unfordable. No pontoons. Every expedient was tried—rafts, felling large trees to span the stream, but to no avail. The Confederates on the south bank opened with musketry and artillery. Finally, some dismounted cavalry crossed on the ruins of the railroad bridge and drove the enemy from the southern bank. During the night of the 19th-20th and early morning of the 20th, two bridges for infantry were put across the creek. The infantry then crossed and marched to the northern bank of Duck River three miles away. During the night the pontoon train caught up between midnight and daylight.

The night of the 20th became severely cold. Wood suspended operations and while the troops rested he waited for the delayed pontoon train. On the morning of the 22nd, the canvas pontoons were put together, and the Fifty-first Indiana was sent across to clear the opposite bank of the enemy. Colonel Streight (of Streight's raid fame. He had been outsmarted and captured by Forrest in May of 1863.) laid down a more permanent bridge. The remainder of the infantry, most of the artillery, and trains were crossed to the southern bank of Rutherford Creek, and encamped for the night. It was here that Wilson told about the infantry lining the roads as his corps marched to the crossing of the river, and cheered the cavalry as they passed. Wilson had never experienced infantrymen praising cavalry before. Wood's infantry rested near Columbia on the 23rd until midday waiting for the cavalry to cross. Instructions were for the infantry to press down the turnpike and the cavalry to operate on the flanks. He moved five miles down the pike and ran into a party of the Confederate rearguard which was dispersed. Here he learned of the composition of the rearguard of the enemy under Walthall and Forrest. Near nightfall Wood halted to await the crossing of the cavalry and bivouacked for the night.[29]

At Nashville, Wilson had stopped action following the fight on Granny White pike about an hour after dark on the 16th. At 5 a.m. on the 17th, Knipe, Hammond, and Croxton moved up a road along Richland Creek to Franklin pike. At Brentwood, Croxton took Wilson pike. Hammond came upon the Confederate rearguard out of Brentwood a short ways out Franklin pike and drove them back to Hollow Tree Gap. Knipe attacked in front while Hammond turned the position and atacked in flank. About 250 prisoners and 5 battle flags were taken, and the Confederates fell back across the Harpeth. One gun was captured. Johnson's and Harrison's divisions had broken camp at 4 a.m. and went out the Hillsboro pike and entered Franklin at about the same time as the rest of the corp. All cavalry units were able to cross the Harpeth while the infantry waited for a bridge to be built. Lee had fallen back two miles after finding Johnson on his flank. Hatch moved out the Lewisburg and Columbia pikes; Knipe on the Columbia pike, and Johnson on the Carter's Creek pike. Knipe attacked in front while Hatch and Johnson attacked the flanks. The enemy's lines were broken and driven back in great confusion according to Wilson. Here he was facing Stevenson's division and Buford's Kentuckians. Colonel Datus E. Coon, commanding Second Brigade of Hatch's division, in the fight three miles south of Franklin says "... a hand-to-hand fight ensued ... on burying the dead three Federal and five Confederate soldiers were found dead within three paces of each other." Nightfall saved the enemy's rearguard from complete destruction according to Wilson.

---

[29]*Ibid.*, pp. 134-37.

Wilson renewed the pursuit early the next morning, the 18th. He encountered the rearguard, now composed of Cheatham's corps, but he says it could not again be brought to a stand. He pushed to within three miles of Rutherford Creek, but the rain, need of rations, ammunition and forage, compelled a halt to let the trains come forward. Wilson had described the Army of Tennessee as a "broken and flying mass," but now Cheatham's corps was sufficiently recovered and reorganized to assume rearguard duties. Wilson's plan had been for those on divergent roads to outflank the main force and rearguard and make prisoners of the broken army. Rain was pouring, but the Confederate skirmish line covered the retreat so skillfully that the numerically superior Federal force was not able to accomplish its goal.

The Confederate rearguard had bivouacked near Spring Hill. This area in Middle Tennessee had been fought over and foraged until it was cleaned. Both men and horses went hungry. The morning of the 19th Wilson pushed the pursuit to Rutherford Creek, but it was so flooded that it could not be forded. The Confederates were between Rutherford Creek and Duck River. Hatch crossed a regiment of cavalry on the ruins of the railroad bridge. There was some skirmishing, but with darkness coming on he recrossed to the north side of the stream.

Here at Rutherford Creek, on the 20th, Hammond, Croxton, and Harrison remained in camp drawing supplies; Johnson and Knipe went back to Nashville with their dismounted brigades to refit; Hatch again crossed on the railroad bridge but found the enemy gone and recrossed.

According to the journal of the Fourth Corps, the mix-up on the Federal pontoon train was explained as follows: "Captain Ramsey, assistant adjutant general, wrote the order for the train and directed it to come out on the Murfreesboro pike instead of the Franklin pike. The train had moved out fifteen miles on the Murfreesboro pike when (the mistake having been discovered) it was reached by a messenger, and the officer having charge of it was ordered to move over to the Franklin pike. He crossed over on a country road which was almost impassable. Captain Ramsey says that when General Thomas gave him the order he had just awakened out of a deep sleep, and said "Murfreesboro pike," and not "Franklin pike."

Ross's Texas Cavalry brigade crossed Duck River on the evening of the 18th when Forrest rejoined the Army of Tennessee from his detached service at Murfreesboro. It had rained all day, and turned very cold. Adjutant Griscom says the 9th Texas cavalry moved in rear of the train and a division of infantry. Cheatham, to secure passage of the trains, had entrenched two miles south of Spring Hill. When Ross and the Texans came up Rutherford Creek with Forrest on the 18th, Armstrong's cavalry brigade and the infantry were skirmishing with the Federals, but no serious collision took place. The trains made it safely south of Rutherford Creek, a very dangerous stream, and late that afternoon the rearguard slowly withdrew across and burned the bridge. Six miles away to the south, the Army of Tennessee was safely crossing the Duck River. It was still raining hard and very cold.

In the journal entry of the Federal Fourth Corps for the 18th, kept by Lieut. Colonel Joseph S. Fullerton, he says: "The enemy very much demoralized. About one-third of what remains of Hood's army is without arms and as many are without shoes. . . . Hood's trains are two days ahead of him. He has but a very few pieces of artillery left." On the 19th, he continues: ". . . the rain that commenced on the afternoon of the 16th still continues. It is raining very hard this morning. The ground is in such condition that a wagon cannot possibly move off of the pike, and it is almost impossible to march infantry off of it. 9:30 a.m., reach the north bank of Rutherford Creek. The cavalry advance reaches the creek before us, and is now engaged in skirmishing with the enemy on the opposite bank." The Confederates held a "high and commanding line of hills on the south side, near to and running parallel to the creek. . . . He has lined the bank with sharpshooters, and we cannot build a bridge at the turnpike crossing on account of them and the artillery." The creek was reported as fifteen feet deep in most places. "The pontoon train has not yet come up and we can hear nothing of it. We have not the tools to build a bridge that wagons can cross on. The rain still continues to fall very fast and the creek is yet rising rapidly. . . .the rain has ceased now, and it is blowing up quite cold."

Generals Kimball and Elliott were instructed to build foot bridges, but both officers reported that it was not possible. The stream was too deep and too swift.

The night of the 19th, Wood received a dispatch from Thomas as follows. "If at all possible you will push forward your command across Rutherford Creek tomorrow morning and move directly against Forrest, who is said to be in camp between Rutherford Creek and

134

Duck River with about 7,000 cavalry. General Wilson will cross General Hatch's division of cavalry on the ruins of the railroad bridge and strike Forrest on the flank, whilst you attack him in front. . . . Take no wagons with you except the necessary ammunition wagons and ambulances. Your supply train can be brought up afterward." A little after 12 noon on the 20th both Kimball and Elliott had foot bridges across the creek, which indicates that a little prodding from higher-up the command structure can be encouraging. Wilson was crossing his cavalry over the ruins of the railroad bridge before noon. By 2 p.m., the head of Wood's infantry column had reached the north bank of Duck River, and part of Wilson's cavalry was there also. The journal goes on to report: "The enemy has left Columbia; his infantry left, the last of it, last night. Forrest's cavalry is yet near Columbia. A few of his men, pickets, etc., can be seen on the other side of the river. The enemy took up his pontoon bridges over Duck River at daylight this morning (Dec. 20). The river is very much swollen; is too deep and swift to bridge with timber, and we will have to wait for the pontoon train to come up, as it will be impossible to cross Duck River today, the corps will be put in camp on the bank of the river, in the timber on the left of the turnpike. The cavalry is going into camp on the right of the pike. 3 p.m., it ceased raining about midnight last night, and has not rained until this hour, and now it commences to rain hard, with a prospect of raining all night. . . . Have just heard from General Thomas. He reports that the pontoon train will be up tonight. This corps has already been delayed thirty-four hours waiting for the pontoon train to cross the Harpeth River, Rutherford Creek, and now Duck River. The enemy has, therefore, gained so many hours in his retreat. . . . 12 Midnight, it is still raining hard. The roads off of the pike are impassable for wagons; they cannot be moved at all."[30]

At 7 a.m., the 21st it was snowing. George E. Cooper, surgeon, and Medical Director, Dept. of the Cumberland in his report says this concerning the weather: "The weather during the pursuit was of the most disagreeable character. Rain fell for four successive days, and when this ceased the weather grew severely cold. This was followed by rain, rain, rain, and as a sequence mud. Probably in no part of the war have the men suffered more than in the month of December, 1864, when following Hood's retreating army from Nashville to the Tennessee

---

[30]*Ibid.,* pp. 158-61.

River. The result of this weather and the hard marching was, as might have been looked for, severe affections of the pulmonary viscera, fevers, rheumatism, and diarrheas, which served to fill the hospitals in this vicinity to their utmost capacity."[31]

While the Federals were trying to force the barrier of Rutherford's Creek on the 19th, the Confederate train and Hood's main force were already south of the Duck River.

Hood had hoped, and originally intended, to remain in Tennessee for the winter along a line about the Duck River. He had already sent prisoners, wagon trains, sick and wounded, and large herds of cattle and hogs to that vicinity. When he arrived at Columbia he realized that his shattered army was in no condition to face the pressures of the victorious enemy. He therefore, made plans, after consulting with Forrest, to cross a wider river barrier—the Tennessee. The retreat was continued and he moved out of Columbia with what remained of his beaten army.

Before crossing Duck River the rearguard withstood two attacks upon them that were easily beaten back. They then crossed the river and remained at Columbia that night (18-19th). Forrest met with General Hood and assumed command of the rearguard. His plans were developed and orders issued from the Warfield house, home of Major A.W. Warfield, CSA, a few miles south of Columbia.[32]

General Forrest asked for a force of infantry to be added to his cavalry rearguard, and that Major General Edward C. Walthall, Stewart's Corps, be placed in command of the infantry. Major D.W. Sanders, General Walthall's Assistant Adjutant General gives this account of Walthall's selection for this post of duty:

> On the morning of the 20th of Dec., 1864, General Hood sent a member of his staff to Gen. Walthall, who had established his headquarters at the residence of Nimrod Porter, near Columbia, with the request that he should call at army headquarters, and the writer accompanied him. On the pike, as Walthall approached army headquarters, he met Gen. Hood on his horse in company with Dr. Darby, who was the medical director of the army. Hood said to Walthall substantially as follows: "Things are in a bad condition. I have resolved to reorganize a rearguard. Forrest says he can't keep

---

[31]*Ibid.,* p. 111.

[32]This historic house still stands, and there is a state historical marker alongside the highway near the entrance.

Warfield house, south of Columbia. Here, on Dec. 20, 1864, Major General Forrest issued orders for covering the retreat southward of the Army of Tennessee.

the enemy off of us any longer without a strong infantry support, but says he can do it with the help of three thousand infantry with you to command them. You can select any troops in the army. It is a post of great honor, but one of such great peril that I will not impose it on you unless you are willing to take it, and you had better take troops that can be relied upon, for you may have to cut your way out to get to me after the main army gets out. The army must be saved, come what may, and, if necessary, your command must be sacrificed to save it.

Walthall, in reply, said: "General, I have never asked for a hard place for glory, nor a soft place for comfort, but take my chances as they come. Give me the order for the troops and I will do my best. Being the youngest Major General in the army, I believe my seniors may complain that the place was not offered to them, but that is a matter between you and them."

General Hood said: "Forrest wants you, and I want you."

General Forrest rode up during the conversation and said: "Now we will keep them back."

And General Hood gave verbal orders for General Walthall to take any troops he wished.

Edward Cary Walthall was born in Virginia in 1831, but moved with his parents to Holly Springs, Mississippi at the age of ten. He studied law and passed the bar examination, then practiced in Pontotoc before being elected to public office. He held several political offices before the war. In 1861 he joined a Mississippi regiment and became Lt. Colonel of the 15th Mississippi and later Colonel of the 29th Mississippi. He fought at Mill Springs and in the Kentucky campaign. He was promoted to brigadier general to rank from 1862. Due to illness he missed the Battle of Stones River, but fought in every major engagement of the Army of Tennessee from Chickamauga until the surrender. He is perhaps best remembered as commander of the infantry of the rearguard on the retreat from Nashville. He surrendered in North Carolina and was paroled May 1, 1865. He was senator from Mississippi from 1885 until his death April 21, 1898.

Word spread that Forrest was to command the rearguard with Walthall as the infantry commander. Men rushed to headquarters to volunteer, such was the popularity of these two great leaders. Desertion and willful surrender almost ceased entirely. As Lieutenant Rennolds, Fifth Tennessee Infantry said: "No higher compliment could be paid to Henry County's gallant soldiery than that both the Fifth and Forty-sixth

Tennessee were selected to form part of this heroic band, that day and night stood as a stonewall between the remnant of Hood's army and their victorious pursuers."[33]

The Federals began to shell Columbia. Forrest, under a flag of truce, made a personal request to General Hatch to cease shelling the town since no Confederates were there. He explained that only sick and wounded Federals were there, and that the shelling would only result in injury to women and children. Hatch acceded to the request and the shelling was discontinued. Forrest also requested that the prisoners he had on hand be either accepted for exchange or parole, but his request was denied by Thomas. Many of these unfortunate men died as a result of the exposure on the retreat.

After leaving Columbia, the pursuit was a cavalry show for the Federals all the way to the Tennessee. The pursuing infantry under Wood never made contact with the Confederate rearguard.

In the selection of troops for the infantry portion of Forrest's rearguard five other brigades were ordered to be added to Walthall's own three. He reported to Forrest with the following brigades: Brigadier General W.S. Featherston's; Colonel J.B. Palmer's; Strahl's commanded by Colonel C.W. Heiskell; Smith's commanded by Colonel C.H. Olmstead; Maney's commanded by Colonel H.R. Feild; Brigadier General D.H. Reynolds'; Ector's commanded by Colonel D.H. Coleman; and Quarles' commanded by Brigadier General George D. Johnston. Walthall then consolidated these depleted units so that they would be more manageable and compact: Palmer's and Smith's brigades under Colonel Palmer; Maney's and Strahl's under Colonel Feild; Reynolds' and Ector's under Brigadier General Reynolds; Featherston's and Quarles' under Briadier General Featherston. The total number of men in these eight brigades now numbered only 1,920, 400 of whom needed shoes. Also to show how depleted and fragmented the Army of Tennessee was, these eight brigades would have once constituted over thirty regiments. From the returns of strength submitted at the time, the breakdown of these pitiful remnants of once-teeming

---

[33] Edwin H. Rennolds, *A History of the Henry County Commands* (Jacksonville, FL: N.p., 1904; repr. Kennesaw, GA: Continental Book Company, 1961), p. 113.

regiments and brigades was as follows: Palmer—616; Featherston—498; Feild—278; Reynolds—528, far less than the 4,000 Forrest felt he needed.[34]

Ralph J. Neal, Co E, Twentieth Tennessee said in the history of his company: "The companies had now become so small that the regiment was but little more than a few messes. Some of the companies had no commissioned officers left; but every man and officer had an individuality that made it a remarkable set of men. Every one of these knew his duty just as well as if he had borne a commission; He was just as prompt to do his duty as was the officer. They were quite different from the young men and beardless boys, who left home nearly four years ago. Time had made them men. The usage and customs of war, and its privations had inured them to such hardships as but few men could bear, and made them veteran soldiers. . . . Those remaining were physically perfect. . . ."[35]

Forrest, now with about 1,600 effective infantry and 3,000 cavalry was to face a pursuing force of over 10,000 cavalry and possibly 30,000 infantry. The very fact that Forrest was present and "Forrest's men" were now in the rearguard would act to curb Wilson's boldness. Captain Walter A. Goodman, Asst. Adjutant General on General Chalmers' staff, noted "that at no time in his whole career was the fortitude of General Forrest in adversity, and his powers of infusing his own cheerfulness into those under his command, more strikingly exhibited than at this crisis. Defeated and broken as we were, there was not wanting many others as determined as he to do their duty to the last, and who stood out faithfully to the end; but their conversations was that of men who, though determined, were without hope, and who felt that they must gather strength even from despair; but he alone, whatever he may have felt, (and he was not blind to the dangers of our position), spoke in his usual cheerful and defiant tone, and talked of meeting the enemy with as much assurance of success as he did when driving them before him a month before. Such a spirit is sympathetic, and not a man was brought in contact with him who did not feel strengthened and invigorated, as if he had heard of a reinforcement coming to our relief."[36] On the 20th and

---

[34]*OR,* pp. 728-30, 757.

[35]McMurray, pp. 147-48.

[36]Jordan and Pryor, p. 647.

21st nothing of importance had occurred. Forrest was to hold Columbia as long as he could. By the night of the 21st-22nd the Federals had finally got their pontoon train, and had effected a crossing of Duck River between one and two miles above town. Several hundred had made the crossing when Forrest directed Walthall to start the infantry on the pike leading toward Pulaski. Walthall's command traveled light. He had already sent all wagons, except ordnance wagons and a few others to transport cooking equipment, to the rear with the army train.

Jackson's and Buford's cavalry divisions covered the rear while Chalmers' was on the right flank. Detachments of scouts patrolled the left. The infantry held to the pike. Many of Walthall's infantrymen were barefooted, but the ever resourceful Forrest, commandeered escort wagons, and when the men were not fighting off pursuing cavalry, they rode these wagons to save their bleeding and frozen feet. The infantry under Walthall had moved from Duck River to the vicinity of Lynnville on the 22nd, and taken up a position as a support for the cavalry which operated in front.

About two and a half miles from Lynnville the rearguard occupied a good position between the large hills. This position was held until sunrise the 24th when the retreat was resumed. Another stand was made on the same day south of Lynnville, and there was desperate fighting between there and Pulaski. Walthall withdrew his infantry to Richland Creek to hold the crossing for the cavalry if they should be hard pressed and need to cross before night. He stayed there until 8 o'clock that night, (23rd) then withdrew seven miles to the outer line of earthworks near Pulaski.

The 24th was a day of constant skirmishing. A severe engagement took place south of Lynnville, where Ross' Texans were rearguard. The Sixth Texas did outstanding service here throwing back a heavy enemy charge. Armstrong's brigade supported a six piece battery of artillery which swept the pike. Chalmers and Buford were on the left and Ross' brigade was on the right. The Federals forced a crossing, but were met by Jackson's division. There was heavy fighting for several hours, and a strong stand was made by Forrest near night. It was here that the gallant Kentuckian, General Abraham Buford was wounded. In the fight at Richland Creek, the Federal disposition was Hatch on the turnpike while Croxton was on the flank. In the fighting along Richland Creek, after Buford was wounded, Chalmers assumed command of his unit and merged it with his own. Both commands were about the size of a brigade. Wilson says it was interesting to note that the two leaders, Buford on the Confederate and Croxton on the Federal side, in this hand-to-hand fight, were both Kentuckians from the Bluegrass country. "With bugles blowing and guidons fluttering in the wind" the fight lasted until darkness ended the fray.[37]

Abraham Buford was born in Kentucky in 1820. He attended Centre College, then entered West Point in 1837. He graduated in 1841. Saw service in the Mexican War and was brevetted for gallantry at Buena Vista. He later served on Frontier duty, and resigned in 1854 after attaining the rank of captain. He raised cattle and thoroughbred horses on his farm near Versailles, Kentucky until joining the Confederate army in 1862. He commanded three Kentucky infantry regiments as brigadier general. In 1864 his troops were mounted and he served under Forrest. During the Nashville campaign he was with Forrest around Murfreesboro, but when Hood retreated south, Buford formed part of the rearguard. He was wounded at Richland Creek on the 24th, but returned to duty in early 1865, and was with Forrest in Alabama.

After the war, he returned to his farm in Kentucky and again raised thoroughbreds. Business reverses, loss of his home, and the death of his wife and only son depressed him to the extent that he committed suicide June 9, 1884.[38]

Captain Samuel T. Foster, Company H, 24th Texas Cavalry (dismounted) had been wounded on December 13th before the Battle of Nashville as heretofore mentioned. He had been evacuated first to Franklin, then to Columbia, and on December 21st he was in a church-hospital in Pulaski. He continues to tell his story in his diary: "December 21—I notice a general whispering consultation among the doctors, and it is plain to see there is something up.

As soon as one of them comes my way I asked him what was up? He said they had received orders to leave all the wounded here that are not able to walk out of Tennessee. Which of course includes me. I told the doctor that I must go out some way.

---

[37]James Harrison Wilson, *Under the Old Flag,* 2 vols. (New York: N.p., 1912), 2:128-29.

[38]Faust, pp. 88-89.

In the afternoon I learned that the Texas troops will pass in front of the church, so I wrote a note to the Sergeant in charge of the Brigade ambulances, asking him to send me an ambulance. I gave the note to one of our nurses and told him to go to the door, when he saw a flag with a star in it to go and hand the note to the first man he met. In about 20 minutes an ambulance was at the door and the Sergeant come in enquiring for me. He helped me in the ambulance, and drove me out to the camp.

The men were all glad to see me, and helped me out, built fire, etc. I told them what orders the doctors had received, but that I must go out of Tennessee with them.

Two of my company hunt around the country all night for a horse for me, but failed to get one—

December 22—Early this morning my prospect for going with the army looked gloomy. Can't get a horse nor mule to ride.

Ordered to move at 12 o'clock and am still a foot, not able to walk one step and it very cold. . . ."[39]

Cheatham's corps, crossed Rutherford Creek and bivouacked on the south bank on the 18th. On the 19th they fought the Yankees nearly all day along the creek, and late in the day they withdrew across Duck River. Stewart's corps stayed on the north bank of Duck River and withdrew and crossed the river about daylight on the 20th. Everything was now across.

The march of the main army was resumed on the Pulaski pike in the following order: Lee's corps in front commanded by Stevenson; Cheatham's corps next; with General Stewart bringing up the rear. The head of the column camped within two miles of Pulaski and the other corps to the rear in order of march. The main force had now, on the 21st, reached Pulaski while the rearguard was still being formed at Columbia under Forrest and Walthall to cover the retreat.[40]

Captain Samuel T. Foster, the wounded Texas officer at Pulaski, resumed his story in his journal dated Dec. 22: "Just before 12 one of my men comes and says he has found a horse, bridle, and saddle for sale. He

---

[39]Foster, pp. 153-58.

[40]OR, p. 673.

142

belonged to one of the doctors that are going to be left in charge of the hospital here. We commenced negotiations for the horse and outfit and close a trade for him for $800.00 which I considered cheap.

About 12 noon we move off, going south. Very cold, ground covered with snow, and the wind whistles. At about 8 miles we camp in the woods. The men build fires, assist me in getting down, and made me as comfortable as possible." The captain made his get away, but the next day or so he had to leave off riding his horse to keep from fainting due to the pain. A man rode his horse, while he got in an ambulance. On Christmas Eve he again rode an ambulance. Dressed his wound and could pour water through the bullet hole. He was not healing well. Some of his men got some whiskey and they all had a jolly Christmas Eve. The men also got some good bread for them to eat. Christmas day was dark and gloomy with light rain. The wounded captain reminisced. He opined that the missing in his outfit would outnumber those present. Hood in early 1863 commanded a division in Virginia. Now he commanded only a remnant of the Army of Tennessee as a result of his battles around Atlanta, Franklin, and Nashville. The captain wrote: "He might command a brigade—even a division but to command the army he is not the man. Genl Joe Johnston has more military sense in one day than Hood ever did or ever will have." On Christmas day Captain Foster arrived at the Tennessee River, with Cheatham's Corps seven miles above Florence. He could hear the fire of the Yankee gunboats below. The day after Christmas was spent building breastworks. Cheatham had placed batteries a mile below the crossing site, and Granbury's brigade began crossing at 8 a.m. About 11 o'clock there was heavy shelling, but it didn't last long. The captain writes: "General Cheatham is entitled to the credit of putting those batteries below the pontoon. Hood is not here."[41]

At Richland Creek, on the 24th, Captain John W. Morton, commanding Forrest's artillery, "placed one section of artillery across the bridge near a bluff, and another to the right of the road on the approach to the bridge. These guns were supported by Buford's and Chalmers' divisions of cavalry and Ross' brigade of Texans, which were part of Jackson's command." These two sections greatly helped in checking Wilson's troops. The retreating army had previously removed the

---

[41] Foster, p. 153.

bridge flooring, and now the artillerymen had to replace it to get their pieces across by hand. They led the horses across, then destroyed the bridge. That night, both the pursued and pursuers went into bivouack in the vicinity of Pulaski.

The next morning Forrest slipped away early and was on the march before the Federals left camp. It was here that Wilson says there was some delay while cooking breakfast before moving out. "The enemy, having nothing to cook, lit out by daylight. There was indeed no choice for them but to imitate the French in the retreat from Moscow—to take a drink, tighten their belts, and hit the road to the rear at the best gait they could make. It was but little better for the victors, and so both sides were under way as soon as it was light enough to see their hands before them."[42]

As they "lit out" one Confederate described it as "making tracks for the Tennessee River at a quickstep known to Confederate tactics as 'double distance on half-rations.' "

When the main army approached Pulaski, the weather became most severe. Rain fell in sheets and froze in a layer over the mud. The wagon train bogged down as well as the artillery. Forrest impressed oxen to help haul his wheeled vehicles. The infantry found marching next to impossible. One member of the retreating force recalled in later years: "Heavy rains alternating with snow and ice now set in. To add to our suffering our clothing was worn threadbare and many were actually without shoes. These constituted the barefoot brigade, and were compelled to cover their feet with rawhide that being the only material at hand. —As we neared Pulaski the weather grew more and more inclement and added to the severity of the hardships we underwent. An exhausting day's march, prolonged far into the night, a halt in the forest, where not only the ground was frozen hard, but the very trees were coated with ice, so that we could neither build fires to warm ourselves and dry our clothing, nor obtain the benefits of a little sleep, while our rations of the plainest food were extremely scanty. . . ."[43]

At Pulaski, Jackson's Confederate cavalry division held on to the town until the last moment. The covered bridge across Richland Creek

---

[42]Wilson, *Under the Old Flag*, 2:143.

[43]John P. Dyer, *The Gallant Hood* (New York: Bobbs-Merrill Company, 1950), p. 303; A. J. Lewis, "From Nashville to Tupelo," *New Orleans Times-Democrat*, March 12, 1893.

had already been set on fire when they had to withdraw "very rapidly." The hair, beard, and eyebrows of some of the troopers were singed as they galloped through the flaming bridge cover.

The pike ended at Pulaski. Here the rearguard left the pike and took the road to Bainbridge on the Tennessee. These roads away from the pike were barely passable, and the wagon train and artillery were moved with great difficulty. They also overtook wagons from the train of the main army that had been slowed due to the muddy condition of the road. These were assisted and carried with the train of the rearguard where possible. A heavy mounted force of the enemy began to press vigorously and boldly on the dirt road. Anthony's Hill, seven miles southwest of Pulaski was selected by Forrest for a stand. General Wilson in his official report says: "The country on the right and left of the pike, very broken and densely timbered, was almost impassable. The pike itself, passing through the gorges and hills, was advantageous for the enemy; with a few men he could compel the pursuing force to develop a front almost anywhere."[44]

Hood had sent a message to Forrest to hold Anthony's Hill until the army could get across Sugar Creek fourteen miles further on. On the 22nd, the main army had moved out of Pulaski on the Lamb's Ferry road. Stevenson's corps moved out in rear of the pontoon train, and camped about eight miles from Pulaski, or a mile beyond Anthony's Hill.

General Stewart's corps followed next and bivouacked in rear of Stevenson's corps, about six miles from Pulaski. Cheatham's corps camped on Richland Creek, on the southern edge of the town. Richland Creek curves around in an arc so that it was crossed twice—once about seven miles north of Pulaski toward Columbia where the heavy fighting took place on the 24th and where Buford had been wounded. Then again on the south edge of Pulaski as it makes its way toward Elk River near the Alabama line. Hood's headquarters was at a Mr. Jones in Pulaski from December 20th to include the 22nd. At daylight on the 22nd the wagon train moved out toward Bainbridge on the Powell's Ferry road.[45]

---

[44]*OR*, p. 566.

[45]*Ibid.*, p. 673.

In falling back through Pulaski, on Christmas day the First Tennessee Infantry, as part of the rearguard under Walthall, marched near the spot where a young member of the regiment, Sam Davis, had been unjustly hanged by the Federals as a spy a little over a year before on 27 Nov. 1863. His "manly deportment" and brave and stoic demeanor on the gallows are still remembered by admiring Tennesseans. He was a true Confederate martyr. Farther along, beyond Pulaski at Minor Hill, the army would pass near his place of capture.

At the first crossing of Richland Creek, seven miles north of Pulaski, Ross' Texas Brigade had held the Federals in check until all of Forrest's forces had crossed the creek. They then withdrew through Pulaski and again crossed Richland Creek on the outskirts of the town. On Christmas Eve, the Texans camped one mile from town after having fought at Lynnville and Richland Creek which they had forded under heavy fire. They were without forage or rations. Captain Griscom's diary entry for Christmas day tells of the fight at Anthony's Hill:

December 25, 1864—Rejoin the brigade 5 m S of Pulaski on Lamb's Ferry road—Wait for trains etc. to pass—Armstrong's Brig is driven from Pulaski—Dismounts and fights & draws them back to where we are—Walthall's Div Infy were posted here—Armstrong's Cav on left—Ross took position on right & 9th Texas extreme right as Cavalry—where they fight a heavy Cavalry fight while Feds charge infy—are repulsed & charged in turn—Infy capturing a 2 gun battery & about a brigade of Cav horses—28th Miss (Cavalry) of A(rmstrong)'s Brig is winner by 100 horses—9th was supported by Ross on their right dism't'd drive enemy back—our forces moving off bring up the rear about 2 miles to where A(rmstrong)'s Brig is formed—turn them over to them—move back to Sugar Creek & camp at 10-½ PM—Armstrong's Brig falling back beyond us leaving a regiment of pickets out—Rains and so muddy—Col Jones sltly (wounded) R. Russell Co "A" w'd'd Lt. Jouett Co "B" & Capt Alderson Co F sltly w'd'd—loosing a few horses also—[46]

On Christmas day the Texans had alternated with General Armstrong's Mississippians as rearguard, and there were frequent brushes with Wilson's advance troops. At Anthony's Hill, Ross was on the right, and he tells of the infantry charge that drove the Federals back with the capture of a gun. He says the check was so "effectual that he (the enemy) did not again show himself that day. This done, we retired leisurely, and after night bivouacked on Sugar Creek."[47]

---

[46] George L. Griscom, *Fighting with Ross' Texas Cavalry Brigade, CSA,* edited by Homer L. Kerr (Hillsboro, TX: Hill Junior College Press, 1976), pp. 197-98.

[47] *OR,* pp. 771-72.

On Anthony's Hill, Morton's artillery had been double-shotted with canister. He waited until the Federals were at close range and then opened with deadly effect. The infantry also poured in deadly volleys, and the gorge was filled with smoke of battle. When the enemy broke and fled, the old "Rebel Yell" could be heard echoing in the cold woods as the Confederates pursued.

Walthall describes the infantry action:

> The enemy with a heavy mounted force, as soon as we got on the dirt road at Pulaski, began to press us with boldness and vigor. It was determined to turn upon him, and as an advantageous position for this, a line was selected (25th) on Anthony's Hill, about seven miles from Pulaski. Here Featherston's and Palmer's commands, with a brigade of cavalry on either flank, were put in ambush to await the enemy's approach, Reynold's and Feild's being reserved for support. So broken is the ground at that point, and so densely wooded, that there was no difficulty in effectually concealing the troops. A line no thicker than a strong line of skirmishers was exposed, which the enemy promptly engaged, and when it proved stubborn he dismounted part of his troops and made a charge. When the attacking force neared the troops lying in wait for them the latter delivered a destructive fire, and a section of artillery (Morton's) belonging to the cavalry, concealed nearby, opened upon it with considerable effect. The enemy retreated in disorder, and my command, by prompt pursuit, captured a number of prisoners and horses and one piece of artillery. (Wilson said this was the only gun ever taken from his cavalry.) About sunset we withdrew from this position, and at 11 o'clock reached Sugar Creek, where we camped.[48]

The rearguard camped on Sugar Creek on what was left of Christmas night. The march that night to Sugar Creek was a fourteen mile nightmare. "The roads were now as bad as ever an army encountered, and the horses had to be pushed through mud and slush every step of the way, often belly-deep, and never less than up to their knees. The men marched barefooted in many cases, often waist deep in ice-cold water, while sleet beat upon their heads and shoulders; nevertheless, by one o'clock that night, they had reached Sugar Creek, fourteen miles from Anthony's Hill. There the stream was clear, with the pebbly bottom; and the men were brought to a halt, in order to wash the mire from their ragged clothing, and, building fires, were suffered to remain at rest until daylight."[49]

---

[48]*Ibid.*, p. 747.

[49]Jordan and Pryor, p. 651.

General Wilson in his report describes the terrain and action around Pulaski and at Anthony's Hill:

> The rebels retreated that night (24th) to the vicinity of Pulaski, but the next day (25th) were driven through that place, closely pressed by Harrison's brigade. The bridges across Richland Creek were saved by the celerity and good management with which Colonel Harrison handled his command, so that, without delaying, he continued the pursuit, and by 2 p.m. came up with the enemy strongly entrenched at the head of a heavily wooded and deep ravine, through which ran the road. The country was so difficult and broken that the men of Harrison's brigade were necessarily in weak order, but nothing daunted, they pursued the enemy's skirmishers back to their fortified position. Here they were compelled to halt, and while the troops of Hatch's, Croxton's, and Hammond's commands were marching through the woods to their support, a few hundred of the enemy's infantry, for the first time since the battles about Nashville, sallied from their breastworks and drove back Harrison's attenuated skirmish line and captured one gun of Smith's battery (I, Fourth U.S. Artillery). They were promptly driven back, but succeeded in getting the captured gun off.[50]

Wilson's troops had driven Armstrong's brigade through Pulaski, and his advance under Colonel Harrison had arrived at Richland Creek on the south edge of town on the 25th. Forrest's men were just leaving. The Confederate pontoon train had passed through Pulaski on the 23rd, and the Federals were uncertain where the planned crossing of the Tennessee would be made.

The turnpike had ended at Richland Creek in Pulaski and from there on the roads would be country dirt roads, now mud. The Federals double-teamed their artillery and all wagons. They found the road south of Richland Creek "covered with broken down wagons, abandoned artillery, ammunition, etc., left by the enemy." According to citizens reports, mules were taken from these wagons and put to the pontoon train.

At 3:30 (25th), Wood received a dispatch from Wilson asking for infantry support since Forrest had given him a check. Wilson had telegraphed Wood: "We are four miles from Pulaski, on the Lamb's Ferry road, and have met a slight check. If you bring up your infantry, we may get some prisoners, and I think I shall be able to drive Forrest off."[51]

---

[50]*Ibid.*, p. 567.

[51]*OR*, Series I, Vol. 45, Part 2, p. 348.

Colonel Thomas J. Harrison, commanded the First Brigade of the Sixth Division in Wilson's Cavalry Corps. He being the chief Federal actor in the Anthony's Hill fight, tells his side of the story. This brigade consisted of the Sixteenth Illinois, the Fifth Iowa, and the Seventh Ohio Cavalry regiments. On Christmas day he led the advance in pursuit of the Confederates, and moved out of camp ten miles north of Pulaski at 5 a.m. Eight miles north of Pulaski he struck the Confederate rearguard, either Ross' Texas or Armstrong's Mississippi brigade, since they alternated on the rearguard position that day. The Confederate cavalry retired only at the last minute and when about to be overwhelmed. Harrison tells of driving the enemy from every position, and that upon reaching Pulaski the Fifth Iowa charged through town and saved the covered bridge over Richland Creek which had been fired. He forced the Southerners back seven miles to the head of a narrow gorge where they had taken position on a high hill behind strong barricades. The position was hidden by heavy timber. Harrison dismounted the three regiments and deployed them as follows: Seventh Ohio on the right and the Sixteenth Illinois on the left of the Fifth Iowa. They moved upon the position, and were met by the fire from a masked battery of three guns. Two lines of Walthall's Confederate infantry charged over the works with a column of cavalry down the main road. Harrison says he fell back about half a mile, and receiving support drove the enemy back. ". . . regret to state that Company I, Fourth U.S. Artillery, were obliged to abandon one gun and limber at this time. The stand made by the enemy at this point was to save his train, as we had driven his rearguard sharp upon it. In the hasty evacuation of Pulaski the enemy threw two cannon into the creek, burned a locomotive and train of five cars loaded with arms and ammunition, and it is reported he left near town two locomotives in good order. For six miles below Pulaski the road was strewn with abandoned artillery ammunition, and burning and abandoned wagons. I think he saved some twenty wagons entire."[52]

Wilson would later write of the fight on Anthony's Hill: "Just before sundown on Christmas Eve (*sic*), Forrest in a fit of desperation, made a stand on a heavily wooded ridge, at the head of a ravine, and by a rapid and savage counter-thrust drove back Harrison's brigade and cap-

---

[52]*Ibid.*, Part 1, p. 602.

tured one gun, which he succeeded in carrying away as the sole trophy of that desperate campaign."[53]

Capt. John W. Morton, Chief of Forrest's Artillery, tells of an incident at Anthony's Hill:

General Armstrong's troops had expended all of their ammunition, and he had asked permission from Forrest to withdraw, but was told to hold on a little longer. A second time Armstrong asked permission to pull his men out of their exposed position, and again Forrest had him remain. Finally the point could no longer be held, and Armstrong's men fell back from their untenable and exposed position. As he rode by General Walthall and General Forrest he said to General Walthall, with tears streaming down his face, "General Walthall won't you please make that d————d man on the horse see that my men are forced to retreat?" Forrest, with unusual gentleness and understanding, told him he was gaining time for Hood's main body to get across Sugar Creek. He then looked at his watch and said, "It is about time for all of us to get out of here."

When Forrest fell back after the Anthony's Hill fight both the Federals and the Confederates marched along parallel roads for the same crossing on Sugar Creek. The Yankees were slow to move out for fear of another Forrest ambush. Rain mixed with sleet made the night march miserable, but the Southerners moved on, following their great leader. The weather worsened. The main army, the trains, artillery, and now followed by the rearguard had made the roads a sea of mud. It was frozen, but not sufficiently to hold the weight of a horse. Horses sank knee deep at every step. Wilson later wrote: ". . . Untold hardship of advance, battle, and retreat. Men and horses had suffered all the rigors of winter, snow, rain, frost, mud, and exposure. During the night the temperature would fall so as to make ice form half an inch thick and this was far too thin to carry horses without breaking through. As a consequence, the roads were worked up into a continuous quagmire. The horses legs were covered with mud, and this, in turn, was frozen, so that great numbers of the poor animals were entirely disabled, their hoofs softened and the hair of their legs so rubbed off that it was impossible for them to travel. Hundreds lost their hoofs entirely. . . ."[54]

This particular area in Middle Tennessee which had been occupied by both armies for an extended period offered little in the way of sustenance for man or beast.

---

[53]James Harrison Wilson, *Battles and Leaders of the Civil War,* 4 vols. (New York: Century Company, 1887), 4:471.

[54]Wilson, *Under the Old Flag,* 2:142-43.

Wilson later said additionally: "The men of both forces suffered dreadfully, but the poor cavalry horses fared still worse than their riders. Scarcely a withered corn blade could be found for them, and thousands exhausted by overwork, famished with hunger or crippled so that death was a mercy, with hoofs dropping off from frost and mud, fell by the roadside never to rise again. By the time the corps found rest on the Tennessee River, it could muster scarcely 7,000 horses fit for service."[55] Forrest would have been extremely pleased to have mustered 7,000 men and horses—at any time!

The Journal of the Army of Tennessee shows the army wagon train had moved out of Pulaski toward Bainbridge at daylight on the 22nd. The rearguard could not have been "sharp upon it" as reported by Harrison. The journal for the next three days is quoted: "December 23—Army headquarters on Powell's Ferry Road, six miles from Lexington, Ala. The army, after the day's march, camped as follows: Stevenson's Corps at the intersection of the Lamb's Ferry road with the Powell road, four miles from Lexington; General Stewart in rear, on the Lamb's Ferry road; General Cheatham moved on the Lawrenceburg road.

December 24—Army headquarters at Mr. Joiner's, eleven miles from Bainbridge road. Stevenson's corps reached and camped on Shoal Creek and Stewart's in his rear. General Cheatham has not yet come in to the main road from the Powell road.

December 25—Army headquarters at Bainbridge, on the Tennessee River. The pontoon was being laid across the river as rapidly as the arrival of the boats would allow. General Cheatham came into the main road this morning, and in rear of Stevenson's corps moved to the river, where a line covering the bridge was formed. Cheatham occupying the right and Stevenson the left. General Stewart's corps, upon arriving at the point where Cheatham's corps came into the main road, was put into position so as to protect both roads."[56]

Colonel W.D. Gale, Asst. Adjutant General of Stewart's corps wrote his wife that "Every mind was haunted by the apprehension that we did not have boats enough to make a bridge." The road from Pulaski had been "strewn with dead horses and mules, broken wagons and

[55]Wilson, *Battles and Leaders,* 4:472.

[56]*OR*, p. 673-74.

worse than all, broken pontoons. We counted as we passed them, one, two, three to fifteen."

The main army was arriving at the Tennessee and the pontoon bridge was started while Forrest's rearguard was still battling Wilson's troopers at Anthony's Hill on Christmas day. The Confederates had a pontoon train under a very capable engineer officer by the name of Captain Robert L. Cobb, but did not have enough pontoons to bridge the Tennessee. Major H.N. Pharr tells the story of how Cobb "saved the Army of Tennessee" at Bainbridge:

> After Hood's disastrous defeat at Nashville, we (the engineer battalion) put him over the Duck River at Columbia. We were there informed tha the General had selected Bainbridge as the point at which he would attempt to recross the Tennessee, and were ordered to hasten forward with the battalion. At the same time, Capt. Cobb was dispatched with his company of pontooniers, mounted on mules, to Decatur, Ala., to bring down if possible, several pontoon boats that had been captured there, as we did not have enough. The whole corps of engineers felt that upon his success depended the fate of the army, and we all knew that to run the Muscle Shoals at that stage of water, in such frail boats, was a hazardous task.
>
> We approached the river late on the second afternoon, with that grand old army disheartened, disorganized, wrecked, behind us, and the broad Tennessee river before, while the roar of artillery in the distance told plainly that the rearguard was being pressed by the victorious foe.
>
> Just then the chief engineer rode rapidly up, his face all aglow, his fine gray eyes sparkling, and exclaimed, "Cobb has come! Cobb has come!" A wild cheer for Cobb went up from the old battalion, for all felt that the army was saved.[57]

The rearguard reached Sugar Creek at 11:00 o'clock Christmas night after the hard day's fight at Anthony's Hill. The muddy fourteen mile march in a heavy mixture of rain and sleet with a brisk north wind was almost more than these weather hardened veterans could take as they trudged with heaviness toward Sugar Creek. The goal was to reach the crossings before the Yankees. The weather became worse as the night went on, and the horses plowed through mud from knee-deep up to their saddle girths. Some of the men were barefooted.

The ordnance train with the main army had been parked at Sugar Creek while the mules had been used to help transport the pontoons on

---

[57]*Confederate Veteran,* Vol. 3, no. 8 (August 1895), 249.

to the river. The mules were returned in the night and the ordnance train left early on the 26th before the arrival of the Yankees.

About daylight, Reynolds and Feild's brigades of the rearguard were aligned in a narrow ravine about 200 yards south of the creek and built barricades. The infantry was in deep sedge grass, and there was also a heavy fog which helped conceal them. A small screening force out front was purposely exposed to draw the enemy. The other two brigades of infantry were about a half mile back as a reserve. The cavalry brigades were grouped as follows: Ross' Texans on the right with Armstrong's Mississippians on the left of the first line of foot troops. Chalmers was posted along a parallel road leading to the crossing. At half-past eight the Yankee cavalry could be heard splashing through the creek and began to form in line. The screening force fell back to the breastworks when encountered by the enemy who were dismounted at that point. They came to within thirty paces of the breastworks. Upon a signal shot by Morton's artillery, the infantry poured a deadly stream of fire which caused them to break in confusion. Morton's artillery further aided in the repluse. Walthall's infantry followed them through the icy creek. Most of the horses of a dismounted regiment were captured. The Federals were driven back through their horse-holders and some prisoners were taken. Ross' Texans pursued the routed men for about a mile. They proved to be from Hammond's brigade. Forrest held the line for about two more hours after the pursuit was ordered back. The fog had concealed the creek, and many of the Federals had plunged over the steep bank into the water. Some were shot and others captured.

Here at Sugar Creek was the last fighting in Hood's ill-fated Tennessee campaign, and Walthall's infantry, Forrest's cavalry, and Morton's artillery "were the last guns of the Army of Tennessee that found echo in battle" on Tennessee soil during the war. When Forrest withdrew he left a picket at the creek until 4 o'clock that afternoon. The march of the rearguard resumed at 9 o'clock for the Tennessee, and that night of the 26th and 27th Forrest camped sixteen miles from the river.[58]

Wilson brushes off the fight at Sugar Creek. He says:

At the latter place (Sugar Creek) they took up a strong position and held it until General Hammond had developed his forces and got ready to attack.

---

[58]Jordan and Pryor, p. 653.

Hastily withdrawing they continued their march throughout the night.

It had now become evident that no effort on the part of my command could again bring Forrest to risk another engagement. Having neither rations nor forage, and learning that the main body of the rebels had already reached the south side of the Tennessee, I directed the corps to halt. . . .[59]

1st Lieutenant J.E. Tunnell, commanding Company B, 14th Texas Infantry, Ector's Brigade leaves the following report of the action at Anthony's Hill and Sugar Creek: "On Christmas day we left Pulaski setting fire to the bridge there when we left. The rascals came up, put the fire out, crossed over and attacked us on the first hill (Anthony's Hill). We gave them a good drubbing, however, capturing some of their artillery. We made a forced march then to Sugar Creek, only a few miles from the Tenn. R., wading the creek in a late hour of the night and bivouacked at the edge of the valley, half a mile or more from the creek.

At daylight we were aroused and informed that the Yankees were on our side of the creek. A dense fog rested upon the valley. After waiting for some time for them to make an attack, which they failed to do, we were ordered to charge them, and did it very successfully. In trying to cross the creek on their big cavalry horses, the banks on our side were so high they could not ascend them and our boys captured many large, fine horses. When they were driven across the creek General Ross' Cavalry Brigade charged and drove them for miles. Our brigade got a good Yankee breakfast from the saddle pockets on horses killed and captured. From thence to the pontoon bridge on the Tenn. R. our brigade was largely mounted."[60]

The pontoon was completed at daylight on the 26th. Forrest was fighting Wilson's troopers at Sugar Creek at about that time. Morton's artillery had played its usual prominent role at Anthony's Hill as well as at Sugar Creek. Forrest liked to have his artillery well up front and Captain Morton was the man who could put it there and he knew how to use it. The men called his guns the four "Bull Pups." Forrest was very proud of his young artillery commander, but such was not the case when Morton first reported to him for duty in 1862. Captain John W. Morton, Jr.,

---

[59]*OR*, p. 567.

[60]*Confederate Veteran*, Vol. 3 (July 1904), 319.

was a seventeen year old student at Western Military Institute at Nashville when the war began. He first enlisted in an artillery company, was elected First Lieutenant of Porter's Battery, and later was captured when Fort Donelson fell. He was later exchanged.

When he first reported for duty to Forrest, that rugged leader burst into sharp language befitting a cavalryman, and said: "I'd like to know why in the hell Bragg sent that tallow-faced boy here to take charge of my artillery? I'll not stand for it!" But he did and Morton stayed.

Later, in a letter dated May 10, 1865 Forrest wrote: "... He was ordered to report to me by General Bragg, to take charge of my horse artillery in November 1862. His appearance was so youthful and his form so frail that (wishing stout active men for my service) I at first hesitated to receive him. . . . the gallant and efficient manner in which he handled his guns won my confidence and esteem. . . ."

Robert A. Jarman, Co. K, 27th Miss. Infantry, Brantley's brigade of Lee's corps, retreated with the main army from Pulaski. He says the retreat began in earnest after Pulaski. Brantley's brigade

arrived at Shoal Creek and told to wade on Dec. 24, 1864. Four inches of snow. Some rolled up their pants, but when water touched their naked legs no coaxing or persuasion could get the brigade in until General Brantley started across on his horse. The horse slipped and fell, ducking him good, then the men took to the water like ducks, laughing as they went. The water was very, very cold, but there was a row of fence fired for us to warm by on the south bank. After warming a short while we were told for every man to get a piece of fire, as we were going into camp close by.

Next morning up early for the Tennessee where they began putting in a pontoon bridge just below the shoals where there used to be a little town called Bainbridge. The first thing to do was to lash two or three pontoon boats together and use them as a ferry boat to cross over some artillery and horses to go towards Florence and protect our bridge from Federal gunboats until the army could cross. We had the bridge completed by 3 o'clock that night, when at once the wagon trains started over. . . .

After the wagon train had crossed, our division was crossed over on Tuesday, December 27th, and as soon as the division was over, I got a leave of absence for 24 hours to visit my paternal grandmother who lived about 4 miles off. I got to grandma's just after dinner, but had a good dinner fixed for me and left next morning, rejoining my command. After dark that night, when I called for Co. K, and Reid, Co. F, who had carried my gun and accoutrements for me, poured out the contents of my haversack, and after supper pulled out several twists of home-made tobacco and then for a smoke by all hands."

155

After a short furlough when they reached Tupelo, Jarman later rejoined his unit in North Carolina, but was too late for the Battle of Bentonville.[61]

The Federals did not follow the Confederates to the Tennessee after Sugar Creek, except for a small force under Colonel Spaulding. On the 27th Wilson dispatched 500 of his best mounted men to try to pass through or around to the river. Spaulding picked up a few Confederate stragglers as prisoners, worn out from the long march. When he reached the river the last of Hood's forces had crossed, and the pontoon bridge had been taken up in the night.[62]

Walthall's infantry took up the march to the river from Sugar Creek around 9 a.m. on the 26th. At 1:00 p.m. the cavalry withdrew, except for the pickets, and were put in movement for the river. The infantry troops also bivouacked sixteen miles from the river on the 26th and 27th. Next day they reached Shoal Creek, and after crossing over took position to guard the crossing. Here the cavalry passed them, and moved on to the river. There is no mention that either the infantry or the cavalry cheered the other as the cavalry marched past. The Federal Commander Wilson, had experienced this at the crossing of Duck River when the Federal infantrymen had cheered his cavalry. Well might either Confederate force have cheered the other for a job well done! On the 27th at Shoal Creek Walthall reverted to the command of his corps commander, General A.P. Stewart.[63]

On the 27th Reynold's brigade, of Walthall's Division, had been left to hold the position at Shoal Creek while the remainder of the unit moved up at 10 p.m. to "occupy the works covering the pontoon bridge, from which the rear division of the main army had just withdrawn." They remained there until daylight, the 28th, when all crossed the river except for 200 men furnished to assist in taking up the bridge.

In his report of Jan. 24, 1865, General Forrest says: "I am also indebted to Major General Walthall for much valuable service rendered during the retreat from Columbia. He exhibited the highest soldierly

---

[61]*Civil War Times Illustrated,* Vol. 12, No. 2 (May 1973).

[62]Wilson, *Under the Old Flag,* 2:128-29.

[63]*OR,* pp. 724-28, 758-59.

qualities. Many of his men were without shoes, but they bore their sufferings without murmur and were ever ready to meet the enemy."

On Sunday, Christmas day, Cheatham's corps reached Shoal Creek. They had a difficult crossing due to deep water and a rough ford, but succeeded in fording and bivouacked between the creek and river. They built breastworks and took position to guard the bridge.

On the 26th would begin the crossing of the Tennessee on Cobb's pontoon bridge the torn, shattered and vanquished remnants of some of the most renowned regiments, brigades, and divisions of the western Confederate army.

In his report General Bate says his division crossed the river on the evening of the 25th, but this is surely in error since the Journal of the Army of Tennessee for December 26 to January 2, 1865, inclusive, states: "The pontoon bridge was completed by daylight on the 26th instant, and the army was occupied two days in crossing." On December 26, the Itinerary of the Army of Tennessee states "Pontoon bridge completed today and the army commenced crossing. Headquarters at Bainbridge." Also the itinerary of Cheatham's corps for Monday, December 26—"The pontoon across the river was completed this morning after working on it all night, General Cheatham supervising in person, and about sunrise the trains began to cross. By night most of our wagons and artillery had crossed. . . . Two gunboats came up the river in the afternoon to within two or three miles of the bridge, but were driven back by our batteries."[64]

Cheatham went over to near Bainbridge and got some much needed sleep, and left word for his troops to start crossing at 3 o'clock the next morning. It took two days for the army to cross. Lee's and Cheatham's corps crossed on the 26th and Stewart's and the cavalry on the 27th—28th. Stewart's corps was left to cover the crossing and was the last to move across on the morning of the 28th. The last infantry outfit to cross was the brave and depleted ranks of Colonel David Coleman's Thirty-ninth North Carolina from Ector's small band of heroes, commanded by a captain.

---

[64]*Ibid.*, p. 732.

Among Cheatham's troops to cross on the 26th were the fine old Arkansas regiments of Cleburne's command. Six months ago, almost to the day, on the 27th of June, Lieut. Colonel William H. Martin had leaped atop the head-logs on Kennesaw Mountain and waved a white flag to temporarily halt the slaughter of the Yankees in his front. He offered a truce long enough for them to remove their wounded. The woods had caught fire from the cannon blasts. The temperature was over 100°, and the leaves and underbrush extremely dry. There was the horrible danger of the helpless wounded dying from incineration. Colonel Martin was now gone—severely wounded in Hood's reckless fighting around Atlanta. In that action, too, six other colonels and Lieutenant Colonels from the Arkansas regiments were either killed or wounded. Now the depleted and exhausted ranks of the 1st, 2nd, 5th, 13th, 15th, and 24th regiments were consolidated into one regiment under command of Colonel Peter V. Green.

Forrest's cavalry crossed on the evening of the 27th. The Seventh Tennessee Cavalry of Chalmers' division went across on the sleet-covered pontoon bridge at midnight December 27th, leading their horses.

Apparently the artillery planted by Cheatham down river kept the gunboats at bay, plus "the natural timidity of a deepwater sailor in a shoal-water river." If Admiral Lee had made more of an attempt to bar passage, Hood might not have been able to cross.

After the pitiful remnant of the once proud Army of Tennessee was across, ". . . there was not a man of all that battle and weather-tempered band who did not feel a sense of relief at the moment." The pontoons were taken up on the 28th.[65]

The wounded Texas captain, Samuel T. Foster of the 24th Texas Cavalry (dismounted), had made it out of Tennessee with Granbury's brigade. On the 27th, he was traveling down the river toward Tuscumbia. His wounded leg was mending very fast. Still very cold. On Jan. 1, 1865, he was near Corinth, Mississippi. The weather was clear and cold with sleet on the ground. It had rained and sleeted on Dec. 30 and was bitter cold.[66]

---

[65] Jordan and Pryor, p. 654.

[66] Foster.

On December 29, 1864, Thomas issued General Orders No. 169, announcing the end of the campaign:

SOLDIERS: The major-general commanding announces to you that the rearguard of the flying and dispirited enemy was driven across the Tennessee River on the night of the 27th instant. The impassable state of the roads and consequent impossibility to supply the army compels a closing of the campaign for the present.

Although short, it has been brilliant in its achievements and unsurpassed in its results by any other of this war, and is one of which all who participated therein may be justly proud. That veteran rebel army which though driven from position to position, opposed a stubborn resistance to much superior numbers during the whole of the Atlanta campaign. Taking advantage of the absence of the largest portion of the army which had been opposed to it in Georgia, invaded Tennessee, buoyant with hope, expecting Nashville, Murfreesboro and the whole of Tennessee and Kentucky to fall into its power an easy prey, and scarcely fixing a limit to its conquests, after having received the most terrible check at Franklin, on the 30th of November, that any army has received during this war, and later met with a signal repulse from the brave garrison of Murfreesboro in its attempt to capture that place, was finally attacked at Nashville, and although your forces were inferior to it in numbers, it was hurled back from the coveted prize upon which it had only been permitted to look from a distance, and finally sent flying, dismayed and disordered, whence it came, impelled by the instinct of self-preservation, and thinking only how it could relieve itself for short intervals from your persistent and harrassing pursuit, by burning the bridges over the swollen streams as it passed them, untl finally it had placed the broad waters of the Tennessee River between you and its shattered, diminished, and discomfited columns, leaving its artillery and battle-flags in your victorious hands, lasting trophies of your noble daring and lasting mementos of the enemy's disgrace and defeat.

You have diminished the forces of the rebel army, since it crossed the Tennessee River to invade the State, at the least estimate, 15,000 men, among whom were killed, wounded, or captured 18 general officers.

Your captures from the enemy as far as reported, amount to 68 pieces of artillery, 10,000 prisoners, as many stands of small-arms, several thousand of which have been gathered in, and the remainder strew the route of the enemy's retreat, and between 30 and 40 flags, besides compelling him to destroy much ammunition and abandon many wagons, and, unless he is mad, he must forever relinquish all hope of bringing Tennessee again within the lines of the accursed rebellion.

A short time will now be given you to prepare to continue the work so nobly begun.

In his report of Jan. 20, 1865, Thomas wrote: "He (Hood) had formed a powerful rearguard, made up of detachments from all his organized force, numbering about 4,000 infantry, under General Walt-hall, and all his available cavalry, under Forrest. With the exception of his rearguard, his army had become a disheartened rabble of half-armed and barefooted men, who sought every opportunity to fall out by the wayside and desert their cause to put an end to their sufferings. The rearguard, however, was undaunted and firm, and did its work bravely to the last."[67]

Some of Thomas' conclusions are open to debate, but his remark pertaining to the rearguard is universally concurred in by everyone. From the beginning of the rout the brave rifles of the infantry of Lee's corps withstood the initial shock charges of Wilson's victorious cavalry along the pike until relieved by Cheatham's corps on the 18th. Lee, the army's youngest Lieutenant-General and corps commander did a mas-terful military feat at the beginning of the retreat and saved Hood's shat-tered army. From Columbia to Shoal Creek, the incomparable Forrest had commanded the rearguard and was "a tower of strength, animating the rearguard with his own sublime courage. . . ." Both rearguard per-formances, together with the part played by Chalmers', Buford's, and Armstrong's cavalry before reaching Columbia, and later under Forrest, were deserving of the highest praise from the enemy leader. Thomas' estimate of the strength of Walthall's infantry force, however, was twice its actual strength.

Major General Clayton, commanding a division in Lee's Corps said that the retrograde movement to the Tennessee was "a most painful march, characterized by more suffering than it had ever before been my misfortune to witness."[68]

Private Nelson Rainey of General W.H. Jackson's cavalry divi-sion was with the rearguard on the retreat southward and described con-ditions: "The weather was very cold . . . rain, half sleet, then snow half sleet on the rocky frozen roads. We all suffered. The infantry most of all. Not half of these poor boys had blankets, very few overcoats. More than half without shoes, their feet tied up in gunny sacks or old cloth. We have all read in history that Washington's barefoot soldiers left bloody tracks

---

[67]*OR*, p. 42.

[68]*Ibid.*, p. 700.

on the ground. I saw such instances, plenty of them, on this retreat. The boys were hungry too, all hungry. At one place, our company commissary officer, Bill Eanes, found a pen of fairly fat hogs. We had a day's ration of pork which we ate raw—everything too wet to make a fire. At a cabin I parched corn in an old shovel. George and I lived on that for two days."[69]

In all the misery of cold, mud, hunger, wounds, and death, the Confederate soldier in the Army of Tennessee retained his sense of humor. Thomas J. Walker, Company "C," Ninth Tennessee Infantry tells this story:

> During the whole retreat it was intensely cold, raining, sleeting, and snowing. Being in the rear of the army, (he was with Maney's brigade under Walthall as part of the rearguard) I have actually seen blood on the snow from the bleeding feet of those poor barefoot soldiers. I recollect late one evening, I was detailed to go back to draw some rations for the company. A Georgia command was passing. We had then left the pike and were traveling over desperately muddy roads, in places knee deep. The night was very dark and rainy. As the command was passing, I heard one fellow call out, "Oh, Bill, Oh Billy." The response came back, "Joe Jones, you blasted fool! What do you want with me?" This was spoken in a very fretful tone. The reply came back, "Billy, don't you think South Carolina was rather hasty?" The sally seemed to produce a cheering effect. Immediately I could hear joyous laughter and cheerful voices. I relate this incident to show that although under desperate conditions, the noble boys of our army bore their sufferings patiently and with light and merry hearts.[70]

Another oft told incident is from Dr. W.J. McMurray's history of the Twentieth Tennessee Regiment:

> To show the spirit, wit, and fun there was in the Confederate soldier, while half-clad and half-starved and barefooted, and fighting three to one, I will relate this: on the retreat near Pulaski, the roads were muddy and crowded, and every soldier was pulling along as best he could. General Hood and staff were passing, and as they were about to crowd an old soldier out of the road, he struck up this song, where General Hood could hear it,—(to the tune of "Yellow Rose of Texas):
>
> > You may talk about your dearest maid,
> > And sing of Rosalie,
> > But the gallant Hood of Texas
> > Played hell in Tennessee.[71]

---

[69]Bob Womack, *Call Forth the Mighty Men* (Bessemer, AL: Colonial Press, 1987), pp. 496-97.

[70]Walker, 1:72.

[71]McMurray, p. 352.

There were also other versions, to include:

> And now I'm going Southward,
> For my heart is full of woe,
> I'm going back to Georgia
> To find my "Uncle Joe."
> You may talk about your Beauregard,
> And sing of General Lee
> But the gallant Hood of Texas
> Played hell in Tennessee.

In a report sent to Thomas' chief of staff, from Lexington, Alabama on Dec. 30, 1864, General Wood, commanding the Federal Fourth Corps reported the complete demoralization of Hood's army as they made their way across the Tennessee. According to citizens, half of the men were unarmed and everything like organization gone. Two captured Yankees had escaped and reported conditions on the march. One of the prisoners was with Lee's corps to within two miles of the river when he escaped. He said not more than half the corps was armed. Yet, these were the same troops that had fought so tenaciously along the Franklin-Columbia pike on the 16th and 17th. It is hard to believe they deliberately disarmed themselves afterward. He also reported that there was no company, regiment, or brigade organization, and that the men moved in squads of 6 or 8 up to 15-20 men. They halted or marched at their own choice. From Pulaski on to the point of his escape the Southerners had only parched corn to eat.

The second escaped prisoner marched with Cheatham's corps on the old military road. About one regiment could be formed out of the whole corps to guard 140 prisoners. This corps, too, marched in small squads, and he occasionally saw a musket. Both men spoke of the lack of proper clothing for their captors. There was a great lack of blankets, many without shoes, and all of them poorly clad.

Wood concluded by saying: "Feel confident that Hood has not taken across the Tennessee River more than half the men he brought across it; that not more than one-half of those taken out are armed; that he lost three-fourths of his artillery; and that, for rout, demoralization, even disintegration, the condition of his command is without parallel in this war."[72]

---

[72]*OR*, p. 170.

Perhaps one of the most erroneous and ridiculous official statements made during the entire war was one concluding the Confederate Inspector General's report Jan. 8, 1865: "It (The Army of Tennessee) was well clothed and well fed during the campaign in Tennessee." He had previously said: "The spirit and morale of the army was not good after the engagement at Nashville, but had improved before I left it, and no apprehension need be felt for its safety."[73]

General Richard Taylor, son of President Zachary Taylor, commanded the Confederate Department of East Louisiana, Mississippi, and Alabama. It was to his department that the defeated Army of Tennessee returned when they entered Alabama and recrossed the Tennessee. In his memoirs Taylor has this to say about his shock upon seeing the Army of Tennessee at Tupelo, Miss., afer its return from the Tennessee campaign:

> ... At Tupelo... I met him (Hood) and the remains of his army. Within my experience were assaults on positions, in which heavy losses were sustained without success; the field had been held—retreats, but preceded by repulse of the foe and followed by victory. This was my first view of a beaten army, an army that for four years had shown a constancy worthy of the "Ten Thousand," and a painful sight it was. Many guns and small arms had been lost, and the ranks were depleted by thousands of prisoners and missing. Blankets, shoes, clothing, and accoutrements were wanting. I have written of the unusual severity of the weather in the latter part of November, and it was now near January. Some men perished by frost; many had the extremeties severely bitten.

> ... Hood followed the enemy to Nashville, and took position south of the place, where he remained ten days or more. It is difficult to imagine what objects he had in view. The town was open to the north, whence the Federal commander, Thomas, was hourly receiving reinforcements, while he had none to hope for. His plans perfected and his reinforcements joined, Thomas moved, and Hood was driven off; and had the Federal general possessed dash equal to his tenacity and caution, one fails to see how Hood could have brought man or gun across the Tennessee River. It is painful to criticize Hood's conduct of this campaign. Like Ney, "the bravest of the brave," he was a splendid leader in battle, and as a brigade or division commander unsurpassed; but arrived at higher rank, he seems to have been impatient of control, and openly disapproved of Johnston's conduct of affairs between Dalton and Atlanta. Unwillingness to obey is often interpreted by governments into capacity for command.[74]

---

[73]*Ibid.*, p. 676.

[74]Richard Taylor, *Destruction and Reconstruction*, ed. Richard B. Harwell (New York: Longman's, Green and Company, 1955), pp. 216-17.

Thomas, in his report gave Colonel W.J. Palmer, commanding Fifteenth Pennsylvania Cavalry the "credit of giving Hood's army the last blow of the campaign, at a distance of over 200 miles from where we first struck the enemy on the 15th of December, near Nashville."

The Confederate pontoon bridge had been taken up on Tuesday night and Wednesday morning the 27th and 28th. The entire pontoon train consisted of 200 wagons under command of Captain Cobb, the same officer who had floated the captured pontoons down from Decatur. Thursday night, the 29th, the train had camped at LaGrange bound for Columbus, Mississippi with only a small cavalry force from Roddy's command for escort. Col. W.J. Palmer, Fifteenth Pennsylvania Cavalry, caught up with the rear of the train ten miles beyond Russellville, at dark. He met no resistance, and his advance guard rode through to the front of the train, which extended for five miles, and consisted of seventy-eight pontoon-boats and about 200 wagons, with all the necessary accoutrements and material, engineering instruments, etc. All the mules and oxen, except what the pontooniers and teamsters were able to cut loose and ride off, were standing hitched to the wagons. Three boats had been set on fire, but little damage done. A few prisoners were captured, and Palmer camped about the middle of the train and fed his horses. He then started both ways and burned the entire train which took until 3 a.m. He also learned from a negro servant of Captain Cobb's that a large supply train was ahead. The next night he surprised it in camp just over the state line in Mississippi. It consisted of 110 wagons and over 500 mules. He burned the wagons, shot or sabred all the mules he could not lead off or use as mounts for the prisoners. In one of the wagons was Colonel McCrosky of Hood's infantry, who had been badly wounded at Franklin. He left a tent, some stores, and one of the prisoners to take care of him. He then started back and evaded all pursuit.[75]

It is unbelievable that a five mile train of pontoons, and a supply train of 110 wagons and 500 mules was not afforded more protection! Captain Cobb and the engineers had gone to a lot of trouble to secure and transport these boats, to have them go up in smoke. Perhaps, just as well. The Army of Tennessee would never again make a serious river crossing. The end was near. Captain Morton, Forrest's Chief of

---

[75]*OR,* Series I, Vol. 45, Part 2, p. 643.

Artillery, says that his commander felt the battles around Nashville "had really brought the war to a close. General Forrest expressed himself to this effect many times," said Morton.[76] During the long, cold, and dreary marches of the retreat, and at night in the sodden bivouack when the bitter cold would not let sleep come, many men, no doubt, realized that the end was near. The ghosts of regiments that a year ago teemed with men, would now cross the swift shoals of the Tennessee and march on into proud history. Their fame and memory were already firmly established. Regiments, brigades, and divisions, like individuals, have souls and develop personalities down through the years of their existence. In the Confederate Army where a unit took the name of its original commander, this was especially true.

On the 19th of December Grant sent General Logan, Thomas' erstwhile replacement, the following telegram from City Point. Logan was at Louisville on the way to replace Thomas at Nashville. "The news from Thomas so far is in the highest degree gratifying. You need not go farther. Before starting to join Sherman report in Washington."[77]

Grant had had the one hundred gun victory salute fired twice to celebrate Thomas' victory. Lincoln had sent a telegram to Thomas at 11:25 a.m. on the 16th: "Please accept for yourself, officers, and men the nation's thanks for your good work of yesterday. You made a magnificent beginning. A grand consumation is within your easy reach. Do not let it slip." Is there any wonder that Thomas complained of being treated like a school boy instead of a field combat commander?[78]

On the 18th, Grant wired Thomas telling of the two hundred gun salute fired by the armies operating against Richmond in honor of his victory. However from that distance Grant warned Thomas of Forrest.[79]

Grant wired Stanton, the Secretary of War, on Dec. 20: "I think Thomas has won the Major-Generalcy, but I would wait a few days before giving it, to see the extent of damage done. . . ." Grant is still not

---

[76]John W. Morton, *The Artillery of Nathan Bedford Forrest's Cavalry* (Nashville, Publishing House of M.E. Church, South, 1909).

[77]*OR*, p. 265.

[78]*Ibid.*, p. 210.

[79]*Ibid.*, p. 248.

entirely satisfied to reward the general who has won the most decisive victory of the war!

On December 21st, another annoying telegram from General Halleck to Thomas:

"Permit me, general, to urge the vast importance of a hot pursuit of Hood's army. Every possible sacrifice should be made, and your men for a few days will submit to any hardship and privation to accomplish the great result. . . . A most vigorous pursuit on your part is therefore of vital importance to Sherman's plans. No sacrifice must be spared to attain so important an object."[80]

Thomas, apparently tired of the nagging advice from Washington and City Point, now struck back. He answered Halleck that ". . . General Hood's army is being pursued as rapidly and vigorously as it is possible for one army to pursue another. We cannot control the elements, and you must remember, that to resist Hood's advance into Tennessee I had to reorganize and almost thoroughly equip the force now under my command. I fought the battles of the 15th and 16th instant with the troops but partially equipped, and, notwithstanding the inclemency of the weather and the partial equipment have been able to drive the enemy beyond Duck River, crossing two streams with my troops, and driving the enemy from position to position, without the aid of pontoons. . . . I am doing all in my power to crush Hood's army, and, if it be possible, will destroy it; but pursuing an enemy through an exhausted country, over mud roads, completely sogged with heavy rains, is no child's play, and cannot be accomplished as quickly as thought of. . . . Although my progress may appear slow, I feel assured that Hood's army can be driven from Tennessee, and eventually be driven to the wall, by the force under my command; . . . In conclusion, I can safely state that this army is willing to submit to any sacrifice to oust Hood's army, or to strike any other blow which would contribute to the destruction of the rebellion."

After this exchange with Halleck, Secretary of War Stanton hastened to send Thomas this message: "I have seen today General Halleck's dispatch of yesterday and your reply. It is proper for me to assure you that this Department has the most unbounded confidence in your skill, vigor, and determination to employ to the best advantage all

---

[80]*Ibid.*, pp. 295-96.

the means in your power to pursue and destroy the enemy. No department could be inspired with more profound admiration and thankfulness for the great deeds you have already performed, or more confiding faith that human effort could accomplish no more than will be done by you and the gallant officers and soliders of your command."[81]

Congratulations came from various quarters including: Sheridan from the Army of the Shenandoah—200 gun salute and much cheering; George G. Meade, Army of the Potomac—100 gun salute; Admiral S.P. Lee, Commanding the Mississippi Squadron.

Andrew Johnson, then Military Governor of Tennessee wrote to Thomas ". . . The effect of the great victory over Hood's Army at Nashville is being seen and felt in every part of the State; its withering influence upon rebels is more decided than anything which has transpired since the beginning of the rebellion. . . . It is not necessary for me to say you have a nation's gratitude for what you have done. . . ."[82]

Even Grant joined the laudatory chorus on the 22nd: "You have the congratulations of the public for the energy with which you are pushing Hood. . . . If you succeed in destroying Hood's army, there will be but one army left to the so-called Confederacy capable of doing us harm. I will take care of that. . . . Let us push and do all we can before the enemy can derive benefit either from the raising of negro troops or the concentration of white troops now in the field." Grant couldn't bring himself around to congratulating Thomas, and let it go at that. He had to end with an advisory or admonitory ring to his message.[83]

On December 24th, Stanton notified Thomas, "that for your skill, courage, and conduct in the recent brilliant military operations under your command, the President has directed your nomination to be sent to the Senate as a Major-General in the U.S. Army, to fill the only vacancy existing in that grade."[84] Grant had recommended the promotion to Stanton on the 23rd.

---

81 *Ibid.*, pp. 295-96, 307.

82 *Ibid.*, p. 471.

83 *Ibid.*, p. 307.

84 *Ibid.*, pp. 328-29.

On December 29th, Thomas had wired Halleck of his intention to "halt for a short time to reorganize and refit for a renewal of the campaign, if Hood should bolt at Corinth. Should he continue his retreat to Meridian, . . . I think it would be best for the troops to be allowed til early spring, when the roads will be in condition to make a campaign into the heart of the enemy's country. . . ."[85]

Halleck immediately sabotaged the idea of waiting for a spring campaign by wiring Grant at City Point: "I think, from the tone of General Thomas' telegram of last night, that there is very little hope of his doing much further injury to Hood's army by pursuing it. You will perceive that he is disposed to postpone further operations till spring. This seems to me entirely wrong. . . . If Thomas was as active as Sherman, I would say march directly from Decatur to Talledega, Montgomery, and Selma, living upon the country, . . . But I think Thomas entirely too slow to live on the country."[86]

This stirred Grant's petulance again and he replied to Halleck that he had no idea of keeping idle troops any place. On December 31st Halleck lost no time in so informing Thomas that "General Grant does not intend that your army shall go into winter quarters; It must be ready for active operations in the field."[87]

Under a flag of truce on December 27th, Wilson sent Hood an official copy of a dispatch from Washington, D.C. announcing Sherman's capture of Savannah, Ga. "This done that you may furnish the troops of your command more recent, as well as more reliable, intelligence concerning operations in Georgia than that imparted to them during the late campaign in Tennessee."[88]

There was no pursuit and no rearguard action during the entire war to compare with that during Hood's retreat. The pursuit was vigorously executed, while the rearguard action, by a series of bold stands, protected Hood's shattered force from annihilation. In rain, dark of night, sleet, mud, snow and swollen streams, both the pursued and the pursuer

---

85 *Ibid.*, p. 403.

86 *Ibid.*, pp. 419-20.

87 *Ibid.*, p. 441.

88 *Ibid.*, p. 382.

showed great fortitude, but the pursuit failed because of the heroic stands made by Lee, Chalmers, Forrest and Walthall.[89]

General Orders No. 33, War Department quoted a joint resolution of thanks to Thomas and the army "under his command for their skill and dauntless courage, by which the rebel army under General Hood was signally defeated and driven from the State of Tennessee."[90]

There seems to have been a pattern among Northern officers to always report their opponents as "superior in numbers." Thomas seems to have been of that opinion as concerned both the Atlanta Campaign and the Tennessee Campaign. Wood, in his report says: "Thus was closed for the Fourth Corps one of the most remarkable campaigns of the war. The enemy, superior in numbers, had been driven by assault, in utter rout and demoralization from strongly entrenched positions, pursued more than 100 miles, and forced to recross the Tennessee River."[91]

December 28, 1864—4 p.m. Wilson says: "I have just received a dispatch from Colonel Spaulding, one mile and a half from Bainbridge, saying the rebel rearguard crossed the Tennessee last night and took up the pontoon bridge before daylight this morning.[92]

Colonel W.D. Gale, Stewart's Asst. Adjutant General, wrote: "Thus we toiled on till Christmas Day, cold, drizzly and muddy. We camped on the bank of Shoal Creek, and our corps (Stewart's) formed line of battle to protect the rear and let all cross, if the bridge could be made. Roddy had captured the enemy's pontoons at Decatur, and they were floated down over the Shoals. The bridge was made and the crossing began. Then began the fight with the gunboats, which tried to destroy our bridge. They were driven back and we crossed. "All is well that ends well." Every wagon, every cannon, every horse, every mule, the hogs, beeves, cavalry, infantry, and finally every scout crossed over. . . ."[93] The battered and emaciated remnants of Hood's Army of Tennessee had now crossed to the south side of the Tennessee.

---

[89]Robert Self Henry, *First with the Most Forrest* (New York: Bobbs-Merrill Company, 1944), pp. 416-17.

[90]*OR,* Series I, Vol. 45, Part 1, p. 51.

[91]*Ibid., p. 138.*

[92]*OR,* Part 2, p. 397.

[93]Bromfield L. Ridley, *Battles and Sketches of the Army of Tennessee* (Mexico, MO: Missouri Printing and Publishing Company, 1906; repr., N.p., Morningside Bookshop, 1978), p. 415.

On the 28th the pontoon was taken up, and the march resumed down the Memphis and Charleston railroad. At least, the railroad bed was not muddy. A circular was issued from Hood's headquarters directing further movements, as follows: Lee's corps to move to Rienzi, on the Mobile and Ohio railroad, Cheatham's corps to move to Corinth, and Stewart's corps was to remain at Burnsville until further orders.

Cheatham's corps, after crossing, moved through to Tuscumbia and camped in the mud along Cane Creek. By January 1, 1865 they had reached Corinth by way of Burnsville and Iuka. From Jan. 1 to 9, spent in Corinth. January 10-13, they were on the road to Tupelo by way of Rienzi. The wagon train had to go a circuitous route by way of Verona due to the condition of the roads. They reached Tupelo at 3 p.m. on the 13th.[94]

Admiral S.P. Lee reported that: "Foggy weather and a rapidly falling river prevented my reaching and destroying Hood's pontoons at Bainbridge, six miles above Florence."[95] There is no mention of the Confederate artillery on either bank planted by Stewart and Cheatham.

On January 3, Stewart and Stevenson (commanding Lee's corps) were ordered on to Tupelo. Stevenson's corps arrived on January 7 and Stewart's corps arrived on the 9th.

General Beauregard arrived at Tupelo on Jan. 15 to visit the army, and concluded his report as follows:

> Untoward and calamitous as were the issues of this campaign, never in the course of this war have the best qualities of our soldiery been more conspicuously shown; never more enthusiasm evinced than when our troops once more crossed the Tennessee River; never greater gallantry than that which was so general at Franklin; and never higher fortitude and uncomplaining devotion to duty than was displayed on the retreat from Nashville to Tupelo.
>
> The heroic dead of that campaign will ever be recollected with honor by their countrymen, and the survivors have the proud consolation that no share of the disaster can be laid to them, who have so worthily served their country, and have stood by their colors even to the last dark hours of the republic.[96]

---

[94] *OR*, Series I, Vol. 45, Part 1, pp. 674-732.

[95] *Ibid.*, Part 2, p. 507.

[96] *OR*, Series I, Vol. 45, Part 1, p. 651.

When the Fifth Tennessee Infantry, Cheatham's corps, reached Corinth, Lieutenant Edwin H. Rennolds says: "We found Lieutenant J.L. Lemonds awaiting us with wagon loads of clothing, etc. which he had collected in Henry County for us. . . . Many of us were made happy by the sight of warm clothing, so sadly needed, and made doubly valuable because we knew that the hands of loved mothers, sisters, and wives had toiled to prepare it for us. . . . Nearly all of the West Tennessee soldiers were granted thirty day's furlough, and in groups, small and large, we turned our steps homeward. The country through which we passed had so long been in an unsettled condition, and had been held alternately by both belligerants, that we were often at a loss to know whether those we met were friends or foes. However we failed to meet any bushwhackers, and all reached home safely. Here we met a royal reception and were treated like lords. Dinners and parties were the order of the day, and mothers, sisters, and sweethearts vied with each other in making our stay pleasant. But, alas! all earthly pleasure must have an end, and all too soon we must turn our faces toward the post of duty and say farewell to loved ones. So, some on foot and some on such ponies as our relatives and friends could furnish us, we started for our place of rendevous (West Point, Miss.)."[97]

Various regiments of Forrest's Cavalry were furloughed to collect absentees, procure clothing, mount themselves, and recruit. All men were instructed that if they returned with a deserter or a recruit, well mounted, they would be given a twenty day furlough within the next twelve months.

Reorganization of the cavalry also took place. The 7th, 12th, 14th, 15th Tennessee regiments and the 26th battalion were each so reduced in numbers that on Jan. 3, 1865 at Rienzi they were consolidated into one regiment. On the 5th of January they were granted 20 day furloughs and headed, joyously for their homes in West Tennessee. J.P. Young, Company A, 7th Tennessee says they gave three cheers for "their esteemed commander, General Chalmers," then "turned their horses' heads by companies toward their homes."

Private Emmett Hughes, Company E, 7th Tennessee Cavalry, who lost a brother and a brother-in-law on the campaign, wrote to his sister from Rienzi, Mississippi on January 4, 1865. His letter indicates the depleted condition of Forrest's cavalry.

> . . . I send you these few lines to let you know that I am unwell and barefooted and no chance to get anything. If Billie Myric don't start before you get this send me a pair of boots if you can get them if not a pair of shoes.

---

[97]Rennolds, pp. 114-15.

If you can't get any new ones send me some old ones . . . anything to keep my feet off the ground. Sister this has been one of the hardest trips that is on record. I am broke down my horse broke down sick & six men left our company last night Their is only ten men with the company and forty seven with the Regiment We were expext to be sent home any day until this morning and we learn the Yankees are crossing Tenn river as we have to stay here to see what they are going to do if they advance we are going to fight them if not we will be furloughed for twenty days. . . .

The Federals did not cross the Tennessee at this time and the troopers were granted twenty days furlough to recruit, refit, and remount. On March 3, 1865, Hughes wrote another letter from Verona, Mississippi. Morale had improved as well as conditions within the command: "Our camp is now pitched near Verona and this is March, 1865 . . . Our regiment is filling ranks every day. The Tennessee boys are coming in and we number four hundred. We are drawing better rations now, peas, bacon, potatoes and meal. Our horse's fare is rough, damaged corn and no fodder . . . We expect to go to Selma, Alabama. Barefooted as I was, I was not willing to surrender."[98]

Kate Cumming, the famous Confederate nurse, in her journal entry for January 20, 1865 wrote:

Hood's army is really demoralized; our loss in everything has been very great, and had it not been for our brave cavalry, scarcely a man would have been left to tell the tale. We have lost nearly all of our artillery. The company of which my brother is a member—Garrity's battery—lost one man (Edward Haggerty) all their guns excepting one.

My brother writes that the scene on leaving Tennessee was extremely depressing. On their entering it, the ladies received them joyfully, and were ready to do anything in the world for them. When they left, the grief exhibited was enough to melt a heart of stone. He says the recollection of them makes him miserable. We have been told by many that the devotion of the women to the wounded at the battle of Franklin is beyond all praise. They gave clothes of all kinds to the well soldiers.

I have heard nothing before this to equal the sufferings of the men on this last retreat. Many of them were without shoes, and the snow was lying heavily on the ground. The flesh actually dropped from their feet. I heard of one man who has been compelled to have both feet amputated from this cause.[99]

---

[98]Henry, pp. 282-85.

[99]Kate Cummin, *Journal of a Confederate Nurse,* ed. Richard B. Harwell (Baton Rouge, LA: Louisiana State University, n.d.), pp. 253-54.

On January 3, General Hood asked Richmond for permission to furlough the troops in the Army of Tennessee from the Trans-Mississippi area for 100 days. Hood the same day, notified the Secretary of War that "The army has recrossed the Tennessee River without material loss since the battle in front of Nashville." On January 8, the War Department in Richmond wired both Beauregard and Hood to repress "the proposition to furlough the Trans-Mississippi troops, the suggestion merely is dangerous; compliance would probably be fatal; extinguish, if possible, the idea." The Trans-Mississippi troops remained on duty without furloughs.

On January 2, Forrest had written to General Taylor, the Department commander, stating the needs of his command. He says that the Army of Tennessee was badly defeated and greatly demoralized, and to save it during the retreat from Nashville he was compelled to almost sacrifice his own command. He goes on to request that he be given permission to go to Richmond for official purposes as well as recreation himself, since the latter was much needed. Apparently no action was taken on Forrest's request to make the trip to Richmond. "In the retreat he was a tower of strength, animating the rearguard with his own sublime courage, keeping the harrassed and famished soldiers together under the colors and personally standing in the ranks with musket and bayonet. He was the last to recross the frontier. . . ."[100] The above quote, of course, pertains to Marshall Ney, "Bravest of the Brave," who commanded Napoleon's rearguard on the dreadful retreat from Moscow in 1812, but could just as well apply to General Forrest, as he led the rearguard in the "fearful winter retreat from Nashville." He had safely escorted the gaunt ranks of what was left of the Army of Tennessee to the south bank of the Tennessee River.

Beauregard reached Tupelo on January 15, two days after Hood had sent the following terse message to the Secretary of War in Richmond: "I respectfully request to be relieved from the command of this army."[101] On the 15th the Secretary of War notified Hood that his request had been complied with, and for him to report to the War Department in Richmond. Lt. General Taylor was named commander of the Army of Tennessee, January 23rd. The message relieving Hood was dated the 15th, but not received until the 17th. On the 16th Hood

---

[100]*Enclyclopedia Brittanica* (1951 ed.), Vol. 16, p. 405.

[101]*OR*, Series I, Vol. 45, Part 2, p. 781.

had sent the following message to President Davis: "If I am allowed to remain in command of this army, I hope you will grant me authority to reorganize it and relieve all incompetent officers. If thought best to relieve me, I am ready to command a corps or division, or do anything that may be considered best for my country." General Taylor arrived at Tupelo and assumed command of the Army of Tennessee on January 23. Hood relinquished command and departed. Soon after assumption of command by Taylor, the army was broken up and sent to Johnston in North Carolina, while some troops were sent to Mobile. Beauregard had reported that the army did not number 15,000 infantry. On this same date Hood sent a message to President Davis: "I wish to cross the Mississippi River to bring to your aid 25,000 troops. I know this can be accomplished, and earnestly desire this chance to do you so much good. Will explain my plan on arrival. I leave today for Richmond."[102]

—VALEDICTION—

The tattered columns of the hard-luck Army of Tennessee were much dispersed. Some eventually surrendered in Mississippi and Louisiana, others served and died in the defense of Mobile, Alabama and a few made it to North Carolina to meet the end with General Joseph E. Johnston. Johnston estimated that only 5,000 troops from the Army of Tennessee ever reached North Carolina. On April 4, 1865, a young aide to General A.P. Stewart, at Smithfield, North Carolina, made the following observations:

> I witnessed today the saddest spectacle of my life, the review of the skeleton Army of Tennessee, that but one year ago was replete with men, and now filed by with tattered garments, worn out shoes, barefooted, and ranks so depleted that each color was supported by only thirty or forty men. Desertion, sickness, deaths, hardships, perils and vicissitudes demonstrated themselves too plainly upon that old army not to recur to its history. Oh, what a contrast between the Dalton review and this one! The march of the remnant was so slow—colors tattered and torn with bullets—that it looked like a funeral procession. The countenance of every spectator who saw both reviews was depressed and dejected, and the solemn, stern look of the soldiery was so impressive—Oh! it is beginning to look dark in the east,

---

[102]*Ibid.,* p. 104.

gloomy in the west, and like almost a lost hope when we reflect upon the review of today.[103]

The mills of battle and of grim starvation ground it into dust; yet even then there remained a valor which might well have inspired that famous legend which was one of the conflict between the church and its assailants in earlier ages, that after the destruction of their bodies their fierce and indomitable spirits continued the desperate struggle in the realms of air. The Southern army was worn away as a blade is worn by use and yet retains its temper while but a fragment exists.[104]

What remained of the Army of Tennessee was surrendered to Sherman by Johnston on April 26, 1865 at Bennett's House, near Durham Station, North Carolina.

Once Hood was safely across the Tennessee—"The remnants were safe, but the Army of Tennessee had died in front of the gap at Franklin and on the hillsides at Nashville."[105]

---

[103] Ridley, p. 456.

[104] *The Old South,* Thomas Nelson Page, pp. 45, 50.

[105] *The Gallant Hood,* Dyer, p. 303.

APPENDIX I
BRIGADIER GENERAL
THOMAS BENTON SMITH, CSA
AND
COLONEL WILLIAM LINN MCMILLEN, USA

Thomas Benton Smith was born at Mechanicsville, Tennessee February 24, 1838. He had an only brother, John, in Company B, Twentieth Tennessee who was a color bearer, and was killed December 31, 1862 at the Battle of Murfreesboro. Here, the flagstaff of the Twentieth was shot in two twice during the battle. Five of the six color guards were either killed or wounded. The regiment suffered 55% casualties. At that stage of the war, Thomas Benton Smith was colonel of the regiment (date of rank May 8, 1862), having advanced from second lieutenant, Company B. He was educated in local schools, and at age 16 was sent to the Nashville Military Institute, whose commandant was Bushrod R. Johnson from Ohio, later Major General, CSA and division commander, Army of Northern Virginia. As a young boy, Smith had shown a turn of mind for things mechanical. At age fifteen he obtained a patent for a locomotive pilot, and later worked in the railroad shops in Nashville.

There is mention that Smith was a cadet at West Point for a year, but a search of the "Register of Graduates and Former Cadets" for the years when he would have attended does not show his name.

In early 1861, Smith helped raise a company at Triune, Tennessee which merged with a group raised by General Joel A. Battle. This unit became Company B., Twentieth Tennessee, and it was due to him as a lieutenant that the regiment became most proficient in drill and discipline.

At Corinth, Mississippi, after the Battle of Shiloh, the Twentieth Tennessee was reorganized and Thomas Benton Smith was elected Colonel. He was twenty-four years of age.

Dr. Deering J. Roberts, in his biographical sketch, in the history of the regiment, describes Smith as follows at this time: "At the head of this

176

regiment, as he appeared in 1862, Colonel Smith was the physical embodiment of a magnificent soldier, with mental attainments and inclination that made him admired and respected by all who came in personal contact with him. Splendidly built, on grand proportions, a little over six feet tall, muscular, erect as an Indian, of a somewhat dark complexion, deep gray eyes, quiet and courteous in demeanor, cool, calm, and collected on all occasions, whether in genial conversation or in the thickest storm of shot and shell, with a most kindly interest in every man in his command, at all times approachable by any subaltern or private in the line, yet commanding the respect and esteem of those superior to him in military rank, he was the beau ideal of a soldier." He was severely wounded at Murfreesboro, a bullet wound across his breast with the ball passing through his left arm. This was his most serious injury due to enemy action during the war. He was again wounded at Chickamauga.

At Missionary Ridge, his brigade commander was wounded, and he assumed command of the brigade, which was Bate's old brigade. Bate had been promoted to major general Feb. 23, 1864 as a division commander. Smith commanded the brigade "during the succeeding winter at Dalton, and throughout the long and trying campaign from there to Atlanta. At the end of this one hundred days, July 29, 1864, while in front of Atlanta, he received his commission from Richmond as Brigadier General, CSA. . . ."[1] He was the army's youngest brigadier general.

Afer the fighting around Atlanta, Smith's brigade followed Hood on the Tennessee campaign. He participated in all the fighting on that campaign to include the Battle of Nashville where he was captured while defending Shy's Hill. About 160 yards from his place of capture one of the most dastardly, unchivalrous acts of the war took place. While being escorted to the rear by three Federal soldiers, General Smith, an unarmed prisoner of war, was approached by Ohio Colonel William Linn McMillen, 95th Ohio Infantry[2] who began to curse and abuse him. Smith made no reply, other than to tell the poltroon that, "I am a disarmed prisoner." He then was wantonly and repeatedly struck across the head with a sword by McMillen and fell to his knees.

---

[1] W. J. McMurray, *History of the Twentieth Tennessee Regiment,* (Nashville, Publication Committee 1904) pp. 395-96.

[2] "Generals in Gray," Warner, LSU press—1959, "Note 444—that it was this particular officer and not others of similar name who have been at various times blamed, was demonstrated by the author (Warner) in an article published in the District of Columbia Civil War Round Table News Letter (November 1952).

The victim of this cowardly attack was taken to a Federal field hospital where a surgeon examined him. He was told that he was at the end of his battles for the surgeon could see the brain oozing through the wound. His death was expected at any moment, but he survived, and was sent North as a prisoner of war to Fort Warren, Mass. He remained there until the end of the war.

Lieutenant J.W. Morgan, Company F, Twentieth Tennessee, and Private Monroe Mitchell, Company B, were witnesses to the attack on General Smith.

After his release from prison, he returned home and tried to resume work for the railroad, but had to be committed to the Tennessee State Hospital for the Insane at Nashville. He was an inmate patient there until his death sixty years later on May 21, 1923, at age 85. An otherwise useful life for Tennessee and the South was wasted due to this cowardly act of the Ohio Colonel.

General Smith attended the reunions of his old unit after the war. It is said that he could call the roster of the Twentieth Tennessee from memory on these occasions.

Various reasons for McMillen's attack on General Smith have been offered:

"His combativeness cost him his sanity and threatened his life. . . . He was acosted by the Colonel of an Ohio regiment whose men had suffered heavily in opposing Smith's brigade. The enraged officer repeatedly struck the captive across the head with his saber. . . ."[3]

As a matter of fact, for both days of battle at Nashville, McMillen's regiment suffered very light casualties:

> officers killed—none
> officers wounded—none
> enlisted men killed—1
> enlisted men—wounded—8[4]

Another writer suggests that "his assailant was thought to have been momentarily insane from the heat of battle."[5]

---

[3]*Historical Times Illustrated Encyclopedia of the Civil War,* Ed. Faust, p. 698, (Author of the biographical sketch of Smith, Edward G. Longacre).

[4]*OR,* XLV, Part 1, p. 443.

[5]"The Battle of Nashville," Walter T. Durham, *Journal of Confederate History,* Vol. 1, No. 1, Summer 1988, p. 138.

William Linn McMillen was born in Ohio in 1829. During the Crimean War, he had been a surgeon in the Russian army. In 1861, he had also been a surgeon with the First Ohio regiment. He was commissioned Colonel August 16, 1862 of the 95th Ohio. His actual combat experience during the war was limited, and he was unfortunate in having faced on separate occasions, two of the Confederacy's finest combat officers. The first was Patrick R. Cleburne at the Battle of Richmond, Kentucky, August 29-30, 1862, where the Federals were routed and Colonel McMillen afterward was tried by court-martial for cowardice in the face of the enemy after he and most of his regiment were captured. After the battle First Lieutenant T.P. Jones commanded the 95th Ohio. He says the total strength of the regiment on the morning of the battle was 975. After the battle, the lieutenant says: "I gathered on the road around Lexington 168 of the privates and 3 commissioned officers that were in the battle. With these and the 65 privates left at Lexington to guard camp, I moved in the column to the camp near Louisville. The total number now in camp is 4 commissioned officers and 233 privates. Of these of the regiment who have not reported to camp near Louisville, 100 escaped to Ohio, 550 were taken prisoner and paroled, and the remainder killed, wounded, and missing."

McMillan was shot in the hand and captured. We next hear from him at Camp Chase Sept. 23, 1862, then at Camp Wallace October 31, 1862 in command of paroled forces. Lt. Colonel James B. Armstrong, 95th Ohio, signed the court martial charges against McMillen. There were three charges and several specifications "affecting the courage of Colonel W.L. McMillen. . . . It is hoped a speedy investigation of the matter may be had, for reasons best understood by the regt and prayed for by lookers on," according to Armstrong. On October 28, 1862, Armstrong wrote to the Secretary of War asking where he should send charges of a capital nature "for alleged cowardice in the presence of the enemy at Richmond, Ky., and for unsoldierlike conduct otherwise. The social position of the colonel in Ohio seems thus far to baffle any attempt to procure a court martial, as it seems, though I hope it is a mistake."

A letter from Armstrong on November 21, 1862 forwarded the charges apparently to the Commanding General, Department of the Ohio in Cincinnati. He sent along a list of witnesses. An investigating officer, Major F.F. Flint, 16th Infantry, was appointed and proceeded to Columbus, Ohio "with the view of ascertaining whether or not the charges and specificaitons against Colonel McMillen of the 95th Regt. O. Vols. are sufficiently well grounded to order a court martial ... I am of the opinion that the charges are sufficiently well grounded to justify the convening of a court martial. . . ." The charges were delivered to McMillen and acknowledgment received November 29th 1862.

A witness to the rout and accompanying disorder wrote the following letter to General Horatio G. Wright, Commanding the Department of the Ohio, Cincinnati, Ohio:

Longansport Ind Dec 1, 1862

Major Gen. Wright

Cincinnati, Ohio

Dear Sir

I see by todays Gazette that Col. McMillen of the Ninety-fifth Ohio demands an investigation of his conduct while in command of his reg. If I am not mistaken he was in command on the retreat from Parris & Cyntheanna. I was at Cyntheanna the day they retreated from there and I must say I never saw the like before or since There seemed to be no discipline in the 95th Whatever Officers and men were running in every direction. There was almost a general destruction of every thing and no enemy in sight We could see about 1½ miles in the direction the enemy were reported to be coming and when the train started there was no enemy in sight They even left their picket I considered it the worst skedaddle of the Seson (*sic*) I was with the Ninth Ind. When the rebels run from Phillip' Laurel Hill & Carrick's ford. and with the Fifty fifth Ind as 1st Lieut. of Co. B during the Ky. campaign last summer and I never saw such a skeddadle with no cause whatever, I think the more things is investigated the more damaging it will be to the Col.

Yours

John T. Powell
Late 1st Lieut Co B 55 reg Ind vol.

The exact wording of the charges and specifications is not known, but McMillan was acquitted by a general court martial. This court martial was convened in compliance with General Orders No. 24, Headquarters Army of Kentucky, dated November 21, 1862, of which Brigadier General Henry M. Judah was president.*

After his exchange and court martial, McMillen spent some time guarding railroad trestles and bridges in Indiana.

---

*Material pertaining to McMillen's court martial is from the National Archives.

His command was next assigned to General W.T. Sherman's XV Corps as part of the Army of the Tennessee. He participated in the engagement at Jackson, Mississippi on May 14, 1863 where troops of the 95th Ohio saw brief action against slight resistance. It has been said that McMillen and his men "were the first Union troops to enter the city." They found Jackson empty since Joseph E. Johnston had evacuated the city—a strategic blunder. He took part in the assault on Vicksburg on May 19 before the start of Grant's siege. November 1863 found him around Memphis where he was given command of the First Brigade, First Division, Sixteenth Army Corps. It was from this station that his next combat exprience was to take place, and unfortunately for him his opponent would be Major General Nathan B. Forrest CSA, at the Battle of Brice's Cross Roads in North Mississippi. This battle was fought June 10, 1864 between Forrest's cavalry and a force of cavalry, infantry, and accompanying artillery under Brigadier General Samuel D. Sturgis.

McMillen was given command of the 6,000 infantry contingent, although many of the officers and men opposed this choice by Sturgis, "because McMillen was known to be a heavy drinker."[6]

Forrest was greatly outnumbered, yet he scored a brilliant victory. Federal losses were 223 killed, 394 wounded, and 1,623 missing. Forrest captured the entire train of 250 wagons and ambulances, 16 of 18 cannon, and 1,500 stands of small arms, and 184 horses. Forrest had 96 killed, and 396 wounded.[7] The Federal forces, in a state of panic, were utterly routed by less than half their number and pursued for a number of miles.

A board was appointed on June 25, 1864 to "look into the disaster to the late expedition under Brigadier General Sturgis." The report of the board is included in 73 pages of the Official Records (Vol 39, part 1). One of the questions asked of various witnesses was if any general officer or brigade commander was intoxicated during the expedition? Name them. Colonel McMillen. Question: To what degree was he intoxicated, and was it so as to unfit him for duty? Answer: He was so much so that to prevent exposure I got his aides-de-camp to get him to a

---

[6]Bearss, Edwin C., *Forrest at Brice's Cross Roads,* Morningside Book Shop, Dayton, OH, 1979.

[7]*Enclyclopedia of the Civil War,* Faust, Ed., p. 79.

house and place him in bed that night. . . . Question: While Colonel McMillen was in this condition was he in a position to be observed by other officers and men of the command? Answer: He was, at one time. In attempting to get from the cars he fell to the ground and had to be assisted to rise.

Various officers testified that a lack of confidence in their commanding officers was one reason for the disaster at Brice's Cross Roads. Lt. Colonel C.G. Eaton, commanding Seventy-second Ohio Infantry stated emphatically that the officers he referred to were Brigadier General Sturgis and Colonel McMillen. Question: What did this want of confidence arise from? Answer: With Colonel McMillen, it arose from the men seeing him in a beastly state of intoxication. . . .

Captain H.W. Buckland, Seventy-second Ohio Infantry was on McMillan's staff. Question: Did you see General Sturgis or Colonel McMillan drink any liquor on the day of the battle? Answer: I did once, at the house where we halted when we first heard of the fight going on.

Lieutenant George W. Maurer, One Hundred and fourteenth Illinois Infantry was asked by the board: What was the feeling among the troops as regards confidence in their commanding officers? Answer: All that I heard express themselves did not have confidence in their commanding officers above their regimental commanders. . . . The reasons given were: It was generally reported through our brigade that General Sturgis and Colonel McMillen had been drinking pretty hard on the trip. . . .

Captain J.M. Johnson of the same regiment was asked if he knew of any general officer or brigade or regimental commander being intoxicated on the expedition? Answer: Yes, Sir, I do. Colonel McMillen. . . . The soldiers saw him in this condition.

One private soldier, Andrew Armstrong, same regiment as the above two officers, testified as follows: Question: Did you see any general officer or colonel drink any intoxicating liquor on the day of the fight? . . . Answer: Yes, Sir, I saw General Sturgis and Colonel McMillen with a bottle of whiskey about sundown that day where we formed our last line. . . .

Private Armstrong was asked if he saw any general officer or colonel intoxicated at any time after the expedition left Memphis? He

182

replied: Yes Sir. I saw Colonel McMillen intoxicated on the cars, and saw him fall out of the car at the place where the troops left the train. I saw him fall once after he got off the cars.

The expedition that Sturgis and McMillen had embarked upon to "return with Forrest's hair" took ten days to get from Memphis to Brice's Cross Roads, but only one day and two nights were used on the return trip.

By the end of the year 1864 McMillen was at Nashville as part of Major General Andrew J. Smith's Sixteenth Army Corps and a participant in the Battle of Nashville. He was breveted for his part in the battle as a Brigadier General (USV). After the war, General Orders No. 67, dated July 16, 1867 appointed him "Major General by brevet in the Volunteer Force, Army of the United States, for gallant and meritorious services to date from March 13, 1865."

Many officers held brevet commissions higher than their ordinary rank, usually for gallant actions or meritorious service in combat. "About 1,700 Federal officers held brevet rank as brigadier or major general. The confusion caused by the awarding of numerous brevet commissions was great, and the abuse led to the discontinuance of brevet awards in the army.[7]

McMillen was mustered out of the service on August 14, 1865 at Louisville, Kentucky. After the war, he apparently was a carpetbagger in Louisiana as a planter and legislator. "In 1872 and 1873 he was sent to the U.S. Senate but not admitted, and later was New Orleans' postmaster."[8]

He died in 1902, twenty-one years before General Smith, his intended victim. Various reasons have been considered for his vicious and unwarranted attack on General Smith. His prior record could indicare that intoxication may have been the excuse for atrocious conduct.

---

[7]*Encyclopedia of the Civil War,* Faust Ed., p. 79.

[8]*The Civil War Dictionary,* Boatner, p. 537.

COLONEL WILLIAM L. MCMILLEN

BRIGADIER GENERAL THOMAS BENTON SMITH, C.S.A.

Nathan Bedford Forrest

Nathan Bedford Forrest was born in Bedford County, Tennessee in 1821. He was born into a poor family and by age 16 was responsible for the support of his widowed mother, and his nine younger brothers and sisters. By 1860, it has been said that he was a millionaire business man. When he enlisted in the Confederate army June 1861, he has been described as follows: "There was six feet-two of him, lithe and powerful of build, with steady eyes of deep gray-blue set wide in a lean, high-cheeked, swarthy face crowned with thick, wavy, iron-gray hair and set off with a short black chin beard—altogether a man of striking and commanding presence."[1]

He had very little formal education and no military education whatsoever, but became one of the most feared and respected cavalry commanders on either side during the war. He was a natural military genius.

At Fort Donelson he refused to surrender his unit and marched them safely out the river road. He was wounded at Shiloh on April 8 on rear-guard duty. On July 21, 1862 he was appointed brigadier general, and became famous for his cavalry raids. After the Battle of Chickamauga Forrest clashed with Bragg due to the latter's failure to follow up on the Federal defeat. He returned to West Tennessee and raised another force. In June 1864, he fought the Battle of Brice's Cross Roads Mississippi and routed a Union force about three times his own number. In October the same year Forrest made the raid on the Johnsonville, Tennessee Federal Supply Depot on the Tennessee River. Total damages estimated to be $6.7 million.

He then joined Hood's Tennessee Campaign and covered the retreat from Columbia to the Tennessee in a masterful way that elicited praise even from the Federal commander. In the waning days of the war, he was not able to stop Wilson's raid into Alabama. This was his only lack of success during the entire war. He surrendered with Taylor May 4, 1865.

After the war he resumed a planter's life and also was engaged in railroad building.

He died in Memphis in 1877, acknowledged by officers on both sides as perhaps the greatest soldier the war produced.

---

[1] Robert S. Henry, *First With The Most Forrest* (Indianapolis: Bobbs-Merrill, 1944), p. 13.

Major General Nathan Bedford Forrest, C.S.A.

John Bell Hood

John Bell Hood was born in Kentucky June 1, 1831. He graduated from West Point in 1853. He served in the farmous 2nd U.S. Cavalry commanded by Colonel Albert Sidney Johnston. Other officers in this regiment who would later on become famous were Robert E. Lee, George H. Thomas, and William J. Hardee. Before he resigned in 1861 to join the Confederacy, he had been wounded in Indian fighting. He was appointed Brigadier General March 6, 1862 and given command of the "Texas Brigade" which gained fame as "Hood's Texas Brigade." Hood was brave and courageous in battle and respected by his men. In October he was promoted to Major General and given command of a division under Longstreet. He was severely wounded in his left arm at Gettysburg. At Chickamauga he commanded several divisions in Longstreet's left wing. He was again badly wounded and lost his right leg. Promoted to Lt. General to rank from Sept. 20 1863, he commanded a corps under Joseph E. Johnston. Because of his wound, he had to be strapped to the saddle and aided in mounting and dismounting. He succeeded Johnston as commander of The Army of Tennessee in July 1864, but after a series of disastrous battles around Atlanta, the city fell Sept. 1, 1864.

Hood then withdrew north along Sherman's line of supply, hoping to draw the Union commander away from Atlanta. Failing in this maneuver, the Tennessee Campaign was planned which failed disastrously when he lost the battle of Nashville which all but destroyed The Army of Tennessee. After his retreat from Tennessee, he was relieved at his own request and never again held field command. After trying to reach the Trans-Mississippi Department, he surrendered at Natchez, Mississippi May 31, 1865. He died of yellow fever in 1879 in New Orleans.

General John Bell Hood, C.S.A.

George H. Thomas

Thomas was born in Virginia in 1816. He graduated from West Point in 1840 and was assigned to the artillery branch. A Virginian, when he failed to follow his state during the Civil War, he alienated both friends and family. His pre-Civil War service included the Seminole War, frontier duty, and the Mexican War where he won two brevets. In April 1862 he was appointed Major General USV. He fought at Mill Springs, Ky., Shiloh, Corinth, Perryville, Stones River, and at Chickamauga. At the latter battle he won the title "Rock of Chickamauga" when his men held their ground. He then fought at Missionary Ridge and Lookout Mountain where his troops made a good showing. He was second-in-command on Sherman's Atlanta Campaign. He was in charge of the defenses of Nashville when Hood invaded Tennessee, and methodically built up the forces at Nashville, and endured much harassment from Stanton, Halleck, and Grant prior to the Battle of Nashville. For the Nashville victory he was made Major General, Regular Army and given the Thanks of Congress. After the war he was in command of the Military Division of the Pacific. He died in 1870 in San Francisco.[2]

---

[2]Patricia L. Faust, ed., *Encyclopedia of the Civil War* (New York: Harper and Row, 1986), pp. 754-55; Mark M. Boatner, *Civil War Dictionary* (New York: David McKay Company, 1959), p. 836.

Major General George H. Thomas, U.S.A.

James Harrison Wilson

James Harrison Wilson was born in Illinois Sept. 2, 1837. He graduated sixth in the West Point class of 1860 and was a classmate of Stephen D. Ramseur, North Carolina, later Major General CSA. Like Ramseur, he was a major general five years after graduating from the military academy. At the beginning of the war he was on frontier duty, but transferred back east where he held various assignments. He was promoted to brigadier general Oct. 30, 1863, and from February— April 1864 headed the newly created Cavalry Bureau in Washington. It was during this time that he urged a reorganization of the cavalry and that the Spencer carbine replace the muzzle loaders. E.P. Alexander, CSA, said that this weapon "fully doubled the efficiency of the cavalry against ours with only muzzle loaders."

In late 1864 he was with Thomas at Nashville on the right flank of the numerically superior Federal army, and was instrumental in turning Hood's left. Pursuit was hampered by weather, but he doggedly followed the Confederates to the Tennessee River on their retreat.

On his Raid to Selma with 13,500 troops he routed the Confederates and captured Selma April 2, 1865. Forrest, for the first time had been bested in the field by a Federal commander.

After the war Wilson resigned his commission in 1870, but returned to the service when the Spanish-American War began. He retired in 1901 as a brigadier general. He died in 1925.

Major General James Harrison Wilson, U.S.A.

SELECTED BIBLIOGRAPHY

Primary Sources: Unpublished
Diaries, Letters, eyewitness Accounts

Brownlow, James P. Papers, ca. 1915. Battle of Nashville, 1864. Tennessee State Library and Archives.

Cheatham, Benjamin Franklin. papers, 1834-93. Battle of Nashville, 1864. Tennessee State Library and Archives.

Claiborne, Mollie M., and Charles H. Eastman. Statements—Hood's Headquarters, 1864. Battle of Nashville, 1864, Confederate Collection. Tennessee State Library and Archives.

Cooke, Samuel Alonzo. Memoir, 1907. Battle of Nashville, 1864. Tennessee State Library and Archives.

Eastman Family. Papers, 1849-1865. Battle of Nashville, 1864. Tennessee State Library and Archives.

Federal Collection. Battle of Nashville, 1864. Tennessee State Library and Archives.

Harmon, J.W., 1860-1865. Diaries and Memoirs. Confederate Collection. Battle of Nashville, 1864. Tennessee State Library and Archives.

Primary Sources: Published

Buck, Irving A. *Cleburne and His Command.* Ed. Thomas Robson Hay, 1959. Jackson, TN.

Cox, Jacob D. *Atlanta and the March to the Sea.* New York: Charles Scribner's Sons, 1882.

Cumming, Kate. *Kate: Journal of A Confederate Nurse.* Ed. by Richard B. Harwell. Baton Rouge, LA: LSU, 1959.

Dinkins, James. *1861-1865, By An Old Johnnie.* Facsimile reprint by Morningside Bookshop, 1975.

Edwards, E.E. *Diary.* Greencastle: Indiana Archives of DePauw University, December 1864.

Evans, Clement A. *Confederate Military History.* Vol. 10. Atlanta: Confederate Publishing Company, 1899.

Foster, Samuel T. *One of Cleburne's Command.* Edited by Norman D. Brown. Austin: University of Texas Press, 1980.

Griscom, George L. *Fighting with Ross' Texas Cavalry Brigade, CSA*. Ed. Homer L. Kerr. Hillsboro, TX: Hill Junior College Press, 1976.

Hood, John B. *Advance and Retreat: Personal Experiences in the United States and Confederate Armies*. Privately printed by Hood Orphan Memorial Fund, New Orleans, 1880.

McMurray, W.J. *History of the Twentieth Tennessee Regiment Volunteer Infantry*. Nashville, TN: Publication Committee, 1904. Reprint, Nashville, TN: Elder's Bookstore, 1976.

Morton, John W. *The Artillery of Nathan Bedford Forrest's Cavalry*. Nashville, TN: M. E. Church South, Publishing House, 1909.

Rennolds, Edwin H. *A History of the Henry County Commands*. Jacksonville, FL: 1904. Reprint, Kennesaw, GA: Continental Book Company, 1961.

Ridley, Bromfield L. *Battles and Sketches of the Army of Tennessee*. Mexico, MO: Missouri Printing and Publishing Company, 1906. Reprint, Dayton, OH: Morningside Bookshop, 1978.

Taylor, Richard. *Destruction and Reconstruction*. Ed. by Richard B. Harwell. New York: Longman's, Green and Company, 1955.

U.S. War Department. *The War of The Rebellion: A Compilation of the Official Records of the Union and Confederate Armies*. Washington, D.C.: Government Printing Office, 1881-1900.

Van Horne, Thomas B. *History of the Army of the Cumberland*. Cincinnati: Robert Clarke and Co., 1875.

Watkins, Sam. *Co. Aytch*. New York: Macmillan, 1962.

Wilson, James Harrison. *Battles and Leaders of The Civil War*. 4 vols. New York: Century Co., 1887.

_____. *Under the Old Flag*. 2 vols. New York: B. Appleton and Co., 1912.

Secondary Sources: Books

Alexander, E.P. *Military Memoirs of a Confederate*. New York, 1912. Reprint, Bloomington, IN: Indiana University Press, 1962.

Anderson, Ephraim McD. *First Missouri Confederate Brigade*. St. Louis: Times Printing Company, 1968. Reprint, Morningside Bookshop, 1972.

Boatner, Mark M. *Civil War Dictionary*. New York: David McKay Company, 1959.

Connelly, Thomas L. *Army of the Heartland.* Baton Rouge, LA: LSU, 1967.

_____. *Autumn of Glory: The Army of Tennessee, 1862-1865.* Baton Rouge, LA: LSU, 1971.

_____. *Civil War Tennessee—Battles and Leaders.* Knoxville: University of Tennessee Press, 1979.

Daniel, Larry J. *Cannoneers In Gray.* Tuscaloosa, AL: University of Alabama Press, 1984.

Dyer, John P. *The Gallant Hood.* Indianapolis-New York: Bobbs-Merrill Company, 1950.

Faust, Patricia L., Ed. *Encyclopedia of The Civil War.* New York: Harper and Row, 1986.

Foote, Shelby. *The Civil War: A Narrative.* New York: Vintage Books, 1974.

Hay, Thomas Robson. *Hood's Tennessee Campaign.* New York: Walter Neale, 1929. Reprint, Morningside Shop, 1976.

Henry, Robert Self. *First With the Most Forrest.* Indianapolis: Bobbs-Merrill Company, 1944.

Horn, Stanley F. *Tennessee's War 1861-1865.* Nashville, TN: Civil War Centennial Commission, 1965.

Johnson, Curt, and McLaughlin, Mark. *Civil War Battles.* New York: Fairfax Press, 1977.

Jordan, Thomas, and Pryor, J.P. *The Campaigns of Lieut. Gen. N.B. Forrest and of Forrest's Cavalry.* New York: 1868. Reprint, 2nd ed., Dayton, OH: Morningside Bookshop, 1973.

McAulay, John D. *Carbines of The Civil War 1861-1865.* Union City, TN: Pioneer Press, 1981.

McCaffrey, James M. *This Band of Heroes.* Austin, TX: Eakin Press, 1985.

McDonough, James Lee, and Connelly, Thomas L. *Five Tragic Hours—The Battle of Franklin.* Knoxville: University of Tennessee Press, 1983.

Page, Thomas Nelson. *The Old South.* New York: Chatauqua Press, 1982.

Swinton, William. *Decisive Battles of The Civil War.* New York: Promontory Press, 1986.

Williams T. Harry. *P.G.T. Beauregard—Napoleon In Gray.* Baton Rouge, LA: LSU Press, 1954.

Womack, Bob. *Call Forth The Mighty Men.* Bessemer, AL: Colonial Press, 1987.

Wyeth, John Allen. *That Devil Forrest.* New York: Harper, 1959.

Secondary Sources

Articles, Journals, Letters, Newspapers
Letters, Newspapers

Civil War Times Illustrated, May 1973, Vol. 12, No. 2.

Confederate Veteran Magazine, Nashville (40 vols.), 1893-1932.

Dowd, John T. *The Pillaged Grave of a Civil War Hero.* Nashville, TN: Mini-Histories, 1985.

Durham, Walter T. *Journal of Confederate History,* Vol. I, No. 1, Sept. 1988.

"John Bell Hood's Tenn. Campaign," 1861-1865, written by Elbert L. Watson; presented at the Okla. Civil War Round Table, May 27, 1965. Confederate Collection, Sketches. Battle of Nashville, 1864. Tennessee State Library and Archives.

Johnston, John. *Reminiscences of The Battle of Nashville.* Ed. by Tim Birgess. Paris, TN: Guild Bindery Press, *Journal of Confederate History,* 1988.

Walker, Thomas J. *Confederate Chronicles of Tennessee,* Ed. E.B. Bailey, Nashville, TN: Sons of Confederate Veterans, 1986.

Index

Index (Continued)

Index (Continued)

Index (Continued)

Index (Continued)

Index (Continued)

Index (Continued)

Paul H. Stockdale is a native of Tennessee. Since retirement he has lived in Texas where he and his wife have restored 1850 Waverly Plantation. He is a graduate of LSU where he studied under the late T. Harry Williams. Member of Brazos Valley Civil War Roundtable, and Sons of Confederate Veterans.

ACKNOWLEDGEMENTS

Maps by Bernice Shaver

Photos courtesy Carter House
Franklin, Tennessee

TO ORDER THIS BOOK

Write to: P.O. Box 34
            Chappell Hill, Texas 77426